Vipassana Meditation
& Ayahuasca

"At the beginning of this century, we face a meta-crisis that is stimulating a renaissance of the human spirit. In *Vipassana Meditation and Ayahuasca*, Clint Sidle reveals one of the most significant encounters of our time: the meeting of the sophisticated Buddhist psychospiritual technology of the bodhisattva with the jungle dharma of the grandmother master plant teacher Ayahuasca. In sharing his exploration of these two spiritual paths, he reveals their mutually reinforcing benefits for deeper psychological integration, contemplative realization, and human maturation. Whether you are a practitioner of the Buddha Dharma or this plant medicine, you will find this informative integration of great value."

JOHN CHURCHILL, DOCTOR OF
CONTEMPLATIVE PSYCHOLOGY, DHARMA TEACHER,
AND TRADITIONAL CHINESE MEDICINE PRACTITIONER

"This is a much-needed contribution to the global spiritual literature, highlighting two distinct but mutually reinforcing traditions that have been separated by time and distance for thousands of years."

ALONSO DEL RIO, PERUVIAN SHAMAN AND
MUSICIAN AND FOUNDER OF AYAHUASCA AYLLU

"*Vipassana Meditation and Ayahuasca* is a unique and captivating book that weaves together Clint Sidle's Buddhist training and practice with his skillful use of the visionary plant medicine Ayahuasca. Deeply grounded in his many years of spiritual inquiry, the author takes us along for the ride as he reveals the promises and pitfalls of living an awakened life. This guide has many practical suggestions for anyone seeking a more authentic way of living as well as for the experienced practitioner in need of a spiritual tune-up!"

JOHN ORR, FORMER THERAVADA BUDDHIST MONK AND
TEACHER AT THE DEEP SPRING CENTER IN ANN ARBOR

"In today's world, where the spiritual quest has become more challenging than ever with the rapidly expanding offerings of self-exploration, there is a dearth of books that explore the connections and synergies between Indigenous shamanic practices and the contemplative traditions of the East. I am delighted that Clint Sidle's *Vipassana Meditation and Ayahuasca* fills this gap, and I hope that it becomes the cause for other works on this topic to appear."

LAMA OLEG, DIRECTOR OF RANGJUNG YESHE
OF RUSSIA AND COLOMBIA

"An uplifting and enlightening read! Adding to the conversation about whether temporary, ceremonial-based visionary states can create lasting personal change, Clint Sidle weaves the wisdom teachings of Tibetan Buddhism with his experience with the Shipibo Ayahuasca tradition of South America to show their mutually reinforcing benefits for becoming a more integrated human being. Drawing on a lifetime of spiritual practice, exploration, and study, Clint motivates us to consider stepping into the life that awaits us. Deftly weaving insights gained from his Ayahuasca journeys and his deep grounding in Tibetan Buddhism, he inspires and guides the reader on the path of self-discovery and wisdom."

RAFAEL LEON LOPEZ, PRACTITIONER OF TRADITIONAL
AMAZONIAN PLANT MEDICINE AT
MÁMA ABUELA'S SPIRITUAL CENTER

Vipassana Meditation & Ayahuasca

Skillful Means for Transcending the Ego and Opening to Spiritual Growth

A Sacred Planet Book

C. CLINTON SIDLE

Park Street Press
Rochester, Vermont

Park Street Press
One Park Street
Rochester, Vermont 05767
www.ParkStPress.com

Park Street Press is a division of Inner Traditions International

Sacred Planet Books are curated by Richard Grossinger, Inner Traditions editorial board member and cofounder and former publisher of North Atlantic Books. The Sacred Planet collection, published under the umbrella of the Inner Traditions family of imprints, includes works on the themes of consciousness, cosmology, alternative medicine, dreams, climate, permaculture, alchemy, shamanic studies, oracles, astrology, crystals, hyperobjects, locutions, and subtle bodies.

Cataloging-in-Publication Data for this title is available from the Library of Congress

ISBN 979-8-88850-043-9 (print)
ISBN 979-8-88850-044-6 (ebook)

Printed and bound in the United States by Lake Book Manufacturing, LLC

10 9 8 7 6 5 4 3 2 1

Text design and layout by Priscilla Harris Baker
This book was typeset in Garamond, with Futura, Gill Sans, Harman Script, Legacy Sans, and Meno Banner

To send correspondence to the author of this book, mail a first-class letter to the author c/o Inner Traditions • Bear & Company, One Park Street, Rochester, VT 05767, and we will forward the communication, or contact the author directly at **clintsidle.com.**

To My Teachers

Vipassana Instructors:
*S. N. Goenka, Joseph Goldstein, Jack Kornfield,
Sharon Salzberg, Ruth Denison, Anagarika Munindra,
John Orr, Larry Rosenberg*

Tibetan Lamas:
*Khenchen Palden Rinpoche, Khenpo Tsewang Rinpoche,
Thinley Norbu Rinpoche, Tulku Sang-nyak Rinpoche*

Ayahuasca Curanderos:
*Ricardo Amaringo, Alonso Del Rio,
Rafael Lopez Lobos*

Contents

Introduction

Out beyond ideas of wrongdoing and rightdoing,
There is a field. I'll meet you there.

RUMI, TRANSLATED BY COLEMAN BARKS
AND JOHN MOYNE[1]

This book offers an approach to spiritual growth to those who have become stale on their path and seek renewal, as well as those newly inspired and looking to enter onto one earnestly. It shares my experience of the entheogen Ayahuasca as a skillful means for creating a spiritual opening, and the promise of both *Shamata Vipassana* meditation and the fundamentals of Tibetan Buddhist thought as an uplifting pathway in a proven spiritual tradition. It is at once an invitation to a psychoactive intervention, a meditation manual, and a philosophical guide for inspiring entry to and sustained growth on a road to awakening.

Ayahuasca as a Skillful Means for Opening and Renewal

As a skillful means, the use of entheogens—such as cannabis and datura—as a spiritual aid is well documented in the Buddhism of Tibet. Often called *amrita*, or nectar, they were used in certain ceremonial situations. The ancient Buddhist *Guhyasamaja* and *Chakrasamvara* tantras from India described the use of entheogens as a skillful means for destroying evildoers in tantric rituals and medicines. Longchenpa (1308–1364), who systemized many of the teachings of the Buddhist Nyingma lineage in

Tibet, pointed to their use in his commentary on the original texts of the tradition. Jigme Lingpa (1730–1798), who condensed Longenpa's teachings into a practice manual and is considered one of the most important scholars and visionaries of the lineage, refers to their use in his autobiography. And, finally, the Third Dodrupchen (1865–1926), also a leading visionary as well as a teacher of many great masters of his time, called them the nectar of liberation in ancient practice.

So although the evidence for the use of psychoactive plants in Buddhism in ancient India and Tibet is clear, unlike in South American and other indigenous spiritual traditions worldwide, today it has all but disappeared. For a time, however, it seemed to have served as an effective occasional skillful means but never a central aspect of the path.

For me, Ayahuasca proved to be a remarkable catalyst. It made clear my self-deception, provided insight into the source of my psychoemotional obstacles, and pointed to a clear vision for a way forward. I found it impossible to hide behind any façade or false pretense, as the effects of Ayahuasca laid bare the emptiness of my normal frames of self-reference and opened my heart and mind viscerally and authentically to a much vaster view. Of all the psychoactive plants tried in my search for meaningful, mind-expanding experiences in youth and midlife, including LSD-, psilocybin-, and peyote-assisted sweat lodges and Native American Church ceremonies, I found Ayahuasca to be the most potent, and the grandmother of them all. As interest in the psychotherapeutic and spiritual effects of Ayahuasca has grown rapidly among North Americans and Europeans, I want to offer a perspective on its use from a long-term Buddhist practitioner.

Not for the faint of heart, Ayahuasca brings an onslaught of truly visionary experiences that totally crack open your world and place you well beyond any normal frame of reference. It challenges everything you know, and its powers are renowned for their physical, psycho-emotional, and spiritual healing effects. Unlike other psychedelics, this "medicine," as is it commonly known, puts you on an uneasy edge that brings forth a natural healing from within. As such, it is non-habit-forming. Some people have bad trips, but these are few among the ceremonies conducted by traditionally trained facilitators called *Curanderos*.

Critics argue that, when used as a spiritual aid, there is a difference between the temporary states of mind that Ayahuasca induces and the ingrained traits of your psychological makeup—*states and traits*—and that it is much easier to change the former than the latter. To that I say yes, but occasional practice of meditation does the same. Others argue that Ayahuasca provides insight but is not necessarily *developmental*. That is also mostly true. However, that is the very reason for taking Ayahuasca—to wake up, and to be inspired to take on the regimen of a proven spiritual path—and this it does very well.

Shamata Vipassana and Tibetan Buddhist Philosophy as a Pathway

For a sustainable developmental path, I offer not the entirety but simply the main principles of Buddhist philosophy according to the Tibetan tradition and a progressive sequence of Shamata Vipassana meditation techniques for bringing them to life.

Tibetan Buddhism generally divides the Buddha's teachings into three main vehicles called the *Hinayana*, *Mahayana*, and *Vajrayana*. Each of these varies according to the karma, needs, capacities, and proclivities of different people. The Hinayana focuses on foundational teachings of the Buddha, such as the four noble truths and the practices of mindfulness and awareness for individual liberation. The Mahayana emphasizes the same but adds compassion for the liberation of oneself and also for all other beings. The Vajrayana encompasses the first two but adds many other skillful means for fully activating and revealing our inherent inner nature that is both stainless and free.

Known as the diamond vehicle or the quick path, the Vajrayana holds out hope for enlightenment in a single lifetime, and the Shamata Vipassana meditation practices I offer here are from the Vajrayana perspective.

The first challenge of the Vajrayana, particularly for Westerners, is that it possesses such an amazing array of philosophical teachings that it can be difficult to absorb. There are four main schools in Tibetan Buddhism—the Nyingma, Kagyu, Geluk, and Sakya—and in the Tibetan Nyingma canon alone, for example, there is the *Kangyur*, a collection of teachings given by the Buddha himself, as well as the *Tengyur*, a set of commentaries on those original teachings. All told there are roughly 5,300 texts with over seventy-three million words across four main lineages, each having sub-lineages emphasizing different texts with similar but different meanings. These teachings also come with ornate rituals, mantras, and recitations that are initially completely foreign to Westerners.

All of this is indeed precious but can be overwhelming for a newcomer. I struggled with this over the years myself in study and experience, trying to understand and internalize the philosophy, methods, and techniques and how they fit and work together. In both earlier times and, to a lesser extent, today, in a society dominated by monastic life, Tibetan monks and nuns spent their youth studying the teachings. That is an investment of time not available in our culture, and the tradition has not been very good at adapting and providing pith and principle simply and clearly.

Many have made serious attempts, most prominently the Dalai Lama, Dzongchar Khyentse Rinpoche, and Chogyam Trungpa Rinpoche, along with Khenchen Palden Rinpoche and Khenpo Tsewang Rinpoche and others but there is still much room for improvement. Lacking perspective, many Westerners get caught in mindlessly chasing one teaching after another, collecting different empowerments and tenents while not really understanding or internalizing the basics.

The second challenge of Tibetan Buddhism is that many newcomers have little or no foundation in the calm abiding and insight that Shamata Vipassana provides. Without sufficient study and mind training, newcomers can quickly be confused or undone in trying to practice the different sadhanas, visualizations, and rituals encased in a culture so different from their own. Shamata Vipassana is the foundational meditation practice for each of these. It is, after all, what was originally taught by the Buddha himself, and it is typically offered in some form as an entry point to the Vajrayana. However, the offerings coming from within the tradition itself tend to be sporadic at best and rarely done in a way that is sufficient for developing the stability of mind necessary for fruitfully onboarding a new Western practitioner.

As a result of both these challenges, many fail to engage authentically, or they drop out entirely.

So, my motivation in sharing Shamata Vipassana meditation practices and the philosophical principles of Tibetan Buddhism is to address all of the above. I want to share them as an entryway that is inclusive of all three vehicles. I want to share them in a way that lays the groundwork for approaching the more advanced visualization, inner yogic, and choiceless awareness practices of *Dzogchen* and *Mahamudra*. I want to share them in a way that addresses the self-deception that can derail practice and obscure genuine insight into the true nature of one's mind and being. Finally, I want to share them in a way that ensures the promise for internalizing and practicing in a fully authentic way and places you on a constructive and fruitful path.

Other special and in some ways unique features of the book include its focus on:

- How the development of psycho-emotional wellness is critical to balanced spiritual growth
- How the ego can play both *restrictive* and *supportive* roles on the path
- How Shamata Vipassana naturally progresses from a more to a less fabricated form and prepares you for the more advanced practices
- How the development of awareness and compassion is central to every aspect of the Tibetan Buddhist path
- How compassion is not an automatic outcome of expanding awareness and needs separate cultivation on its own
- How the development of faith helps crack the habitual patterns of the mind (the Cosmic Egg) and opens you to deeper and vaster experiences of your being

The book is organized into three parts and assumes little prior knowledge of Buddhism or any previous meditation experience:

Part I: The Cosmic Fool describes the compelling common sense of the Buddhist philosophical perspective as well as the all-too-common seductive pitfalls of self-deception in its practice.

Part II: Cracking the Cosmic Egg describes my psycho-emotional growth and spiritual renewal resulting from the use of Ayahuasca over the course of three years and twenty-four ceremonies.

Part III: A Path of Awakening applies the lessons learned in a concise yet comprehensive introduction to Tibetan Buddhist philosophy and guided instruction on four progressive techniques of Shamata Vipassana meditation that support it experientially.

As an avid student of Buddhism, I practiced each of the meditation techniques over the course of seventeen years, including at least one seven-to-ten-day Shamata Vipassana retreat annually. On this journey, the method progressed from a structured to a nearly formless style from the Sweeping technique I learned from Sri S. N. Goenka at my very first retreat at his center in Igatpuri, India to the Open Shamata Vipassana method I learned while attending various retreats at the Insight Meditation Society in Barre, Massachusetts and finally to the Open Space Vipassana method I learned in Shambhala Training and by attending a month-long *Dathun* at Karme Choling in Barnet, Vermont.

Since 2017, I have taught these techniques twice a year in programs offered through Namgyal Monastery in Ithaca, New York, the only Western monastery of His Holiness the Dalai Lama. This program includes one hour per week of online meditation instruction and philosophical teachings joined with a personal commitment to practice twenty minutes twice a day for the entire eight weeks of the program. Part III of this book mirrors the content and progression of this program.

PART I

The Cosmic Fool

1

What Makes You a Buddhist

It is not the appearance that binds you, it's the attachment to the appearance that binds you.

TILOPA

What does this quote really mean, and how might it apply to you and me? If you and I are anything alike, then I know there is a constant hunger in you that longs for something. Just stop and look for a moment, and you will find it. You may be successful, yet still you strive. You may be wealthy, yet still you seek gain. You may be loved, yet still you wander. You feel it, don't you? Where does the discontent begin? What do you so long for?

You may sense this hunger, but most of the time you ignore it. Yet every day you bury yourself in it. You get the kids out the door, you put your time in at work, you fight with your colleagues, and then you rush home to do the laundry before watching your favorite show. But then you worry about the things that break, the neighbors who gossip, and your loved ones who nag, so you escape to go shopping or to the movies to avoid the squeeze. All the while, you build fantasies for a life of greater success, more fulfilling work, early retirement, nicer cars, and better friends.

You may never grow weary of this gnawing feeling, however,

because you always have hope. Even if you get fed up with it all, you can always pack up the Airstream, move on, and start over again. Yet you are drawn on by thoughts of when everything will be just right, when you will have the garden and the grandchildren at your home in the country or can escape to a peaceful spot in the forest. You just know that someday it will all turn out and you will reap the quiet wisdom of your golden years.

So you are always preparing for things to get better. But when you do get your ideal home you soon find things wrong with it, or when your perfect semiretirement situation finally works out, you become bored by the lack of excitement. To fill the void, you drink or turn to shopping, cleaning, golfing, fishing, gambling, or whatever addictive behavior it takes to fill the nagging sense of emptiness. You are so caught up in preparing and running after things that you forget to live fully. Then you look back on that time nostalgically, even though you were so wrapped up in doing that you missed it.

For most of us, this endless planning, doing, fixing, upgrading is what we call life. We have many more glamorous words for this drive to do whatever we are compelled to do—yearning, questing, searching, craving, striving, seeking, or thirsting. It is as gross as our drive to find God in our life, as mundane as needing to clean the house, and as subtle as a simple restless energy.

I call it our *hungry spirit*. It is a pervasive energy that is constantly longing for success, freedom, love, or whatever it is we require to find our place in the world. All our worldly concerns are subordinate to it and a means to its end. It helps us find and make meaning and drives us to achieve and do something with our lives. It is the seed of creation and the heart of our very evolutionary urge—it is our life force, our life energy. Every act, every word, every thought reflects it in some way.

What exactly is this hungry spirit really looking for? Aristotle said it is happiness: "It is the meaning and purpose of life, the whole aim and end of human existence." And so we occupy ourselves with it more than with any other single endeavor in our lives. That's why we buy new iPods, iPads, and iPhones for convenience, as well as Viagra, breast implants, and liposuction for confidence. It is also why we constantly seek new jobs, boyfriends, girlfriends, and experiences—like sweat lodges in Sedona and bungee jumping off the Royal Gorge Bridge.

The trouble is that we are never, ever satisfied. This incessant searching and doing often feels empty, because it is empty.

Why?

The things we pursue appear real, but they are not real. Like a mirage that vanishes as we approach, the satisfaction of reaching a goal quickly dissolves as we reach it. So we continuously replace the old ones with new ones. We go from wanting a new dresser to wanting a new house, from a new job to making more money, and from coffee in the morning to wind up to wine in the evening to wind down. We become swept up in the mindless pursuit of a rainbow's end. But as Lily Tomlin once said, "The problem with winning the rat race is that you are still a rat."[2]

The reason is that all our pursuits are just a simple display, an illusion.

To understand this, we need to look deeper. First, consider that all form, including our homes, our gardens, our flesh and bones, and even our thoughts, feelings, and emotions, is made up of something else. It is a combination of at least two or more things coming together. They are compounded or fabricated. For instance, hydrogen and oxygen make water, water and leaves make tea, and tea and bourbon make a hot toddy. Likewise, an insult and pride make anger, loss and attachment make grief, and competition and low self-esteem make jealousy.

The final product, whatever it is—a physical thing, a thought, or an emotion—does not arise except through its relationship to certain conditions or its component parts. It exists only through interdependence. Like our reflection in a mirror, it appears only because we are in front of it. If it were independent, it would appear regardless of whether we were there or not.

Second, this interdependence is subject to constant change. In fact, it is probably safe to say that change is the only constant in life. Think of it—if anything shifts in relation to another thing and everything is inter-dependent, then even the slightest change in one thing changes all. As our physicists argue, this is why, in theory, a butterfly flapping its wings in New York can have an effect on the weather in Tokyo. Likewise, the advent of adolescence can turn a cute, cuddly baby into a miserable teen-ager, sudden praise from the boss can turn loathing into joy, and the self-immolation of a fruit peddler in Tunisia can turn a legacy of tyranny into a movement of hope with ripple effects around the world.

Nothing in life exists in an independent, permanent state. Nothing. Everything from vast empires to tiny apple seeds is made of interdepen-dent and constantly changing parts that wax, wane, and eventually fade away.

In essence, then, life is made up of a constant flux of transitory experiences. They are empty in the sense that they are not permanent or inherently existing in and of themselves and are experienced mostly as a concept, a label, or an interpretation of the mind.

Third, the problem is that we cling to these experiences as if they really are permanent and do exist. This clinging is our hungry spirit speaking—that incessant urge that drives us on—and it is the seed to all of our emotions. When something happens, or when certain causes or conditions arise, they evoke an emotional response. Emotion is an inherent bias that tells us what we like and dislike. Love, greed, anger, joy, sadness, pride, and jealousy are all different forms of like and dis-like, or attachment and rejection. Even indifference, as in not caring, is a reaction, an emotion.

This emotional clinging further distorts and separates us from our experience. Like watching a torch swirled in a circle and seeing it look like a ring of fire, we are fooled, and we solidify the ring as if it were truly real. And so, for instance, we rush to anger when we feel criticized and hold a grudge whether the criticism was intended or not, or we spin a flirtation into a sexual fantasy and even visions of matrimony then hold on to the regret of a lost opportunity when we fail to even reach out.

Look at your body, for example. It is made up of flesh, bones, blood, arms, and legs, but you generalize these constantly shifting interdependent parts by considering it a single "thing" and pasting a label on it. Out of pride and vanity, you fall in love with the idea of the whole and cling to it as permanently existing. Then you spin it out of proportion by becoming obsessed with a flat stomach, a round butt, and a trim physique, so you invest in the gym, diets, exercise regimes, and organic tea to make it fit your idea of beauty. But your body grows old, you lose your beauty, and eventually you die.

Fourth, these clinging emotions come from a basic self-centeredness that arises because we also think of our self as real. We repeat an emotional response each time the same conditions arise (or we think they do), leaving an impression on our minds and hearts like imprints on a page. These imprints then accumulate and form into patterns; these patterns become our habits, ideas, projections, beliefs, hopes, fears, and personality traits that solidify and make up what we believe to be our "selves" and our belief that we —"you", "I"—truly exist. But this is not the real you, this is just the acquired you.

Like the fire ring, you get carried away in thinking this composite of things is the real you. But if you examine all notions of who you are—really investigate them—you will again find just an illusion. When you investigate your body, your feelings, your perceptions, your actions, or your thoughts, you cannot find a truly existing self, or "I," in any of them. This "I" is not your body, your heart, or your brain, nor is it your girlfriend, your home, or your job. You cannot put your finger on it. It is elusive. It's all of those things but at the same time none of those things. These patterns are nothing more than acquired habits, labels, and ways of relating to things that have been shaped and socialized by your parents, friends, media, culture, and so on that you make solid or real.

Like reality itself, then, your sense of self is nothing more than a shifting collection of acquired perceptions, feelings, and beliefs that you hold onto over time. There is no inherently existing "I." The true self is like a vast and expansive palette of open space that has been painted over by the stickiness of "I." In reality, "I" is just another label.

We can also understand this emptiness of "I" by comparing our views to those of others. In some cultures, the public display of bare breasts for instance, is considered an immoral act, while in others it is a thing of beauty. But as we all know, beauty is in the eye of the beholder. What might have made a woman beautiful in ancient China was small feet, whereas in some places in Africa it was a long neck, in North America a curvy figure, and in Central America a round one. Likewise, happiness for some might be delicious food on the table, while for others it is an Audi Quattro, and whereas some consider a gentle touch erotic, others prefer it rough. Who is right?

Our different views of the same thing are shaped in part by our different senses of "I," which in turn are shaped by our cultures, families, and upbringing. They are tightly held habitual patterns that exist at both the individual and collective level and are self-reinforcing. Yet if any of it were real—the way we perceive the world or our belief in "I"—these experiences would be the same for each of us. Nonetheless, we believe them to be real and manage to harden and aggregate them into tribes, cultures, nation states, and other forms of prejudice.

Finally, and here is the most essential point, all this clinging causes suffering. But most of the time we don't even know we are suffering. We are caught up in the illusion we create from our vanity, ambition, and insecurity, that then develops into an excessive pride in our looks, acquisitions, and achievements, and that we run after like a child trying to catch a rainbow in a soap bubble, only to be constantly disappointed. Whatever we do, it is never enough.

As a result, we become the victim of a small mind, a stream of chatter that reinforces an image we already have of ourselves and our world—of wishing, craving, choosing, defending, and deciding right or wrong—and whenever that chatter stops, it is a relief, like the silence that comes after the constant drone of a jackhammer in the background stops. We become tightly spun in a cocoon made of our projections, imaginations, hopes, and fears that makes possibilities much smaller than they truly are. We live behind bars of fear and convention, and we become stuck. We are in a box—and we don't even know that we are in a box.

Thus, out of strong individual and collective habit, you, like me, confine yourself to the safe and narrow. You cling to your cocoon and then suffer when you can't adapt to changing conditions. Every time your perceived reality does not match up with your acquired hopes or desires—all of which you think are real—you suffer. When someone treats you poorly, or you didn't get the promotion, or the cashier is too slow, or your boyfriend does not call you back, you suffer. At times you may even suffer irrationally. You might get angry with your girlfriend because you think she should be angry and is not. Or you might worry that she is too possessive, and then worry again when she isn't. So back and forth you go, whipsawed on emptiness.

On the other hand, you may argue that not all emotion is suffering. What if events go in your favor? What about love and joy? But if you love someone or something, you may fear that they may leave you, that they do not love you as much as you love them, or that you love them too much. So whether it is love, joy, peace, happiness, or another positive emotion, there still remains a seed of discontent. As long as your positive feeling is dependent on someone or something else, there is a basic insecurity about it or a fear that it will not last or that you may lose it. Even if all your dreams come true, that nagging feeling that there should be something more soon returns. It is a suffering of suffering so to speak—a hungry spirit.

In showing us that *"It is not the appearance that binds you, it's the attachment to the appearance that binds you,"*[3] Tilopa gives us not only the view of how we get stuck but also the clue to how to get out and live our lives more fully, because nothing exists as it appears.

The above and the title of this chapter was inspired by Dzongchar Rinpoche's book *What Makes You NOT a Buddhist.* It is framed around what is known as the Four Seals in Buddhism, which form the foundational principles of the spiritual path.

All phenomena are compounded,
Everything compounded is impermanent,
Attachment to impermanence causes suffering,
Nirvana is peace.

If all this makes sense to you, then you just may be a Buddhist.

2

The Cosmic Fool

Let your view be as vast as the sky, and your conduct as fine as barley flour.

PADMASAMBHAVA

There are pitfalls in taking this enlightened approach to life.

After many years of practice, I was still not living it authentically. Why, might you ask? To answer that question, let's step back and unpack the meaning of the above quote.

Self-Deception

Your ego, this hungry spirit of yours, is no different than mine. It is powerful, tricky, subtly evasive, and rarely rests. No matter how pure your intent, its restive tendency still lurches toward turning everything into self-reference. When it does, you easily fall into the trap of self-deception. This is where you think you are getting it, all while still reinforcing your ego and not really growing. It's tough to escape the life-shaping conformities of the ego, even when we believe we are.

Spiritual Materialism

Self-deception starts very simply through what is called spiritual materialism. For instance, you may recently be into yoga and sustainable lifestyles, so you ready yourself with the right mat, the right food, and the right clothes for the inner journey. You find locally made eco-friendly yoga pants as well as yoga props and accessories. You also buy organic teas and beauty and household products and books, along with the other accoutrements of the new lifestyle regime. So you commodify your practice and consume your way to enlightenment. But pure food does not deliver a pure mind, and having organic yoga pants does not necessarily make you a better person.

You may also collect courses, empowerments, retreats, and practices like they were medals and childhood sports trophies, feeding your ever-hungry ego by jumping from one teacher or book to the next like a drunken honeybee flitting from flower to flower. You talk about your latest teacher and pontificate spiritual jargon as if you are selling something. You may even remove yourself periodically from the world to do a deep dive into meditation, but what you are really doing is treating yourself to a short-lived, blissed-out getaway.

You could become so obsessed with your own self-improvement—your story, your victimization, your faults, your fears—that instead of becoming free, you end up caught in an endless self-ruminating loop. I know this one quite well. It is just not true that self-analysis automatically leads to greater health and happiness. At most, it neutralizes them. You are more likely to just self-absorb, proudly wearing your issues like a badge—"this is just the way I am"—or drift into an apathetic self-paralysis—"there is nothing I can do."

More subtly, you could materialize meditation itself. This hungry spirit that strives for peace, calm, and blissful experiences is still none other than your ego looking for itself, constantly searching for something to hold onto. So rather than losing yourself in meditation, the ego self-identifies with the practice of meditation. Instead of "becoming" the meditation, you are "doing" meditation, as an object experienced separately. You are in your mind, not your heart, and so you fail to generate any warmth in your practice. You puff yourself up with pride, find fault with others, cling to spiritual honors, and count up your years of practice without any lessening in your afflictive emotions.

Finally, you may even experience something special, a calm, loving, blissful state, but then you objectify and cling to it as having achieved your goal. You have then just turned it into another concept—in the same way that concepts of illusion, oneness, change, and egolessness become goals. Your ego constantly looks to reinforce itself with something to cling to—especially bliss. It naturally resists letting go of itself and truly experiencing without any agenda.

So it entertains itself by proving you can do certain things, believing you are struggling on the path when the path is not a struggle. Your ego's need for entertainment can take extremely subtle forms. Any time you justify answers, cling to experiences, need to prove or unravel something, try to create or recreate something, or have any fear, hope, loss, or gain around any spiritual experience, you reinforce the ego.

It wants to define the bounds of each of these experiences, like a spider caught in its own web. You need to give up trying to go anywhere or be anything and just be, without any seeking or answer. Only in dropping everything and just being do you experience reality directly, vividly. Otherwise, you ensnare yourself in an interwoven web of identities and subtle strings of self-reference while not even knowing it, like some sort of cosmic fool.

In short, our ego's desire to hold onto its sense of self, a self-consciousness, will use lifestyles, drugs, therapies, and spiritual techniques to reinforce that sense of self, that ego. This is what Trungpa Rinpoche called "spiritual materialism." He said we are often "deceiving ourselves into thinking we are developing spiritually when instead all we are doing is strengthening our egocentricity through spiritual techniques."[1] Enlightenment is not about doing, achieving, and rewarding effort. If it were so, then we would always be subject to ego reasserting itself. *We do not produce enlightenment, we reveal it.*

EXERCISE

Ask your heart, why are you doing a practice in the first place? Are you just creating a spiritual ego?

⊷◉⊶

Spiritual Bypassing

A trickier form of self-deception is spiritual bypassing. This is where you use spirituality to avoid, suppress, or escape an uncomfortable life issue, or where you paste the veneer of a positive spiritual attitude on top of what is still an acquisitive and defensive self-belief. This can never last because under almost any level of stress you automatically default to insecurity and fall back into the ego's defensive mode.

When you do that, you disconnect from yourself as you rationalize your poor behavior based on spiritual beliefs to avoid facing your own fears and insecurities. The difference is so subtle that you usually don't even know you are doing it, and the impact is so powerful that not only can it hurt but it can also nullify spiritual growth.

How does this happen?

My interest in self-deception was first inspired by the work of John Welwood[2] on Abraham Maslow's hierarchy of needs. I had drifted into a certain malaise of "having been there and done that" and was experiencing a growing staleness and loss of inspiration in my practice. I felt stuck, generally alienated, and even hypocritical in certain areas of my life. His commentary gave me some clues as to why.

This hierarchy describes a continuum of a motivational drive that has lesser and greater aspects. It begins at the lesser, lower levels with a sense of deficiency and evolves into the greater, higher levels as a sense of fulfillment. In moving up the hierarchy, we grow from a feeling of self-doubt to one of self-worth, with each stage transcending and including those below.

The bottom three aspects of this drive come from a place of insecurity and lead to the self-protection and self-projection aspects of your being. They tend to be defensive and manifest in negative emotions like anger, selfishness, and jealousy that are based on strong attachments to getting or not getting what you want in the world. It is a necessary function rooted in your *survival instinct*. These qualities can restrict your spiritual journey.

The upper ones, in contrast, come more from a place of well-being. They are made up of positive emotions, such as love, joy, devotion, gratitude, and enthusiasm, that are much more open, inclusive, and outwardly oriented. They broaden your view, connect you to others, extend you into the world, and lead to personal growth and completion. It is a growth toward *selflessness*, designed to help you adapt, and is rooted in your *evolutionary instinct to become more fully functioning in realizing those greater qualities*. Ultimately that drive dissolves altogether upon reaching transcendence, so these qualities help your spiritual journey.

Transpersonal psychologist Ken Wilber calls this drive an evolutionary thread of *spirit in action*, where greater consciousness unfolds at every stage of development in the hierarchy, manifesting more and more at every step in an inherent urge to go beyond what was before.[3]

As we grow up in it, we move from a self-centric to a more open, other-centric view of the world. In so doing, we shift from a place of self-doubt to one of self-worth, all while loosening the grip of the ego. In the end, we don't demolish the ego, *we transcend it* and rest in a fundamental sense of well-being. This is the ultimate aspect of our spiritual journey.

This drive, this evolutionary thread, is our hungry spirit in action, where greater consciousness and acceptance unfold at every stage in an inherent urge to go beyond what was before in pursuit of the spirit, and it ultimately opens to transcendence.

This urge is also the very face and impulse of love. The greater aspect is an awake, selfless love rooted in a sense of abundance and fulfillment, while the lesser is a less mindful, self-centered love of attraction, attachment, and possession based in not feeling enough. *The lesser love strives for the greater through seeking security and comfort, whereas the greater transcends and includes the lesser from an unconditional place of well-being.* As lesser evolves into greater, it provides the psycho-emotional ground for an authentic spiritual practice.

The two indivisible and developmental forces driving this growth are awareness and compassion. There is no unconditional compassion without the awareness of an evolved spirit and no unfettered awareness not based in selfless compassion. Together they are the means and the ultimate ends of spiritual practice.

Growth in this progression, however, is not without its pitfalls. Much of today's self-help and happiness programs, for instance, focus on the self-esteem and other upper levels of this hierarchy. This would be healthy, except where there is not strong ego development at the lower levels. You cannot simply paste positivism on top of underlying insecurities. You cannot pull off patience if you have not owned your anger. The lesser has the stronger grip, so you need release from the lower levels first. Otherwise, you bypass.

For example, do you love out of unconscious attachment or out of a conscious sense of abundance and appreciation? As John Welwood says, the truth is you need to know attachment before you can learn nonattachment. Avoiding attachment and true nonattachment are two different things. If I am attached to something, I need to first identify and own the attachment before I can release it. If not, I bypass and am eventually pulled back. I know both sides of this coin, and with the latter—true nonattachment—there is little residue of self-doubt, resentment, or even hurt. Instead, there is an openness, a richness, and an appreciation.

The pitfalls of bypassing abound, and they are not often enough addressed in the Buddhist tradition. Some examples include:

> Practicing detachment without compassion
> Mistaking indifference for equanimity
> Avoiding connection to sidestep old wounds
> Swallowing anger to be a good person

> Overemphasizing the positive to avoid the negative
> Using reason to escape feelings
> Brandishing spirituality to mask insecurities

In each case, the safety habits of your mind overrule the vulnerable feelings of your heart and you react in neurotic ways.

Instead, you want to align your behaviors authentically with your being and express them in a way which is wholesome, balanced, and authentic. For example, as motivational speaker Jim Rohn said, the paradox of leadership, or psycho-emotional growth in general, is that you want to be:

> Strong but not rude
> Kind but not weak
> Bold but not a bully
> Humble but not timid
> Reflective but not inactive
> Fun without folly
> Proud but not arrogant[4].

In other words, you need to find yourself before you can lose yourself, as the saying goes. If not, the lesser spirit yanks you back in times of doubt and stress. A healthy functioning ego is important for engaging in authentic spiritual practice; otherwise your psycho-emotional growth falls behind your spiritual insight and the shadows follow. You bypass.

Anyone engaged on the path for some time has witnessed this in themselves, in others, and even in some of our gurus.

It is also called premature transcendence, where you try to rise above the raw and messy side of humanness before you have fully faced and made peace with it. Authentic spirituality is not about escaping reality; it is about entering fully into it. Transcendence transcends and includes—not transcends and escapes—what comes before. Otherwise you transcend and deny rather than transcend and own, and what you try to escape comes back and haunts you. It creates a split between where you really are and where you think you should be.

In healthy development, you address both the greater and the lesser, the positive and the negative, the light and the dark; otherwise, all your efforts and progress are short-lived. This makes vulnerability and authenticity central to your practice. As Trungpa Rinpoche said, "before we become the Buddha, we have to become human. Before we wake up, we have to realize we are asleep. And when we face ourselves directly and fully, we soon find we have something to offer."[5]

Only then can true spirituality begin.

Frivolous View, Rigid Conduct

Returning to the opening quote, Padmasambhava forewarned us of all this. *Let your view be as vast as the sky* means to be awake and not automatically assume that our perceptions are as solid as they appear to be. Those perceptions bind us because of our attachment to them. Awareness loosens this attachment, opens other possibilities, and makes situations more workable.

Let your conduct be as fine as barley flour recognizes that we have a living heart and do not live alone. We want to always be compassionate with others. There are also right and wrong actions according to the norms of our world, and our behavior should mirror them in serving the greater good. We might see things as not solid or real, but that does not mean others do.

If you lose your philosophical view in conduct, for instance, you are always accepting and rejecting. You think only in terms of good and evil, right and wrong, and you constantly abide by mindless rules without ever being truly and authentically open as needed in the present. On the other hand, if you lose conduct in the view, then whatever you do does not matter and you become uncaring, frivolous, and undiscriminating. You unmoor from worldly values and relate in a detached way that is not supported in your own development.

So instead of an either/or logic—"Feelings are just perceptions, so it does not matter what I do"—just let that go and accept both: "My feelings are not solid or concrete. They are empty in the Buddhist sense, but that does not mean they do not matter." You balance and integrate both that sense of emptiness with appropriate conduct in your lives to be authentically on the path.

Personal Stagnation

The opening quote has always struck a poignant chord in me but most especially a few years ago. After decades of meditation practice, I felt like I had studied but forgot, I had written but not internalized, and I had practiced but without much change. It was my lament, as I still felt victimized by my impulses, by loves won and lost, and by insights gained and frittered away. Having arrived at the later years of life, I felt stale and stuck. The juice, the warmth, and the joy had gone out of my practice.

Part of this feeling was due to having fallen victim to many aspects of the above. I also felt torn between work that I loved and not wanting to be just my work, needing to pull away from a long relationship that was not working for either of us and then losing two of my gurus at the time who both passed into *Parinirvana* within a short period of time. I needed a renewal.

> *I have alas! Studied Philosophy*
> *Medicine and Jurisprudence too,*
> *And to my cost Theology,*
> *With ardent labor studied through,*
> *Yet here I stand, with all my lore,*
> *A poor old fool, no wiser than before.*
>
> GOETHE'S *FAUST*[6]

PART II

Cracking the Cosmic Egg

3

Introduction to Ayahuasca

*Time to wonder, "Do I dare?" . . . "Do I dare?" . . . disturb
the universe?*

T. S. ELIOT

In the midst of these feelings, I went to Peru on a scouting trip for an
outdoor trek for our university alumni. I was so quickly fascinated by
the culture, architectural achievements, geography, and biodiversity that
I read everything I could about Peru upon my return. Eventually my
interest turned to their native spiritual traditions.

The Three Worlds: Condor, Puma, and Serpent

The indigenous people of Peru believe there are three realms of existence in the human world, symbolically portrayed in the totems of the
Condor, the Puma, and the Serpent. The Condor, the world's largest
bird, with a wingspan of six to ten feet, represents the upper world and
connects us to our spirit, the eternal self above, and it points the way to
ultimate freedom or illumination. The Puma, a four- to-six-foot-long,
black, nocturnal hunter, known for the least ego, represents the middle world of the strength and power of an authentic, manifest self and
serves as the guardian and the embodiment of wisdom in daily life. The
Serpent, the great anaconda of the jungle, represents the underworld of

the inner self and the ability to transmute and transform heavy energy into light through reflection and awareness.

The Three Laws: Love, Service, and Wisdom

The people of Peru also believe that in abiding by the three laws of love, service, and wisdom we align this trilogy of existence with our being. *Love* is the foundation for all three, and it is a love for everything that surrounds us, an open and welcoming acceptance for all of creation. *Service* is the expression of our individual unique gift to offer in this world, a service to the divine in any form whether earth, plant, animal, or human, and returned in reciprocity. *Wisdom* arises when we live with love in service, and it propels us into a consciousness of the divine, where all is one.

I was most intrigued by the Puma, the people devoted to practicing love, self-knowledge, and service in fulfillment of their beliefs, representing a truly integrated and authentic human being.

Ayahuasca

While researching these topics, I learned about the deep shamanic culture and the organic ceremonial psychoactive brew called Ayahuasca that brings the icons of that culture to life. Ayahuasca is better known now to North Americans than it was then. I had experienced hallucinogens in early adulthood but learned that Ayahuasca goes beyond that and induces truly visionary states of alternative realities that feel real and sacred—powerfully and convincingly. There are untested theories that say that instead of adding something to the brain, as in the case of LSD, Ayahuasca releases a visionary molecule, dimethyltryptamine (DMT), that is already there and thus enhances and deepens your normal experience of reality. Whatever the case, it speeds up your brain and makes you "smarter," at least temporarily.

The brew is a combination of two plants that are boiled together for hours. The first contains DMT, but when swallowed alone, a stomach enzyme blocks it. The second plant contains substances that deactivate the enzyme, allowing it to reach the brain. The evidence of Ayahuasca use dates back at least a thousand years. Given the astounding diversity of botanical life in the Amazon, it makes one wonder how this method was ever discovered by an ancient primitive culture. When asked how they know these things, the indigenous people say it came directly from the plants, from dreams, or from observing animals like the jaguar.

People with different cultural backgrounds from across the planet have inexplicably had common visions of the animals of the three worlds, especially the Serpent. Often appearing as a twisting spiral early in the experience, the Serpent taps into something very deep and common to us all. Some claim it is none other than our DNA, something that all life-forms share.

They also report mystical experiences and revelations about their purpose on Earth, the nature of the universe, and how to be the best person they possibly can. It shows them the wounds to heal, which almost always include some aspect of *separation*, *abandonment*, or *shame*, and how to reclaim these disowned parts into a greater sense of well-being and even transcendence. The visionary experience induced by Ayahuasca is commonly viewed as a rebirth or spiritual awakening, and some say they gain access to higher dimensions and beings who act as guides or healers.

The ceremonies are led by a healer, or *Curandero*, who has years of training in working with this plant medicine and its spirits. Its historical use in the Amazon Basin led to the development of mental, physical, and spiritual healing traditions by hundreds of indigenous tribes.

During the ceremony, the Curandero sings *Icaros*, the healing songs they have learned from the plant spirits themselves. These songs are prayers that embody the powers of spirits of plants and animals, ancestors, and elemental forces and channel healing to the participants.

I quickly concluded that Ayahuasca might be the medicine to help me out of my spiritual malaise, so I asked my Tibetan lama for permission to try it. After doing my due diligence, I found a center near Iquitos, in the jungle in northern Peru.

Interestingly, a few weeks after making the arrangement, I received an inquiry out of the blue from Enrique, a Peruvian man wanting consulting help. My eventual work with him would help support my travels there, and I took it as a positive sign for things to come. The synchronicity seemed karmic. I embarked on my first trip with a close friend early the following year.

Preparation and Advice

Preparation for an Ayahuasca ceremony includes a special diet for absorbing the medicine, a safe environment for supporting the visions, and a Curandero, along with a support staff for managing any potential issues. A safe social and physical surrounding is essential for having a productive experience. To help *see* the visions, the Curandero typically conducts ceremonies at night in a darkened teepee-like structure called a *Maloka*.

Choosing a Curandero

In my experience, the Curandero makes *all* the difference. In the indigenous tradition, a Curandero goes through at least eight to twelve years of apprenticeship before ever leading a ceremony on their own. It requires a dedication, a discipline, and a mental fortitude that most people are not evolved enough to hold. It is a noble cause and an honor, so you want someone who is humble, properly trained, and altruistic in motivation. With the growing popularity of Ayahuasca in North America, some who are less qualified now lead ceremonies, so you need to take care in choosing. You especially want to avoid those who may appear attached to the role or obsessed with an image or taking credit for a healing. So examine them carefully before making a choice.

If you feel that you have latent psychological issues, it is also important to consult with the Curandero and others who have experience first, and then make sure you have personal support with you if you do participate. Research shows that Ayahuasca can have a very productive impact on mental health and well-being. In fact, at my very first retreat in Peru, the attendees were disproportionately represented by therapists who had followed their patients to assess the positive outcome for themselves. However, folks suffering from bipolar or schizophrenic disorders or cardiovascular disease, or those who are on antidepressants, *must* consult with the Curandero before ever attending a ceremony.

Working with Fear

Ayahuasca takes you so far out of your reality that it is not for the faint of heart. One Curandero told me he had done over four hundred ceremonies but never once without facing fear. Fear often marks the boundary of our known reality, which Ayahuasca takes you beyond every time. The fear of death and of losing your mind are common. If you can't manage it, then it can overwhelm and dominate the experience.

I instinctively referred to my experience in the feminine, which was probably some Jungian thing but seemed to help. I was told that when in the grip of fear, ask if *She*—Ayahuasca—is there to help; if the answer is no, then visualize throwing a white blanket around the experience. This worked for me. I was also advised to remember to breathe, rub my belly, pour cold water over my head, or ask myself what I am afraid of experiencing. In general, though, my advice is to go with it and trust Her—the medicine is you, your higher self.

Developing Intention

To reap the most from your experience, it is important to have discipline around your intention. Intention has long been stressed as a principal driving force for how anyone experiences their mind on any psychedelic. Ayahuasca opens the mind and frees it from its ordinary patterns, so the mindset with which you enter the experience is crucial for guiding and getting the most out of the experience. This means having a clear question or issue to explore for channeling and guiding your experience. You may have some amazing experiences without intention but miss the progression of revelatory insight that She is there to offer. She responds to what you bring to Her.

In developing an intention, try to maintain a balance between that intention and expectation, and between surrender and engagement. You start by asking what personal challenges or obstacles you face in life because intention cannot transcend where you are right now psycho-emotionally. *She will not go where you are not ready to go—She will not allow you to bypass.*

Then bring that intention to the ceremony and balance your surrender to the experience with this intention. Experiment. If it is off, ask Her what you are overlooking and remain open to changing it in ceremony. You follow what She gives you.

To refine and target the intention over multiple ceremonies, reflect on what comes up after each ceremony and then follow that thread. As you will see, mine evolved over the ceremonies from *How do I fall in love again?* to *What is faith?* to *How do I experience emptiness?* to *Where is compassion?* She answered me each time. But it was a process, and although I share my intentions in the following pages, it is of utmost importance that you work with your own intentions, with where you are right now, and with whatever is most authentic for you at the time. That is the way She works best.

Finally, I should comment about trying to meditate while on Ayahuasca. I have, but it seemed to create a barrier, a mental construct that circumvented the potential for discovering deeper unknowns. So my advice is to let your intention guide your experience and just let it lead where it may.

Progression of Experience

In a series of multiple ceremonies, the typical sequence of experience moves from the *physical* to the *psycho-emotional* to the *spiritual*. You do not advance to the next without resolving to some degree the former. This made sense to me. So you usually start with the nitty-gritty, which may seem less sexy to some but is a prerequisite for later opening. There is, of course, some back and forth, caused in part by the need to clean up unattended patterns and interference from nonceremonial life events. How many ceremonies it takes to progress along this general trend depends almost entirely on your intent, state of mind, and preparation. I experienced this full cycle, and as I walk you through it I will slog through some of my personal stuff before ever getting to the truly spiritual toward the middle and end.

However don't hang on to my experience, as I present it to inspire you to try it on your own. Instead, let Her guide you, as we each get what we need.

Ceremony–Meditation–Reflection

The Curanderos typically separate the ceremonies by one or two days to give you time to take stock and reflect on your experience between sessions. I found this essential—and important for realizing insights otherwise lost or never surfacing because of moving on too quickly to the next ceremony or back to the humdrum of life. I remained quiet and inactive during this downtime. I did a lot of meditation and reflection through journaling and found the three steps—*ceremony–meditation–reflection*—a powerful combination for mining the full depth of the experience. They proved very synergistic, building on and often leading to new insights that were just as important or more than those in the actual ceremony itself.

Finally, I should say that my experience felt more disjointed and chaotic than what I present in the following pages, in which I have connected the dots between the highlights to add clarity to what was indeed an unfolding progression.

With all that as background, I attended my first retreat with Ricardo in the remote jungle of northeastern Peru. Over the next three years, I did twenty-four ceremonies during eight separate retreats. The following narrative is based on extensive notes that I prepared during and right after each retreat.

4

My Experience:
Ceremonies and Reflections

The scariest part of ayahuasca, the thing that scares us the most, is that we might see ourselves.

GERARD ARMOND POWELL

❧ Retreat 1: With Ricardo ❧
How Do I Fall In-Love Again?

Ceremony 1: Connecting
The first ceremony was light on visions and offered nothing deep emotionally or psychologically. However there was a point where I felt She was trying to learn how to communicate with me—like some sort of exchange of information. This is typical, as often it takes one or two ceremonies before the medicine kicks in.

Ceremony 2: Taking Hold
The second one flooded me with geometric forms and codes that were very precise and intricate and at times formed into what seemed a twisting helix, and I wondered whether it was a DNA strand. At one point, I also panicked as I could not breathe when She fully, and almost literally, entered and took full hold in me. I lost control and could not focus.

Toward the end I saw the skin of a jaguar and, for the first time, Her, as She appeared briefly to me as a serpent.

Aligning the Code

It was clear these first two sessions were part of a process of getting to know each other. She was aligning herself with my "code," or my DNA helix, in order to work with me. It was uncomfortable, but over and over the message was to let go, relax, and just go with it.

My resistance made me wonder if my desire for wisdom, or my attachment to it, was blocking me from the very wisdom I sought. Even in my meditation practice, I wondered whether I focus too much on the doer and on controlling the quality of experience without the balance of opening and receiving. Even recognizing that in myself, I still did not know how.

Ceremony 3: No Longer "In-Love"

I struggled with having the right intention. It needs to be authentic for Her to guide, but it is not always obvious. It often needs be detected instead, sometimes even within the ceremony itself. At first, my intention was to become a better, more loving person, but with this ceremony, it became more a question of why I fear falling in love. I was in a relationship at the time, and struggling, verging on breakup.

I had been in love before, but in this relationship I felt loving but not "in-love." I had lost that in-love quality. What was missing was, in part, driven by a feeling of something still missing in myself.

I also felt I had lost my way, as I began to feel disconnected from my lineage and my practice. I had lost that in-love quality there too. I never saw one of my principal gurus again after entering this relationship, and that seemed a karmic signal of things to come.

I recalled that from my early twenties, my life goal was to learn to love. So, I revised my intention to *How do I fall in-love again?* By that I meant, as an outlook, a way of connecting to life in general, and a way of coming fully alive again.

Ceremony 4: Physical Healing and "How Do I Fall In-Love Again?"

This ceremony was a little weird because there was a young man having a bad trip. With the disruption, there was little space for having an introspective experience.

However, as I left the Maloka, I nearly passed out from vertigo as my blood pressure had dropped so low that I needed to sit down. I had stopped taking my blood pressure medications for two weeks prior to the retreat, but now I was suffering from it being too low. So even though it was not apparent, She had been working with me physically. In sharing this with Ricardo, he said that Ayahuasca is always working at multiple levels whether we are fully aware of it or not.

She did not arrive visually until after I was finally back in bed in the bunkhouse, still tripping. There, as I gazed up into the mosquito net above me, She appeared as the serpent curling up as a holograph on my chest with her long neck arching up and her head looking down at me. I then had the chance to ask my question, "How do I fall in-love again?"

She responded, "Through me."

There Are No Secrets

I realized that there are no secrets, no hiding from Her. She is none other than my conscience, always there but now more apparent than ever. She is my innate wisdom, and She will catch me every time in my self-deception and force me to look at and clean up my gaps and inconsistencies. Of course, She is none other than me, and it was an important fact to remember again and again. We are not separate.

She warned that there are never any absolute answers to my questions, that the answers will only bring more questions. However deep I am willing to go, the more willing I am to confront the unknown and ask, the more I would gain from this experience.

✦ Retreat 2: With Alonso ✦
Psycho-Emotional Healing: Love and Discontent

I did not connect well with Ricardo, the Curandero of the first retreat. He seemed to lack the caring and relatability that I felt a person in his position should have and that my Buddhist gurus radiated. It raised some doubt.

I was willing to try again but not with him. I started to look around and asked Duilio, a potential guide for the alumni trek I was still organizing. He referred me to Alonso, near Pisac in the Sacred Valley of Peru.

Although traditionally trained, Alonso does not lead a traditional ceremony. He sings only a few traditional Icaros and does his own creations instead, along with adaptations of other North American songs. He sings in Spanish and in English, plays multiple instruments, and is always accompanied by other musicians. For me, this was a very special and comforting feature of his ceremonies. I was amazed at how, through the selection of his songs, he could judge at any moment exactly where the group was in the ascent, peak, and descent of their experience. When the medicine peaked, he would sing his root Icaro in Quechua, the indigenous language, and it always intensified everything and pushed us a little further. To this day, I fondly recall his music.

There were not many visionary experiences in this retreat, as my mind and heart instead focused almost entirely on the relationship that ended mutually before the retreat. As I said earlier, this may seem mundane and not very spiritual but, in the end, it was a necessary first step in the process of working with Her.

As the outcome of my first retreat was wanting to learn *how to fall in-love again*, I felt exploring my experience in romantic love was the right intention to bring to the ceremony. It seemed perfect, almost fated.

Ceremonies 5–8: I Am Not My Identities

The four ceremonies of this retreat merged around a recurring theme of the emptiness of my personal identities. I saw myself as a shiny protective shell, made up of various accumulated roles and identities that obscured a deeper aspect and protected me from being vulnerable and relating authentically. I realized that shell was my veil, my façade, my cocoon.

These identities formed like bubbles, floating around against a backdrop of a deep, vast, and starlit night sky. They included being a father, a partner, a lover, a friend, a Buddhist, a writer, a coach, a teacher, a loner, a rebel, a traveler, and on and on with so many others. They clouded my vision, and I yearned to just pop them so I could dissolve into the inviting and soothing vastness beyond. Yes, I realized that they were in fact just empty and without substance, but still, I could not get beyond them.

I was still in a shell where I felt I could "see" the emptiness but not experience it, because of the many habits of identity that obscured the deeper part.

Here it is important to define what is meant by *emptiness*, because it becomes a central theme. From the Buddhist point of view, emptiness means that any thought or perception of phenomena is void of any inherent identity or existence except for what we attribute to it through our own mental projections. A tree is not a tree unless we label it so. The thought of a tree is an accumulated habitual pattern learned from our language, culture, and life experience but possessing no separate, inherent identity of its own. There is no "'tree-ness"—it is just as it is without the veil of any socialized mental interpretation or projection. This is true for all of our experience.

Bypassing and the Dichotomies of Self

My reflections during most of the retreat focused on how these identities played out in experiencing love in my life and on my intention of *How do I fall in-love again?* Inspired by the insights of John Welwood,

I found myself bypassing.[1] For much of my adult life, I had felt split in making choices between the lesser and greater parts of myself on the hierarchy of needs—always aspiring to the greater me, but often pulled back by the lesser because that was where I was. Torn by this dynamic, I did not see things with fresh eyes or meet the world vulnerably. I felt fragmented and inauthentic, split between two parts of myself that played out in multiple ways.

Love and Dependence. It was obvious that I had lost my vulnerability, most poignantly in relationships but also in other aspects of my life. It was rooted in an abandonment issue from having lost two of my three most dominant adults in childhood. It was something I thought I had long overcome. Now, in this retreat, I realized that instead of loving, I was still proving myself and covering up the pain with a shiny protective shell of my identity while withholding any real connection. I had lost genuine openness in both relationship and spirituality. In relationships, I developed a distancing to protect myself, most poignantly so in romantic relationships. In spirituality, I lost sight of being vulnerable and instead became puffed up in pride and confidence.

I developed the façade of the impeccable me, always making myself right and others wrong. Some of it was based in fear insecurity—shrink into a cocoon, avoid meeting new people, speak up in a group, be quiet when the truth hurts, and withhold rather than engage. Some of it was based in the opposite, a feeling of entitlement and being dismissive, prideful, elusive, noncommittal, and nonresponsive. The whole package resulted in a tendency toward quietism and independence that I often excused as my desire for freedom. The irony is that it was a cover.

Security and Freedom. I felt torn between the need for security and belonging on the one hand and the need for freedom and transcendence on the other. I looked for the former in relationship before finding it myself. I had bypassed security in my reach for freedom and that bypassing held me in place emotionally, spiritually. What I sought in a romantic relationship, I needed to first find in myself—and once found, I could move on.

Clinging and Distancing. I conflated my feeling of abandonment with attachment and all the lost loves of my life. I never dealt with it authentically. In younger years, abandonment manifested as clinging and neediness. In later years, it turned into more of a feeling of engulfment. So I moved from clinging to distancing. I felt the attachment to close ones as an afront to my "need for freedom." I felt claustrophobic, in a way, and so I distanced and judged based on serving a perceived higher goal.

Authenticity and Self-Deception. I did retreats and assumed they would impact my life automatically. I was lazy. My practice became part of my self-deception instead of a source of opening, learning, and growth. I espoused authenticity but my kindness often came from a place of insecurity rather than a genuine desire to do the right thing. This is disingenuous and inauthentic. The real point is to learn to love, to accept, to open, and to be kind because that is the ultimate and only truth and the definitive expression of our deepest gift.

Relationship and Spirit. I sought romance and spiritual practice but used the lack of relationship as an excuse for not fully stepping into it. It split me in two—part of me wanted to wake up and another part wanted to go to sleep in the arms of my partner. I felt fragmented. Without integrating a loving relationship with spiritual practice, I undermined myself as a lover, as a servant, and as a person. These three—love, service, and wisdom—the very laws of being in this indigenous tradition, have never been aligned in me.

Integration—Love and Awakening

But something also moved in the breakup. Somewhere during the relationship's gradual demise, I also learned to grow and to move closer to loving unconditionally. The ceremonies woke up something that had been percolating in me for a while. It was like I suddenly discovered that I had long worn out an old shoe—*I had to keep breaking my heart until it opened.* This was clear from how the breakup unfolded. I remained open through it, and that showed me that I had learned to love and hurt in appreciation simultaneously. I took that as a blessing.

It felt clean. There was no residue, there was no pining, and there was no obsessing about it. I even felt relieved. This told me that I might have finally dissolved the remnants of abandonment. I left the Peace Corps out of abandonment, I married out of abandonment, I left my home out of abandonment, and I indirectly stayed with this relationship too long out of abandonment. But now all that felt dissolved, and I no longer felt compelled to be in a relationship at all. Even that was gone. I felt secure and happy in my being.

This was a long time coming; it's not like I, or She, just flipped a switch and it was done. It was the culmination of a long process of healing that came to fruition in this retreat. It felt like I had resolved what had stopped me from fully stepping onto a genuine spiritual path and resolution had already begun to flow into other parts of my life. I felt liberated from a lifelong burden. I wrote the following to myself:

Journal Entry

That the sadness sometimes found in my eyes is because I will never find home with the echo of freedom always ringing in my ears. I drew life's hermit card, with a touch of sadness. I am both the servant and the seeker of the servant. This is my path.

Recap

In these first eight ceremonies, it seemed She was helping me identify and work through what the Buddhists call cognitive and emotional obscurations. These are habitual patterns of thought and emotion that we cling to as truth but that really have no inherent existence at all. I am not my identities (cognitive obscuration), nor did my father abandon me (emotional obscuration). I knew this intellectually before but now more viscerally with this experience. I had internalized it in some way.

Post-Retreat Reflection: The Crack in the Cosmic Egg

The theme of identities reminded me of *The Crack in the Cosmic Egg,* a book by Joseph Chilton Pearce that I read years ago and had not fully understood at the time.[2] I read it again sensing it was important, and it proved helpful.

From Pearce's perspective, there is no ultimate or universal truth other than the reality-creating function and thought process of the mind. That function is a co-emergent, mirroring process where the realities we discover are just temporary, partial truths, driven in part by the intention driving the discovery process itself. There is no a priori ultimate truth except emptiness, which is where the search ends. In the meantime, whatever truth we find is a temporary construct determined by the interplay of our intention, the perception of our reality, and where we are in our development. What we look for determines what we find, and what we find reinforces the nature of our looking. A change in worldview, for instance, changes the world viewed, so the interchange is self-verifying, circular, and mirroring.

This makes us the determinator, the maker of our own reality. The resulting form of that reality-shaping process is our *Cosmic Egg*—a net of fabricated illusions of both individual and collective norms and identities constructed through our life experience and our socialized way of being. We are dependent on that egg for creating and understanding our reality, and without its fabrications we fear collapsing into a perceived chaos. It makes us smaller than our potential allows.

To crack that egg and break up that reality requires a great deal of courage because to do so threatens our very identity and sense of the self. It demands an undivided focus that risks the ultimate question of who we are and opens us to being seized by something unknown. As such, it requires a powerful and compelling intention and confidence see beyond what is known.

.Pearce says that to do so requires seclusion from the current context to develop an undivided discipline focused on a passionate belief—a complete surrender to the seeking function itself, not knowing what will be found. Taking a leap of faith to leave the habituated self behind is the only way to freedom and the only way to break up the barrier of the mind-made construct of our Cosmic Egg.

This is the reason that a singular focus and discipline based on faith, or devotion, as I know it in Buddhism, is so important. A more ambiguous way simply does not make the crack. It is necessary to have faith and devotion in this discovery process, and to ultimately center that devotion and faith in the function of faith and devotion itself. In cracking the egg, you give your life over, your way of knowing and identifying, in order to find a greater life.

It's the same message as before—you need to lose yourself to find yourself.

✦ Retreat 3: With Alonso ✦
Faith, the Serpent, and a Crack in the Cosmic Egg

Pre-Retreat Reflection: God Does Not Hear an Empty Cry

Following this theme, early in midlife I attended a personal development workshop in the Canadian wilderness where everyone was asked to take a pseudonym in place of their real name. The purpose was to choose something meaningful that revealed something about you without saying anything else about your personal identity.

I picked the name "Job" based on the character in the Bible because I found the story of his unyielding faith in the face of devastating loss inspiring. In the end it turned out to be a prophetic choice, because soon after, and for the next three to five years of my life, I felt I was on the verge of losing everything—spouse, home, wealth, job, even children. So, inspired by where I was in my process with Her, I decided to write about Job.

The key questions of this story are how can we ultimately judge what is truly fair given the limits of our understanding, and how can we as mortals know more than what our life experience allows? Every spiritual tradition makes clear that wisdom lies beyond reason and makes a folly of the hope and fear that dominate our beliefs, our actions, and our reality. Such things make up the first line of defense of our ego, our hungry spirit, our Cosmic Egg, and represent the very things that a genuine spiritual path tries to overcome.

In Job we find that we should bear not in reason but in something that can break through it—a faith and confidence in "God." There is a profound difference between hope and faith. In hope, we cry out in blame, judgment, and pride when things go wrong, whereas in faith, as a genuine child of "God," we trust even though we do not understand. Job never really asks for relief, only for understanding.

Job's accusers themselves become the self-deceivers in this story. They cannot know "God" because they do not yet know themselves. Just because they can recite strings of proverbs, it does not guarantee them wisdom. They may understand the words but not the deeper meaning. They trust the boundaries of their minds but dare not plumb the unknowable depths of their hearts. This is spiritual materialism in the Christian tradition.

To simply obey the laws of "God" or to make "God's" wisdom into laws is to confine them to words and doctrine and not be open to an *authentic belief* or to entering a true relationship with "God." In a genuine spiritual path, there are no laws, only a communion with "God." That communion is not based on the hopes and fears of our ego, but rather on a faith in the wisdom of a greater mystery, a belief in a much vaster way of being and understanding. It requires a great deal of trust and courage to break the boundaries of the ego.

"God" begins where the limits of our understanding end. If we need an explanation or an appeal to reason, we are not a true believer, or someone who trusts. For "God" does not hear an empty cry, only faith.

Based on these reflections, my intention coming into this retreat was relax, let go, and have faith in Her and in the process.

Ceremony 9: Like a Dream

The feeling of all my perceptions being energetic, sensory clumps dominated my ceremony. I wondered whether they were the clumps of the six
senses as known in Buddhism. They were like the bubbles of the earlier retreat but less defined. I could feel them as transparent, cloud-like
veils blocking the experience of a deeper way of perception, of reality. In
Buddhism, our senses are conduits for the perception of reality but not
reality itself, and those perceptions are clouded by the habitual patterns
of the mind. I wondered if that was what I was experiencing.

As before, I again had glimpses of a deep starlit space beyond—a
vast emptiness—but they were few. It felt deeply soothing, like home
and where I wanted to be.

In that longing, at the end of the ceremony I had a vision of peeking
under the scales of the serpent to see and feel Her.

Ceremony 10: Becoming the Serpent

As the medicine kicked in, the serpent appeared and swallowed me. I
was inside, floating in a vast space of undulating geometric forms. I just
went with it. I trusted Her.

I tried to blend with Alonso's music, to become one with it, to listen
without being a listener. Much of the time, I felt completely at one with
the chords. I had no strong sense of self—there was nothing but the
music, and without the music there was nothing. I blended and mixed
with all of it.

Then I noticed a fluttering on my bottom lip. It felt like the serpent's tongue, and I realized I had blended with the serpent, with
Her—*I became the serpent*. It was like she had instructed me to meld
with the music so that I could become Her. It felt like a seduction. My
skin grew cold and clammy, like the way the scales of a reptile might
feel, and my body undulated as that of the serpent.

She then announced, "Now we can go places together."

I started to panic. I felt I was going to lose myself, and that if I did,
I would not come back the same. It felt a little dark. I pulled back, but

She remained with me, and with that, I was happy and confident in Her again.

As the medicine wound down, I felt mutable, and I thought it pointed to what I thought might be egolessness, or some level of it. In tasting it, I became a serpent, but if I could become a serpent, I could become anything—the music, the silence, a rock.

In the end, I realized that *through faith, or belief, She appeared.*

Faith, Devotion, and Full-Hearted Surrender

Given my intention coming in, I was now convinced that only with full-hearted surrender does one crack the egg. *My heartfelt intention created an out-of-the-box experience.* Only with trust, true belief, and genuine devotion in a wisdom not yet experienced does this happen. It does indeed require a leap of faith to break through the reality-creating function of the mind.

> *All phenomena come from circumstances,*
> *Circumstances rely on intention.*
> *So therefore, whatever one wishes,*
> *As it is wished, the result will come.*
>
> UNKNOWN BUDDHIST AUTHOR

Now, despite initial doubts, the synergies between Buddhism and Ayahuasca seemed real. Without the frame of Buddhism, I would not be able to understand, inform, or direct such a compelling experience.

In speaking with Alonso, he said that not many have this kind of experience with the serpent, but he agreed that if you can become the serpent, you can become anything. He warned me to use this experience for gaining greater consciousness and not to venture into shamanism.

He also advised that when I feel I am about to lose myself, my self-concept, to just go with it and trust Her. This is the same advice of my lamas—let the experience simply be and not inform another identity.

This challenge of surrender—through trust, belief, and devotion—now feels key to everything.

✦ Retreat 4: With Alonso ✦
Learning to Fall "In-Love" Again, and How to Meditate

This was a pivotal retreat for me. My intentions entering were:

Emptiness: I want to experience emptiness fully—or whatever this "God" thing is.

Genuine faith: Am I still being driven by the desperation of a childhood wound or by genuine faith? A desperate search rests in looking in a blind, directionless way. A faith-based search rests in trust, looking in a direction for an eventual outcome or revelation, even if not known.

Ceremony 11: Learning to Fall "In-Love" Again

I was trying to relax my mind when about two-thirds of the way through the ceremony my old relationship popped back into my head. It was as if my subconscious said, "You still have more emotional healing to do."

Healing, Integration, and Authenticity

Her process does not work unless you "do the work" too. I was still rationalizing my role and now realized that no matter how self-justified I might feel, I was still not innocent. I was not always authentic, in a way that was self-deceptive. The real question is not about whether the relationship was the right choice or not; it is about making a choice and being transparent in doing so.

Intimacy demanded that I be clean and authentic. Our connection somehow compelled it, and all the synchronicities around it are a testament to authenticity. It was a gift. If I were completely authentic with her—my lover, my friend, my alter ego—I would be free to pursue my path with a clear, undivided heart. In compelling me to be clean with her, she compelled me to be true to me. Even though in the end we came at our mutual understanding from two different points of view, her gift to me was to keep me honest and challenge me to be real everywhere in my life—to be genuinely authentic.

The Cosmic Mirror

This realization helps explain why some are more unaffected by self-deception while others are not. I have witnessed that when someone has little conscience, their self-deception is rarely mirrored in their actions, at least not immediately or in the short term. They seem immune because there is no inner trigger to respond differently. But I do have a conscience, a trigger, a wisdom, an inner guide, and when I don't follow it, the world conspires to point it out.

Sometimes it feels a little supernatural, as in the synchronicity of an unknown and untraceable earring magically showing up in my bed as I was thinking of pulling away, or the inexplicable and never-repeated instance of the word "child" appearing in the electronic display of my microwave after thinking about giving up and just staying in the relationship. The thing I realized is that it was really me pulling that karmic chain of reaction. As Einstein said, "God does not roll dice." There are no pure accidents. My conscience causes my self-deception to arise in these "signs" that reflect back my guilt. My reality is my mirror. I should feel fortunate, as I was awake enough to see it.

This is also true about Her, Ayahuasca. She is me, my inner wisdom guiding me. She is my "straitjacket" for being and remaining authentic and true to me.

Trungpa Rinpoche called this dynamic the "*Cosmic Mirror.*"[3] When we align a wakefulness with virtuous perspective, the phenomenal world gives us messages—our wisdom reflects it back. When we take that leap of faith of *basic goodness*, the world becomes a bank of richness with synchronicities showing the way.

This mirroring only happens when heartfelt intention is aligned with deed. It is a discipline of attunement with that "in-love" feeling, our basic goodness, and a renunciation of the ego through a practice of vulnerability and being raw and on the edge. It is a practice of relaxing, being aware, telling the truth, and letting basic goodness shine through to let what should happen, happen.

When our ego interferes and tries to manipulate or ignore the situation, the store of basic goodness is sealed up in a vault. Our insecurities lead us to believe we are incapable of living our lives properly, so our hungry spirit intervenes. We end up fooling ourselves by faking it or trying to manipulate the circumstance. When we automatically make things either right or wrong, feel hope and fear, and act from a place of need or deprivation, we solidify and make our world smaller. We self-deceive.

Instead, we can stay open and act according to the moment. Integration of the messy parts is not about aligning mind, word, and deed. It is first and foremost about aligning our vulnerability with our authentic being, our essence. From there, we let our hearts and synchronicities guide action.

In-Love Again

Then there is no going back. It becomes subconscious and you cannot control it. As Alonso pointed out, once we start, our world turns upside down because it affects everything—thoughts, actions, words. So let go, and let this life take its course.

This what faith and devotion are about too—trusting my inner wisdom to the point of just letting the façade drop and being fully me, fully vulnerable. Through devotion—this belief in our own basic goodness—we merge with our wisdom mind, with Her, and slowly the blessings, the karmic synchronicities, come. Just like when we put our finger in water and it gets wet, so too if we invest in our mind in wisdom, it reveals our wisdom nature. Our ordinary mind dies and dissolves and our pure awareness, our Buddha nature, our inner teacher emerges.

I don't think I have ever felt more genuine, more open, or more at peace.

Everything feels so fresh, vibrant, alive, and peaceful in my meditation. Have I ever experienced this before? Is this the answer to my question, my very first intention?

I first noticed a shift in my walking meditation that would blossom later, and was stimulated by a post-ceremony high and a little coca leaf tea. I was reading a Buddhist text and decided to try to balance the perception of seeing with the perception of the seen, of the apprehender and the apprehended, and of the subject and the object to create a sense of evenness between them. As I did, I noticed it resulted in a certain emptiness, a certain bliss. This union, or evenness, brought an open and compassionate feeling.

Just as the Buddhist teachings say, everything manifests as the union of *yab-yum*, masculine and feminine, perceiver and perceived, and in that union or one taste, a joy, a bliss, a compassion arose spontaneously. This was truly my experience.

I felt I had fallen in-love again—that fresh, vibrant, and fully alive feeling I had been seeking since the first ceremony. From such a place as this, how could anyone not be naturally good and motivated to do good in the world?

Ceremony 12: Letting Go and Listening

Although the visions were strong, there was not much in the way of a theme. I spent the session trying to meditate on being without ego. Over and over again I tried to reach the subtlety of egoless state of mind, but "I" was always there, even if barely so. I felt I just did not know how.

Then She returned, so I asked her how to meditate. Her answer was "listen passively," with pure reception, without a doer—not only with the ears but with all my senses, all my thoughts: body, speech, and mind. It was a very subtle instruction of letting go and surrendering my impulse to control.

Since the experience of abandonment in childhood, I have learned to always be in control. I coped by being strong, disciplined, and independent, and it affected every aspect of my life. Even in my early meditation retreats, my blood pressure would rise and I would get headaches, because I was going to master this meditation "thing." Even as I tried to lower it, through exercise and diet, I was still controlling, and nothing changed. I felt damned if I did and damned if I didn't.

Control was how I survived. Now, She was saying "let go." To transcend, the hungry spirit needs to let go, even of itself.

At the end of the ceremony, I saw a black puma grow larger and larger as it approached and entered me. As the symbol of the authentic manifest self, I thought this may be emerging in me.

Ego Chasing

In trying to meditate on emptiness, I felt I chased my ego all over the Maloka to no avail, seeing just how subtly elusive it really is and the many ways it manifests. It was a useful exercise but still not egolessness, not emptiness. There was still a driver, a doer, a controller, an ego. I was still in charge.

There are many faces of the ego, and it works in many ways to get attention. It would rather be right than at peace—to stand out, be special, be in control, and be in power. It is never enough because it never feels like enough. It is governed by fear, the fear of being nobody. It attaches and clings. It wants attention but fears disapproval. If it cannot get positive attention, it seeks negative attention, as in playing the victim. It does not seek an end to its problems because the problems are part of its identity—its entertainment—so it repeats its sad story over and over.

So is suspending this need to control as simple as listening, as She said? First, I feel She showed me how to mingle and mix with my perceptions, and now, to help my meditation, She is telling me that to fall "in-love" again, I need to just listen.

Listening

Thich Nhat Hanh often said deep listening, listening to your own experience, is a sacred activity and a form of surrendering, receiving, letting in. He said that *to love is to listen*. Feeling is a form of listening. Feeling is different than emotion—it has a separate intelligence. The word *compassion*, for instance, literally means "feeling with." We cannot have compassion unless we are willing to listen, to feel what we feel, to have an unconditional presence in what we feel.

There is a Buddhist metaphor, "The finger pointing at the moon is not the moon." The finger is needed to know where to look for the moon, but if you mistake the finger for the moon, you never know the real moon. The finger here is the method, the meditation pointing to mind, but not wisdom mind. It is conditioned mind pointing to wisdom mind. Do not get caught in the method; let go. Getting caught in the method, of course, is an aspect of spiritual materialism.

This is my challenge in seeking an experience of emptiness—I am getting in my own way. I am still pointing to the moon, and She is trying show me how to drop it, to relax and to just simply listen.

Recap

I was having some of my deepest meditation experiences during this time. I don't know if it was the medicine, the coca tea, Her instruction, or a combination of everything. Everything seemed lighter, smoother—like glass—and even smoky at times as I simply rested in awareness itself. It felt like becoming fundamentally and authentically me, and as long as I am true to me, then I can not go wrong in my choices.

Ceremony 13: Learning How to Meditate

I took a second dose, and I was so overwhelmed I was nauseous. It lasted well over six hours, which made me think that I was absorbing the medicine more and more. I saw images of the Condor and of Christ but was not sure what to make of either. My intention returned to asking about meditation.

Am I back in control and not truly letting be?

Should I just be more patient?

Pointing-Out Meditation

She continued to point to a different way of meditating, saying something like, "When the energies of perception, the perceiver (the masculine) and the perceived (the feminine), meet equally, then everything appears through bliss (in-love). Then rest in that bliss." To experience this in meditation, then, I balance intention with receptivity, and I rest in the resulting open, vibrant space.

I have been stuck in my meditation because of this. I have been driven by the doer, by control, by the masculine, and it even at times gave me headaches. She tells me to balance that masculine with the feminine and to perceive everything though the bliss of that union.

With that, She had gradually guided me through this progression of experiences to point this out, moving me

from doing → to mixing → to listening →
to balancing → to resting in place

in working with these subtle energies. These energies of *feminine-masculine–bliss*, of course, correspond to *space–energy–bliss*, the three aspects and modes of being and the essential nature of mind in the Buddhist canon.

In effect, She was showing me how to meditate *without the conditioned ordinary mind of subject and object*, of me and it, even if subtly so, and instead to *rest in the pure unconditioned nature of mind itself, the wisdom mind beyond subject and object.* There is a profound difference, which, of course, I knew this intellectually, but She walked me through it experientially.

Resting in Pure Wisdom Mind

Our practice is first to recognize this essence of this union, and then rest in it. It is not meditation—it is nonmeditation! Meditating is conceptual and doing something. Instead our practice is simply allowing, experiencing our empty and cognizant nature just as it is. We recognize our natural essence and rest in undistracted nonmeditation.

There is nothing to do other than to train in being stable in our natural essence. Tulku Urgyen said it is like ringing a bell. If you ring a bell, there is a continuity of sound—you do not have to do anything for the sound to continue. You simply allow that continuity to endure by itself until at some point it fades away. You do not do anything. You just leave it as it is. Then ring the bell again—short moments repeated many times. It is not a willed or controlled act.

Thus it is more like remembering or recollecting your natural essence and then letting it be. It is not abiding in stillness or quietude because there is still an observer and the observed. Any preoccupation with being calm or blissful blocks the recognition of this self-existing wakefulness. The observer and observed disappear.

Recap

In my first experience with the medicine, I asked, "how do I learn to fall in love again?" I experienced it on this retreat, and She showed me a way. She continued to help me clean up and be skillfully on a genuine path in an authentically present way. Then She showed me how to meditate by not meditating. I had had this instruction before, and maybe this was just recall, but nonetheless I had never experienced it so viscerally. I felt incredibly grateful.

✦ Retreat 5: With Rafa ✦
On the Brink of Emptiness and Holograms

This was a short retreat I attended in Atlanta. It was conducted by Rafael, an apprentice of Ricardo, whose retreat I first attended in Iquitos and with whom I felt a heart connection.

Ceremony 14: On the Brink of Emptiness

The effect of the medicine seemed light and it made me wonder if I should be more specific in my questions rather than trying to experience egolessness or emptiness. But I had no other real questions to ask—I just wanted to experience this, or, in other words, feel a sense of oneness.

Although not fully, I at least felt on the brink of it. On that edge, the colors exploded like a gentle but enormous, richly colorful waterfall, and I felt on the cusp of entering a whole new reality, a more spiritual realm than what I have experienced so far.

Ceremony 15: Holograms—She Is Me

This ceremony was a long, slow crescendo that, like that of the previous night, lasted much longer than my experience of others of the past. I visualized my chakras and my being as a star-filled body. This led to feeling invisible, like a dark shadow, hologram, or ghost. Then I started to experience my outer world in a similar way—empty, spacious, and holographic. It reminded me of the Buddhist visualization practices where the body merges with external reality and begins to disappear, like a body of light without flesh. I remained open to this, but it was flashy and not sustained. I facilitated it by incorporating my new lessons in meditation, and I felt good about being able to do this.

Although She was strongly present, She did not appear visually. It felt as if we had merged, and She was me—my wisdom source. When in doubt, I would supplicate the divine source to receive answers, who is the same as She and none other than Me—we are all one and the same.

I saw bird heads, bird wings, and yellow snake eyes. I also saw a black puma's head—the symbol of authenticity—that slowly turned into a marble sculpture and then into a shiny black marble ball. Physically, mentally, I felt wonderful afterwards.

Living Cleanly

I want to be conscious about keeping things clean. If not, insecurities build and the self-deceptions again catch me in the ceremony. In living cleanly, the experience deepens. My conduct and attitude are interdependent with my experience with Her. *It is a reminder to remain authentic.* It feels clean now except for the subtle, almost subconscious clouds that appear in my viewing of the great space. Yet if I remain disciplined, this view of space will clear up too. It feels like I am approaching a genuineness, an authentic presence that is open, raw, and vulnerable.

✦ Retreat 6: With Alonso ✦
Completion, Emptiness, Authentic Presence, and My Path Is Buddhism

A Sign of Well-Being

For years, I have had a recurring dream about my house, how it was always unfinished, needing constant repairs to the foundation or having something further to fix. Dream after dream, I was trying to make it the way I wanted, but there was always something left and more to do. Just before this retreat, I had a variation on this dream. With the help of others, I had finally brought my house to a point of completion. My family asked me why I was still pushing to make myself better. They insisted that they liked the way I am.

Am I already where I want to be, clean? I have not had that dream since then. In fact, all my other recurring dreams of falling, flying, and not finding my way home, among others, have also disappeared. I felt it a sure sign of healing and wellness.

A Sign of Illness

Just prior to this retreat, I was suffering from constipation that had slowly built up over a few weeks and culminated in a total stoppage. I took a laxative, but to no avail. I am very regular and had not suffered from this since decades before, in the Peace Corps. I looked for probable causes, and one of them was colon cancer. This brought up a great fear of death, which at times felt strangely exhilarating. I entered the retreat with this concern on my mind.

Ceremony 16: More Physical Healing

It was a slow start, so I took another dose and experienced modest visions with flashes of jewelry, ornaments, and headdresses that seemed to be of the ancient Incan culture. My intention was to ask if I was sick, and what, if any, other issues were still holding me back that I needed to uncover, unlock, or resolve.

Even though I could feel Her presence, She barely answered any of my questions. She said that She had already answered my questions around emotional healing and meditating and that She would answer the one about being sick later.

Only after I returned to the bunkhouse did it become clear that she was healing me during ceremony. Toward the end, Alonso started to play bells that made me nauseous, like something was being pulled out of me. Even though it is common, I had never thrown up before in ceremony. As I sat alone in the kitchen, I started to dry heave violently. This ended with a single burp that brought up a little sweet-sour-tasting spittle in a color that I imagined to be pink. My first thought was that it was poison, and I spit it out into a bucket. Within minutes, my bowels moved, and I was normal afterward. I felt I had purged something.

Increasing Access

I now feel Her presence often. It feels like a combination of personal well-being and a subconscious wisdom that has gradually surfaced through ceremony, meditation, and reflection.

This may be what She meant by *"Now we can go places together"*— She is there, I can call on Her, and we can find answers together. It is almost as if there are no boundaries, and She is now awake and available. I also realize that to keep it so demands a regular practice discipline.

Listening, letting in, and balancing all proved to be important adjustments to my practice. My heart just jumps now when I have that balance, allowing that "in-love" feeling to arise that I felt missing in my very first retreat with Her. I feel that that "in-love" feeling—bliss—can now become self-abiding. I do not need any other circumstances for it.

Ceremony 17: Completion, a Full Taste of Emptiness, and Authentic Presence

This ceremony was the peak experience for me among all twenty-four.

Before the session, I sat in the Maloka and a wave of love and brokenheartedness swept over me. I started to weep. I felt affirmed about being on the right path. In everything I was doing, the message was the same—I was on the right track with what I had learned through Her and through doing the right things. I was so happy that I began to sing.

I took two doses, and my experience lasted six to seven hours. It started with a vision of a bird's eye that transformed into a black puma, and finally to a black puma-like head that I had seen before. As I mentioned in the introduction, the puma is a symbol of integration and authenticity, and of one who works in service to their beliefs. This is the way I felt. I am a little embarrassed to point this out, but I need to honor Her and my process by making that connection.

We then engaged in a dialogue, recapping the lessons of healing, authenticity, and meditation. With that, She told me my psycho-emotional work was done, complete. She had shown me how to heal, how to practice, and now told me I was good to go on my own. Our work was done.

Not ready to accept that message, I tried throughout the rest of the session to engage Her with different questions and tactics but there was nothing, only light shows. I grew frustrated and asked why. Her response was *"This is not your path. Your path is Buddhism."* She helped me prepare psycho-emotionally and spiritually, but Ayahuasca was not my way.

Nonetheless, in returning to the kitchen in the bunkhouse later, alone and still tripping, I sat down, and the visions exploded. I felt as if I was in another realm. Her presence so strong. I was Her again, but it was so frenetic it was hard to keep focus, as there was no music, no Alonso as an anchor. I was beyond my normal reality, beyond my Cosmic Egg.

To help settle down, I prepared a cup of chamomile tea and took a few sips, and I felt worse. So I drank a little water instead, hoping for a better result—and then

> *I became the water.*
> *I switched back to the tea, and I became the tea.*
> *I was the water, I was the tea, there was no separate sense of "I" or*
> *me at all—nothing—ground zero of the ultimate truth.*

I had disappeared and became totally whatever was sensed. Any separate
self-reference or feeling of "me" or "I" completely disappeared.
It was nondual—no subject or object.

A jolt of fear pulled me back. It was not the same as the taste of emptiness that I thought I had experienced with Her before. This was a deeper experience. I asked if She was there to help, and She assured me yes, but I was scared and on the edge of panic.

Dark thoughts of shamanism flooded my mind. I was a little suspicious because this happened when Alonso was not around to guide. It may have just been paranoia, I was not sure. I spent the rest of the session trying to come down using the techniques that Rafa had taught, to no avail.

I never asked Alonso about this, thinking I could manage the meaning on my own.

Toward the end, I remember Her saying, *"I have now given you a taste and helped you better prepare for your path. Now you are on your own."*

A Pointing-Out Instruction

This ceremony was the most important one spiritually, but it took me some time to fully absorb it. At first I thought it was dark, because it scared me so. However on reflection it seemed closer to a pointing-out instruction of pure emptiness, oneness, egolessness, or whatever we want to call "that one-taste state." Any sense of "I" or any sub-entity of self at all had completely disappeared. Again, there was really nothing.

"Pointing-out instruction" is a phrase used in Buddhism meaning "to reveal the nature of mind and of emptiness," and it usually involves a series of intellectual analyses, guided meditations, and empowerments from a qualified lama. Here, however, I felt She had been guiding me to it in a different way, a much more experiential one, first through physical and emotional healing, then through meditation, and now through one single, visceral stroke, giving me a full-blown taste.

I don't want to mislead here—that taste was flashy, like a small temporary crack in the egg before my ego grabbed on and pulled me back.

It felt like maybe a flash of death, perhaps of the ego. Whatever it was, it was enough.

> *My meditation practice has not been the same since, as I now know the taste and can just go there to rest my mind in that place.*

Fear of Shamanism

Again, my worry was that it also had a taste of shamanism. It was so out of the ordinary that it felt a little dark. By shamanism I mean having special abilities without truly transcending ego. It is said in Buddhism that power, if it comes, is a temptation to be spurned if further progress is to be realized and the ego transcended, and that compassion, not emptiness, is the true ego killer. In that state, the deepest I had yet gone, I felt no warmth, no loving-kindness or compassion of any sort. It was just an empty nothing. The experience was so brief that perhaps it was not enough for compassion to surface.

I had felt great lovingness in other experiences with Her, especially post-ceremony, but not here in this peak experience of the medicine.

This gave me a little pause, and it took some time for me to resolve and understand.

Ceremony 18: My Path Is Buddhism

I took one dose and the message was the same, *"You have what you came looking for. Now it is time to return to your path. You are good to go."*

In my very first retreat with Her, I asked, "How do I learn to love?" and Her answer was, "Through me." I feel She has indeed shown me the way. I have this abundant loving feeling, and my meditation has been the most authentic, open, present, relaxed, spacious, clean, and concentrated it has ever been.

Authentic Presence

I indeed felt renewed. I felt I had shed the crusty, solidified baggage acquired over the decades and become the more fresh, open, alive, and authentic me once again. She was now saying go out, step back on the path, and be fearlessly confident in that.

Trungpa Rinpoche coined the phrase *authentic presence*, meaning having a personal field of power, a quality, where because you have achieved some merit or virtue, that virtue is reflected in your being and in your presence. Authentic presence comes not just from being a decent person in the ordinary sense but from bringing a presence that is an emptying out and letting go in a way that results in an opened heart whose only agenda is to be awake and compassionately concerned for waking others. "When you meet a person who has authentic presence, you find they have an overwhelming genuineness."[4]

This, I feel, is where She has led me.

Dichotomies and the Play of Mind

My perception during this retreat continued to be more spacious and phenomena, less substantial. Everything seemed to exist simultaneously in the same space without constraint or contradiction. It felt equal, and it bled into my post-ceremony reality. It seemed I could feel love and hate for the same person at the same time without feeling a contradiction. I could feel romantic love for more than one person at once without conflict. I could think about sex or about death, right or wrong, good or bad, this or that, and so on—and it is all in the same space, empty and equal, and without compulsion to act or to follow. Everything had a slight quality of being empty, open, and mutable.

I felt free. I realized that I was *no longer torn* between the dichotomies I felt before and the bypassing of the lesser to the greater spirit. The madness of that split just does not seem relevant anymore. I had somehow transcended it.

This reminded me of one of my favorite novels, *Narcissus and Goldmund* by Hermann Hesse, about the interplay of two aspects of ourselves. Goldmund, the artist and wanderer, is balanced by Narcissus, the structured and stable monk. They are the feminine and the masculine and the root to every other dichotomous tension in our lives. I have felt both, often torn between them, and that split, as I said in an early retreat, had driven much of my life.

In contrast to what I was feeling before, there now seemed to be room for both simultaneously in my being, in every dichotomy. I thought things like, "What is sobriety without intoxication? What is love without turmoil? What is freedom without relationship? What is success without vanity?" How can we feel any of these things without the other? But when we choose between them, the satisfaction is momentary and quickly dries up. Then we ache again for the other, constantly paying for one through the loss of the other. But now, all seem equal because they are impermanent and changeable, like billowing clouds passing in the vast expanse of the open sky.

Post-Retreat: My Mother's Passing

Although She told me our work together was done, I was not so sure, so I scheduled another retreat. I felt some unfinished yet undefinable thing still lingering. Then, shortly before the retreat, my mother passed.

✦ Retreat 7: With Rafa ✦
Mom Passes, the Bardo and the Nature of Emptiness, and Cultivating Compassion

Pre-Retreat Event

My mother had been in intensive care and on life support for six weeks after suffering from a stroke. She was completely paralyzed on her left side, bedridden, and unable to speak. As time wore on, we realized that she was not going to improve. Sensing this, at first she mouthed, then angrily demanded to go home. The doctors told her that if she did that she would die from the lack of adequate support. I asked if that is what she wanted, and she nodded yes. The hospital staff and I then arranged to have her taken to my home.

We moved her by ambulance to my home and placed her in my bedroom. She was sedated for the two-hour drive, and we waited for her wake up before dismissing the ambulance crew. My brothers, children, and extended family members were all there. After about an hour, she finally awakened, and we rushed into the room. She looked around at us all, took one last deep breath, then passed away quickly and peacefully, surrounded by her family.

Soon alone again with her, I whispered mantras in her ear. It was magical in a bittersweet way, happening in a way that I felt was perfect and seemingly complete.

To process her passing, I planned a retreat in my home with Rafa. As I was waiting, I soon felt that Mom was still lingering in the Bardo, a term in Buddhism meaning the in-between state of death and rebirth.

Since our family trip to Italy years ago, when we visited our ancestral homes, Mom had become a big fan of Padre Pio. Padre Pio was an Italian Franciscan friar, priest, stigmatist, and mystic during the last century who is now venerated as a saint in the Catholic Church. A friend had given my mother a drop of oil blessed by him at the hospital which I rubbed on her forehead before leaving to take her home, and I also had taken a picture of Padre Pio from her home and placed it near her ashes in my meditation room.

About two weeks after she passed, I was flipping channels passing the time and serendipitously came across a documentary on the life of Padre Pio. At the end, there was a reenacted flashback of conversation between a bishop and a woman who had been a close associate of Padre Pio. As the conversation ended, the bishop said, "Thank you, Amelia."

I sat straight up in my chair because Amelia was also my mother's name. I suddenly realized Mom had been trying to tell me she was still around, and the only way she could communicate that from the Bardo was to manipulate circumstances. Now tuned in, I could feel her presence.

I wanted to help her through the transition and wondered about the right thing to do. So I held her in the clear light in my mind as I repeated mantras and meditated, hoping she would feel what she needed to find and follow an opening for a positive rebirth. This was my practice from then to the opening ceremony of the retreat. I experienced perhaps some of the most powerful formless meditations of my life, as my motivation was the highest it had ever been.

Ceremony 19: Mom Passes, Kaleidoscopic Visions, and the Bardo

Rafa and I both felt Mom pass from the Bardo during ceremony. *Bardo* means "in-between" as in between one state and another. There are a number of such states in the Buddhist belief system, and the most commonly known one is the state between death and the next rebirth. It was the twenty-fifth day since her passing, and people linger in the Bardo for forty-five days on average.

About two-thirds of the way through, I felt she was no longer there. Afterward, I shared this with Rafa. "You felt that?" he asked. He said that he saw her gentle ghost as she came over to thank him before she left at about the same time in the ceremony.

I do not know what if any role we really played in making this happen, but certainly this brought a sense of relief. Everything just pulled and aligned in the right direction. I was amazed at the power that comes from prayer and well-intentioned motivation. It unfolded in a perfect way—our simple support and the synchronicities just seemed so magical and so right. It left me in awe of the power of the mind and heart and what we can do when authentically and positively intentioned.

Prolific Visions

For the rest of the ceremony, I experienced an explosion of prolific, wide-ranging visions, but She appeared only after I had relaxed and given up any judgment of what was right or wrong in terms of what I was experiencing. She said that only She could make those kinds of judgments—my wisdom, not my mind—and encouraged me to remain open and let things unfold naturally without guilt and with positive intention. For once, I listened.

The visions began with my becoming one with an echo in my mind. Then came a flood of perceptions where whatever thoughts and images came to mind spontaneously—from popcorn to pythons to people—appeared instantly as empty holograms. I saw butterflies, first as an outline, then in full multidimensional color. Rafa became invisible—I could see through him, and I had flashes of being able to see through other things too. At one point I saw through the skin and muscle of my hands to the skeletal structure underneath.

The geometric patterns were expansive, colorful, and kaleidoscopic—amazingly so. I again saw the sacred geometry of fractals and DNA strands evolving and then expanding into pure, multicolored light. I was in awe of an amazing and diverse display. Perhaps I was just riding the wave of power emanating from Mom's transition. I do not know.

At the end She appeared in a dark maroon-colored geometric form similar to a dragon's head, and she beckoned me to enter Her realm, and continue to transform myself into different forms. I was too tired and did not follow.

Ceremony 20: Beyond the Cosmic Egg

She came quickly and invited me to follow Her into three or four realms of reality. I thought they might be increasingly subtle levels of being or what are known as *the three kayas*, the three ways of being, or the three aspects of mind, emptiness, and phenomena in Buddhism. She showed me the initial layers, as I turned into a condor and then a serpent, then they exploded into different holographic forms and visions that words cannot easily explain. The experience ended as I became uncomfortable and nauseous again.

I doubted and pulled back. Why the tendency to change form and become different things when what I really wanted was to experience emptiness? Or was She really pointing to another aspect of emptiness?

I repeated the mantra *Om, Mani Padme Hung* to protect my mind from the doubt. It filled the universe with loving-kindness and an infinite multitude of flowers and rainbow light. The recitation of these sacred sounds seemed to explode my visuals, giving a sign of their inherent, magical wisdom.

As I was coming down, I took a drink of water and fully became Her again—the serpent. I even started hissing. I was not afraid but amazed. Still, I asked, what does this mean? No answer.

Later, I was in my bed looking up at the ceiling. I had a vision of ancient parchment paper with writings that first appeared as Sanskrit, then shifted into what appeared to be Dakini language, and then finally into hieroglyphs.

In processing this shifting into different forms with Rafa, it was clear to him that it is all mind, a layer of reality beyond the Cosmic Egg, or perhaps just a more expansive Cosmic Egg. Many of the images may have seemed archetypal, but are most likely still influenced by culture, so still an egg in a way. I do not know. He advised to just accept it as mind, let it play it out, and take what it is She is offering me. Perhaps it was a provisional step to something deeper. I didn't know at the time, and he encouraged me to not cut myself off from the experience before knowing.

The Bardo and the Display of Emptiness

Later, it occurred me that the visions, the changing shapes, and the holograms were an intermediate state, a nonmaterial spiritual reality not unlike the Bardo, a place between normal reality and pure emptiness. There, the habitual patterns of the Cosmic Egg crack open and unfold into a display of new, wider, and spontaneous perception where all sorts of manifestations beyond normal reality arise. The inner essence of our being, our Buddha nature, arises to display the depth of its expansive qualities. Chaotic fields of light arise and crystallize into complex shapes in displays of incredible power and variety.

At times, this display is too much for us as everything is undone. Too uncomfortable, too powerful, too bright, too vivid, too overwhelming, and we want the more habitual, the more familiar. As the display expands, totally untethered from the habits of the body and mind, the more confusing and exhausting it becomes the more we want it to just stop, to locate, to settle, to land. The sense of *me* strives for resolution. We want to cling to certainty, something fixed, reliable, and embodied.

But nothing is real. That is the fundamental fault of the habitual patterns of our mind. We choose the rules and who we want to play with. But the ultimate real truth is that it is the conceivably vast wisdom awareness (awareness of emptiness) from which all arises in infinite variety. Emptiness is the defining feature and its realization the sole purpose of the display. The sole purpose. Everything is possible within emptiness, but we are inherently uncomfortable with it, so we lock back onto our habitual view and shut it down.

This is how I learned to interpret this display. It is not real; the only thing real is the ground, the ground of emptiness. Everything arises from it and merges back into it. The only goal is to realize this, to empty everything out, so to speak, leaving everything open, possible, and accepting, and She had already given me a solid taste of it.

Ceremony 21: Cultivating Compassion

She came immediately and again beckoned me to follow, but Rafa stepped out of the room to smoke tobacco, a cleansing ritual, and I was afraid to go with Her without him there. The opportunity was lost, or so it seemed. Later, I turned into a hawk and filled the room as a serpent.

I again reflected on why compassion was not a natural aspect in any of my visionary experiences. My Buddhist training told me that wisdom awareness and compassion are the two fundamental ego killers. But without the naturally arising presence of compassion, the visions at times felt dark and lacking warmth. Yes, the holograms were empty, but where was the compassion? Without it, how does this path not become shamanistic?

Still tripping, I thought this medicine should be used only with compassion's active cultivation. In Buddhism, this is the case. Compassion in this sense is an arising heartfelt concern for the benefit of all. With this settled in my heart, I decided that when faced with doubt, I should always ask Her, "For the benefit of whom?"

With that, I spontaneously turned into a bird, a black puma, and a serpent in quick succession—Condor–Puma–Serpent—the wisdom icons of the tradition. This told me that She had heard me and said yes! It was a clear affirmation of my resolution. ·

Compassion as a Skillful Means

After this retreat, I researched this insight for confirmation. I read passages by the nineteenth-century Buddhist yogi Shabkar, who said, "After resolving everything as emptiness, don't fall prey to the demon of black freedom." He went even further, saying, "Compassion arises only through cultivation, not simply from waiting, thinking it may come forth by itself in the arising of emptiness."[5] The nature of mind is empty from the beginning, but the pinnacle of true wisdom does not shine fully without being consciously and actively joined with compassion on the path. It is a skillful means to nurture that which is inherent within so that it manifests fully at the end. It is what takes the ultimate cut at the ego and self-possession.

➤ Retreat 8: With Rafa ◆
"You Have Your Path" and Compassion as an Effect

Still undecided about stopping, I held one last retreat in my home with Rafa.

Ceremony 22: "You Have Your Path"

I did not start tripping until two hours after taking the medicine, and it continued for a full eight hours. I threw up four to five times. My experiences had become longer and more holographic, having almost no psycho-emotional content.

She appeared as I started to hallucinate, then I felt a sense of dread and threw up. Am I avoiding Her out of my doubts around compassion? I decided it was just mind and I just needed to embrace Her.

Again She said, "You have your path. I have shown you the way, now just go practice." Is this really Her or me rejecting Her? I couldn't tell. I decided to just relax, open, and engage the experience.

There was nothing much to record as the display began to shut down.

Ceremony 23: Compassion as an Effect

This ceremony was mostly a dialogue as I continued to investigate the roles of compassion and shamanism on this path. Alonso avoided the seduction of power through his music in ceremony. He said compassion is the greatest antidote to the ego, and this of course is the same view as in Buddhism. The insight of emptiness without the guardrail of compassion can lead to egocentric power.

It Is Not Automatic

As I continued to reflect on this theme, I realized that the compassionate aspect of our nature does not arise fully or automatically under the influence of this medicine. Yes, there is a feel-good openheartedness post-ceremony, but it wanes quickly without a steady diet of the medicine. Instead, it needs to be actively cultivated to counterbalance the residual tendencies of the ego.

I feel creating this balance is the only way to use the medicine skillfully, and it not always part of the Curandero's process or teaching, at least as I experienced it. Thus, as mentioned in the introduction to this section, to reap the full potential of the openings that Ayahuasca provides, it must be joined with a discipline of modeling the laws of *love*, *service* and *wisdom* in our attitudes and actions of daily life. Otherwise, it could undershoot the ultimate purpose and go in weird directions. I acknowledge, however, that this may be just my experience, and perhaps simply just the case that I personally do not go there naturally under the effects of the medicine. Either way, the message of balancing—of experiencing emptiness and compassion—on the path was clear.

This is the same in Buddhism. As I said, Buddhists say that compassion is not automatic. It arises coincident with the realization of genuine emptiness and the automatic function of a growing awareness—more as an effect than a cause—so it needs be actively integrated into our practice on the way; otherwise, we again fall short at the end. One of my lamas explained that perhaps 50 percent of our capacity for compassion is realized through meditation alone. That portion is like a sprouting bud that needs to be cultivated actively to bring it to full bloom. Thus the more time we spend nurturing compassion as part of our practice, the more likely it will manifest fully and spontaneously upon realization. If we don't, then there is residual ego, and full enlightenment is missed, and the black freedom that the Buddhist yogi Shabkar warned about ensues. Until then, we practice it with every meditation, nurturing it on the path so there is no hitch when the ultimate is in sight.[7]

As discussed at length in the pages that follow, we need to emphasize both emptiness and compassion, because they are the nascent stuff of which we are made and the embodiment of our inherent nature.

Compassion as an effect is not something I had fully understood before, and it took me a while to fully resolve this subtle point. This also showed why Alonso and Rafa and their insights were perfect matches for me and why I then felt free to write this book.

I feel grateful, protected, and guided by them and my karma.

Ceremony 24: Joy and Beingness

Perhaps because this issue was resolved for me, I was fearless throughout this ceremony for perhaps the first time ever. I was embraced by a sense of joy and beingness that arose spontaneously in the beginning and stayed with me until the very end. The resulting smile on my face for most of the evening brought an accepting fearlessness. Joy and beingness—compassion and emptiness—are essentially the same thing.

She has shown me many possibilities, and in this ceremony the new one was time travel. I went back in time to change something in the present in this life. It was a flash, a vision so to speak, but it gave yet another taste of the possibility and the power that come from loosening habits of the mind and of the infinite potentiality inherent in emptiness.

5

The Three-Year Cycle Ends: Some Takeaways

*We are not human being having a spiritual experience. We
are spiritual beings having a human experience.*

PIERRE TEILHARD DE CHARDIN[1]

Appreciation

With this retreat, my three-year journey with Her ended. Coming in,
I had felt lost and directionless, but at the end I felt renewed and reinvigorated. I realized She is me and that there is an inner wisdom not
automatically at my fingertips, but that is something I wanted to change
without relying on Ayahuasca as the vehicle.

Ayahuasca is a powerful skillful means. I no longer need it to clear
the way for me. That work is done—from the physical, to the psycho-
emotional, to the spiritual, She showed the way. She helped me clean up
my personal baggage, arouse my authenticity, and inspire my devotion;
she showed me nonmeditation, gave me a genuine taste of emptiness,
and pointed out the subtle expression of compassion.

She gave me a huge, comprehensive, and visceral pointing-out
instruction on all those levels. I now have all the experience I need to
go on my own. I had learned some of these things before but never in

such a taste-worthy and internalized way. My sense of worth and well-being returned, and so too did my inspiration for practice and service. I felt more empowered and devoted than ever before.

My devotion, especially, soared. It is genuine and heartfelt, and although understated here, it seemed to have been a key missing piece in my spiritual derailment. It proved to be a compelling force for cracking the Cosmic Egg and inspired a trust and faith to bring that nature to full bloom. She showed me that She is me and is always available through faith, belief, and practice.

Perhaps now I am finally a Buddhist. I am so grateful.

The Virtues of Ayahuasca

To those intoxicated by datura
Various things appear
Hallucinations one and all
Through the intoxication likewise
Of the sleep of ignorance,
The six migrations manifest
To the deluded mind
Now therefore you should understand
They are truly not there.

LONGCHENPA

For me, She brought clarity to the nature of mind that is empty, yet also awake and inherently compassionate. I tasted it. The nature of mind had been more of a concept, even after years of practice. Now I had some experience of it. Without it, those concepts would have remained just something else to hold onto. It also reinvigorated not only my appreciation for the dharma but also my heartfelt devotion to the path and wanting to help others.

It is the reason for this book.

She also helped me see the mentally constructed roles we inhabit, which has allowed me to loosen and strip away much of their hold. What remains is a kind of innocence, a fresh knowing free from conditioning, even of the dharma. Traditional Buddhist practices do not get at the identities we get stuck in. But once seen for what they are, they do not reassemble as concretely as the way they existed before.

She helped me continually probe who I am, look constantly into my being, and not just remain on the surface with method and philosophy. I realized mind is not what we think it is, and even though She did not tell me what it is either, She reopened the gate of curiosity after I had become complacent in my nice, neatly packaged practice.

She said, "There are no answers, only more questions." This invites the mysterious and the unnameable in a forceful way. I chased Her down one rabbit hole after another, and this is my insight and Her blessing. It is a type of freedom I had not yet found in the dharma.

Finally, She served a purpose, and that purpose is a finite one of cracking the Cosmic Egg. After that, She even told me, it was best to rely on the resources of dharma to grow further.

The Synergies with Buddhism

There are clear synergies between Ayahuasca and Buddhism. My Buddhist background directed my intention. This intention informed my experience and helped me glean the most from my journey with Her. Without that support, I could have become stuck wandering in the wilderness. One might say that my intention and background shaped my outcome, making it a self-fulfilling prophecy. Even so, I am good with that because I wholeheartedly trust and believe in its philosophical premise and grounding in the ultimate truth.

Ayahuasca pushed me to experience those principles viscerally in a way that I will never forget and that will always serve in pointing out the ground of our inherent nature. It would have taken me much longer to experience the same profundity had I simply adhered to the structured and methodical approach of Buddhism.

Ayahuasca also forces the issue of psycho-emotional integration, something that Buddhism rarely addresses and that many gurus even disparage. This is a problem especially in the West, where there is a history of some gurus bypassing, causing pain and confusion in their students. She would not allow me to bypass because there was no escape from Her seeing. Psycho-emotional maturity, just like compassion, does not automatically arise with the realization of emptiness.

I need also to reiterate that to capture these synergies one needs to be well-prepared and disciplined in doing the work in and out of ceremony. The reflection shaped the intention and meaning, the meditation deepened the insight, and the ceremony provided the means for cracking the Cosmic Egg. All three are required.

The Limits of Ayahuasca

Finally, as we have seen, She is not going to enlighten us, but She is going to help us wake up. She helps us see the habitual, deluded way of seeing ourselves in the world. She is good at helping us see our Cosmic Egg but not good at showing us how to cast it off. In fact, She may just cast another shell, a shift in perception, that will not lead to the ultimate truth. This is my take, which may not be the same for others. I believe the only reason I broke through and experienced a true glimpse of emptiness is because of the heartfelt intention and perspective of Buddhism that I brought to it.

She also does not seem to naturally cultivate the virtues and warmth of the heart. As I expressed, my biggest concern was compassion. Its emergence is not automatic and must be nurtured with deliberate practices, as it is in Buddhism. Without that emphasis, we fall short in the development of both awareness and compassion, the two fundamental aspects of our intrinsic nature. These are interdependent, as we shall see, making true transcendence less likely if both are not addressed deliberately in either tradition. Again, this is my heartfelt opinion, and I would be remiss if I did not express it.

Another quote from Shabkar supports this point:

Now I have some heart-advice to give to you: a sky needs a sun, a mother needs a child, a bird needs two wings. Likewise, emptiness alone is not enough. You need to have great compassion for all beings who have not realized emptiness—enemies, friends, strangers. You need to have compassion that makes no distinction between good and bad. You must understand that compassion arises through practice, not simply waiting, thinking that it may come forth from emptiness.[2]

I found emptiness through Her, but when I began questioning the compassion, that is when She began to shut down and instead said, "You have your path." I found peace with her, which made me feel better about others, even loving, but it was not the transpersonal compassion that has been my quest most of my adult life. As explained above, we need to actively cultivate that aspect of our being to realize our full human potential.

She of course is me, still my Cosmic Egg, which of course means all of this is fodder for further reflection.

PART III

A Path of
Awakening

6

Longing and the Spirit of Awakening

My sweet Lord
I really want to see you
Really want to be with you
Really want to see you, Lord
But it takes so long, my Lord

GEORGE HARRISON

A few months after the last retreat, I asked my lama for a reboot. He gave me the preliminary practices of the tradition, a version of which I had done before, but this time I experienced it in an entirely new and deeper way. I felt reinvigorated on the path.

Soon after, I was offered an opportunity to teach Vipassana meditation. Nearly half of my decades of meditation practice were in Vipassana, and I participated in an annual ten-day retreat for years, before ever moving on to the Mahayana-Vajrayana. I was privileged to have practiced with some of its foremost teachers.

So this is Vipassana for the Mahayana-Vajrayana—how to approach the highest teachings without getting lost in the tantalizing esoterica, how to distill it into a few principles that help guide development and choices, and how to internalize the common themes without falling victim to spiritual materialism.

The Spirit of Awakening

As you start to walk the way, the way appears.

ATTRIBUTED TO RUMI

This section is adapted from my 2009 book *This Hungry Spirit: Your Need for Basic Goodness.*[1]

What separates this approach from the Hinayana tradition of Shamata Vipassana is the grounding in the missing "propellent" of longing, faith, and devotion in our practice that my Ayahuasca experience pointed out. It nurtures the open-hearted and compassionate aspect of our being that I found missing from the beginning. On this path of the Mahayana-Vajrayana, we cultivate longing, faith, and devotion in our very first steps so as not to miss the ultimate goal in the end.

Faith and devotion are loaded words for Westerners, as they evoke belief systems, whether it be in God, something else, or even nothing at all. But in the Mahayana-Vajrayana, the ultimate function of devotion is simply having faith in the basic goodness of your very nature. Often this begins by cultivating devotion to your teacher, your guru—as a means, and not the end, to finding you. Of course, the common error is idolatry, but the ultimate and definitive purpose of nurturing that longing is to center the function of that devotion in faith itself.

For this longing is none other than your yearning for you and your heart essence. It is perhaps the most extraordinary quality that you have. It provides you with the strength and motivation to give away your life—your way of knowing and identifying—in order to know a greater life. Cultivating it provides the spirit of awakening required to crack your Cosmic Egg.

So instead of looking to the guru, I suggest nurturing that longing in a different way. This is not something found typically in a Vipassana instruction, but again, this is Vipassana for the Mahayana-Vajrayana.

Take a moment, then, and look closely inward. There is a void in you. Just stop and look for a bit and you will find it. You feel it, don't you? As I said before, you may be successful, yet still you strive. You may be wealthy, yet still you seek gain. You may be loved, yet you still wander. Where does this discontent start? There always seems to be something missing. For what do you long so?

Whether you realize it or not, in your very essence, you are already good and complete. Everyone is. In sitting quietly with our mind for a while, we would see it, recognize it, but the hubbub of life and habits of self-concern obscure it. When we touch our essence it is a love for our shared humanity, a trust in human dignity, a belief in our human potential, a faith in a basic goodness that we all share and that is expressed in the very pinnacle of our urge for self-actualization, fulfillment, and transcendence.

This hungry spirit that I have spoken about is none other than the longing of your heart to find itself, and it is never, ever satisfied until it has done so. The interesting thing is that it is supposed to be this way. What seems to be the torment of our existence is really nature's gift compelling us to evolve. Our compulsive urge to "become" never relents until we exhaust it in our growth or derail it through the fatigue of our endless pursuits. Only then may it rest, opening us to take a deeper look and target the highest goal of life. It is nature's big setup to ensure that we grow and evolve to our highest potential.

Unfortunately, this hungry spirit is shaped in our early years by the needs of the lower ends of Maslow's hierarchy and conditioned by the world and the norms of our families, the educational process, and the culture of our upbringing. We unconsciously acquire and accumulate habits based on someone else's terms that put us in a box, a Cosmic Egg, that we do not even know we are in. It makes us smaller than we really are and places us at odds with nature's divine original intent. It is as if we are sleepwalking through life.

Yet that latent dissatisfaction, inherent restlessness, and endless longing that we all feel is none other than the heartbeat of our need to become full and our subliminal need to reveal the vaster, deeper truth of our selves. In that very "burden" of our existence also lies the lifeblood of its "awakening." We can tap our longing to pursue our nature's highest goal because, ultimately, that is our hungry spirit's divine purpose. To launch us to the greater, spiritual opening, we want to reawaken it to transcend the habituated grip of the lesser.

All religions are based on this longing, and they aim it at discovering what is commonly good in us. Not everyone has a belief in something, but everyone has this longing. It is genetically wired to inspire us to evolve. For some it is more accessible than for others because of differences in life circumstances, upbringing, and karma. We each have different thresholds, but we all possess that longing.

To nurture it, you start with whatever you believe in, whatever that object of longing is for you, whether it is the Buddha, God, Yahweh, a guru, Earth, or just your basic goodness. That is where you begin. Over the years, I guided thousands of people in developing their personal mission statements. Without exception, people want to do good in the world. To test this for yourself, when in doubt or when miserable, go do something good in the world and observe how it changes what you feel inside. That is the spirit come to life. That longing, that faith, in whatever your hungry spirit latches onto in its search for your humanity, is your launchpad for pursuing the ultimate truth in you.

As Dudjom Rinpoche said, "Unless you have faith, however many other good qualities you may have, they will not be of much use to you. It would be as if you were very beautiful but blind. So, you need to make an effort to develop faith."[2] Cultivating faith comes through reason and understanding, as well as aspiration and belief.

It leads to conviction and confidence.

It leads to humility and a serene trust in one's nature and the practice.

It leads to commitment and a heightened ability to let go of self-conceit and self-power.

It leads to an understanding that our deeds have an effect, both good and bad, giving rise to charity, morality, and basic goodness.

It leads to a yearning for breaking through the Cosmic Egg to spiritual experiences previously unknown.

It leads to an authentic practice that avoids the false pretenses of spiritual materialism.

There is no better use of this human life than to stretch yourself this way.

So even though that longing, that faith, that feeling of empowerment is not typically part of traditional Vipassana instruction, it can serve as a powerful motivator and inspiration to, first, sustain and deepen a regular practice and, second, nurture from the outset the highest aspects of your nature for the benefit of all, for an open heart is a giving heart. That openheartedness is the lifeblood of the path.

If we want to plant a tree to have flowers or fruit, then we need to plant a seed and nurture it. Similarly, if we want freedom, we must plant the seed of awakening from the beginning, so it roots within our hearts. This is the foundation for cultivating and maintaining progress on the path. With it, we avoid missing the target of a compassionate wakefulness.

The Launchpad

The Mahayana-Vajrayana has many skillful means for doing this, each corresponding to the level of our readiness. Here I introduce a few introductory reflections to anchor your practice in the vast warmth of an awakened heart and to remind you that you can tune into it at any time. The Mahayana-Vajrayana goes much further at nurturing the heart in the beginning of the path, but these will get you started providing the launching point for your journey and for being conscientious about maintaining it as your foundation. With it, you nurture your heart and your spirit, break up the spell of your self-absorption, and begin to align with the essence of who you really are.

The Opening of Sacredness

Without a sense of the sacred, it is difficult to have faith in your potential. If you relate to your natural world as a collection of lifeless processes, it is indeed lifeless to you. If you relate to your body and mind as machines, they are machines to you. But if you relate to them as sacred, they become sacred. This is not some psychobabble—it is the recognition and appreciation of the reality of how we work and really are. In appreciating something sacred outside, that which recognizes that sacredness is the sacred inside.

We are in relationship with everything. That is what life is. We may have friendly relationships that are nurturing and helpful, and that is good. But if we have no sense of the sacred in our relationship with the environment, with people, with ourselves, then the sacred within starts to dry up and die. It needs be enriched and expressed; otherwise, it wanes and withers. It disappears from our lives and our cultures, it becomes an abstraction, and it is reduced to mythology or psychology. It is easy to lose in the busyness of today's world.

Developing joy and appreciation for life opens the door to the sacred. We all possess Buddha nature; we are all made of the same inherent stuff. To help awaken it, spend time in nature, particularly in places special to you. *Begin each meditation with a prayer to open your heart.* End each practice with the wish to be of benefit to all beings. Engage all that you do as a way of benefiting everything, not just yourself. Just do whatever you can to inspire and broaden your mind and heart, and you will come to the mysteries and sacredness of life.

Joy and appreciation are the window, the light, and the dawn of your awakening. Everything follows from them. The research of positive psychology proves this. They are the key and the foundation. They allow us to feel the preciousness of our life. We have the most profound opportunity not only to be alive but also to be awake, willing, and able to make the most of our human experience. Another inspiring quote from Rumi says, "Wear your gratitude as a cloak, and it will feed every corner of your life."[3]

The fact that you are reading this means you are curious to learn another way. This is not accidental. It did not just happen by circumstance. You were curious, you were inquisitive and open, and you drew it to you. When you open your heart and your mind, you open to other dimensions of life. There are so many other things you could be doing, yet you saw, you were motivated to look at another way. So now you are here to learn about this precious practice. This is joy, and this is appreciation for the sacred, and this is the foundation for the practice and for empowering a fulfilling life.

The Blessings of Faith

Faith in the potential of what you have to offer as a human being brings to life your spiritual treasures and gives you confidence. When you feel that faith, that treasure, you feel rich, you feel empowered, and you feel blessed. Faith ignites these qualities. When you have it, you feel comfort and you are grounded and undistracted by the pull of different emotions and habitual patterns. Instead, you embrace openness with a fearlessness and deny identifying with mundane entrapments of the hungry spirit. It brings a calm, peaceful, and relaxed natural state. It is the door, the window to enlightenment. If you want light, you open the door, you open the window.

There is a story of an old woman whose son was a trader traveling to different places for business. She often asked him to bring back a special relic as an inspiration for her practice, but he always forgot. She became so despondent at his forgetfulness that, as he was about to embark once more, she threatened to kill herself if he failed again. Soon thereafter, the son again traveled to India for business, and then set off to return after it was done. As he was approaching home, he remembered that he had again forgotten to bring what she requested. He stopped, looked around, and picked up a tooth from a dog's skull, wrapped it in silk, and told her that it was one of the Buddha's canine teeth. She was delighted and had such great faith in that tooth that she would do prostrations and make offerings to it all the time. From that faith came many blessings, and she became widely renown for her spiritual accomplishment. Of course, the dog's tooth itself did not contain any blessings, but her faith was so strong that the blessing rose from within, setting the condition to draw it to her.

Buddhism identifies four levels of faith:

Interest. First, there is having an interest, which means when you hear about or read books about the dharma, you take an interest. That interest is the beginning of faith, and it opens your mind and heart to wanting to know more. It is the window to enlightenment. Again, if you want light, you open the window.

Yearning. Your interest piqued, you may want to explore and know more. So you begin to learn, study, and contemplate. This strengthens your faith and devotion, and wisdom begins to develop. First you learn through reading and listening, then you contemplate and reflect on your own. You learn to yearn for more and begin to interpret it in your own way. This ultimately brings forth wisdom.

Trust. Then you practice and apply what you have learned. You now know a few new things, so you integrate these into your own experience, and if it feels right and authentic, then you model them in your attitude and your actions. As you do, you internalize and develop a trust that brings comfort. Your faith strengthens, further empowering your practice and your actions.

Unshakeable Faith. Finally you arrive at an unshakeable faith. With unshakeable faith, your longing and devotion become one, and everything becomes complete and fulfilled. Faith becomes a function for its own sake. Nothing is lost or unsuccessful. Your increasing conviction magnetizes and draws blessings to you. You have success in your practice and engagement in life. Everything begins to ignite, and you start to grow.

The blessings of the teachings depend almost entirely on faith and devotion. If you have great faith, you reap great blessings. If you have little faith or little compassion, even with all your intellectual understanding, you receive little or none at all. As Jesus said, "O ye of little faith, why reason ye among yourselves, because ye have brought no bread?" With strong faith, the blessings of the path present themselves everywhere. This is how karma works.

The Ground of Bodhicitta and Basic Goodness

Central to this faith is a belief in the basic goodness of yourself and others. Basic goodness is also called *Bodhicitta* in Buddhist tradition. *Bodhicitta* means "awakened heart" or "compassionate wakefulness." It is the intention to awaken to life so one can awaken others to life.

Although there are many aspects of Bodhicitta, including aspiration Bodhicitta, such as having sacredness and faith, the absolute Bodhicitta that we experience in meditation, and application Bodhicitta that we express through our actions in our world, fundamentally Bodhicitta is the belief that we are all basically good by nature, and our desire to nurture that in ourselves and in others. It is not something we create, but it is something we need to uncover and apply. It gets submerged in defensive and negative obscurations of the hungry spirit and in the notions of who we think we are or who we should be in the world in which we live.

Patrul Rinpoche said, "without Bodhicitta firmly established in our hearts, even if we have memorized and can quote all the texts and teachings, we are merely paying lip service to the dharma."[4] It is the root of enlightenment and at the heart of every practice.

It was Trungpa Rinpoche who first coined the phrase *basic goodness*. He said we each have inherent wisdom that can help us. If we are willing to take an unbiased look in an open and relaxed moment, we will find that despite all our problems and confusion and all our psycho-emotional ups and downs, we have something basically good inherent in us—an essence that is awake and compassionate. Until we discover and own that goodness within, until we activate and engage in our daily life, we cannot hope to improve our lives or the lives of others.

Whereas Western psychology tends to focus on damage and illness, Buddhist psychology would instead start from a place of wholeness and perfection. There is a story where a clay statue of the Buddha sat in a temple in Thailand. Over the years, the monks would tend to the statue, fixing cracks in the clay that had dried in the heat. One day a monk was repairing a particularly large crack and, peering into it, he found a golden reflection. When the clay was removed, the now famous golden Buddha was revealed.

That is how it is for your Buddha nature. For you to recognize it, you first need to peel away the layers of whatever it is that hides us from ourselves. Once you see it, feel it, and exercise it, it begins to break out and shine through the cast of your acquired habitual patterns and the obscurations of your self-centered neuroses of everyday life. It is the stuff of which you are made, and you want to nurture it in your meditation, your reflections, and your conduct. It is your heart essence, and an inherent muscle that you activate, exercise, and strengthen through your good thoughts, actions, and practice every day and in all aspects of life.

You discover it through all of the above—by appreciating the sacredness of your existence, by bringing to life your spiritual treasures through faith, and by embracing your world with your basic goodness of kindness, generosity, and openheartedness. Together, these three, combined with meditation and the actions you take in the world, offer the confidence, the power, and the momentum for the spirit of awakening.

The Four Thoughts That Turn the Mind to Awakening

We have to make an effort to develop faith—by meditating on impermanence four times a day, by reflecting minutely on actions and their effect, by reflecting on the positive aspects of everything, by reflecting on how rare access to

> *dharma teachings is . . . it is important to consider that*
> *other people are—all of them—marvelous, and to be free*
> *of partiality and notions of high and low, and making*
> *faith a habit of your own mind.*
>
> DUDJOM RINPOCHE

As part of my reboot, one of my assignments was a week of reflection on The Four Thoughts That Turn the Mind to Awakening. This is a traditional reflective practice for cultivating the spirit of awakening in the Mahayana-Vajrayana, and it is typically the initial practice. To a great degree, it overlaps the Four Noble Truths but is much more personal. Sometimes called the cause of faith, this practice is a reflection on:

> The preciousness of human life
> Death and impermanence
> The law of cause and effect
> The cause of suffering

You can reflect on our precious human rebirth from two perspectives—the difficulty in finding it and the great meaning this life has. The first one is a little complicated because to think about it, we need to believe in reincarnation. However, you do not need to rely on that doctrine to benefit from it. You can just consider your present life.

The Preciousness of This Human Life

How is it that we have this excellent, specific set of circumstances that has resulted in human life? It is indeed so rare that it is like the chance of a turtle surfacing once every hundred years through a single yoke (as in the circular harness over the head of a beast of burden) floating in an entire ocean or like throwing a raw pea against a windowpane and having it stick. So are you living your life in a way that honors the preciousness of this birth and makes the best use of it? Being human, you have the greatest potential of all creatures on earth. You have an intelligence and moral capacity for knowing what to leave aside, what to take up, and how to help yourself and others in your search for happiness and reaching your fullest potential. Reflecting on this begs you to take a responsibility not just for yourself but also the whole.

Impermanence

The only constant in life is change. All things, whether your body, thoughts, or phenomena are in a continuous change subject to both growth and decay. Everything is impermanent and changing from moment to moment, like a mirage or a dream, bringing countless new opportunities and possibilities to change and grow. Reflecting on this brings you down to earth and relaxes the grip of your lesser spirit to see what you really need. It gives you a perspective on what is most meaningful in motivating yourself to be the best you can possibly be.

The Law of Cause and Effect

Everything is interdependent. That means everything you do not only affects you, your family, and others close to you but also causes a ripple effect into the extended world beyond. This is known as karma. Understanding this, you learn to take responsibility for all your thoughts and actions. Karma is complex—the way you accumulate it and experience its results depends on many different things. A positive action brings a positive result, a negative action brings a negative result, and it is always operating directly or indirectly. If you keep this in mind, then your thoughts and actions become more peaceful, more thoughtful, more open.

The Cause of Suffering

As we have already seen, if left on its own, this hungry spirit is never, ever truly satisfied. So instead of looking outward, learn to look inward. Many think external forms of personal success, achievement, and acquisition bring happiness, but you all know from your very own experience that they do not. It never lasts, so you go for more, and the more you have the more you want. This incessant desire masks the true happiness that you seek. Often it is so subtle or subliminal that you don't even notice it. Even when you feel happy, you can't acknowledge it because you are afraid of losing it. True happiness can only be found from the inside, never from the outside.

That week of reflection turned into a reflective habit for me, as I started writing my thoughts down as part of my process. I continued revising and editing them, and the following is an abridged version that I provide as an example. I customized it a little to reflect what felt natural to me.

Since I am open to the possibility of reincarnation, I also began with a separate section called Tantra.

The Four Thoughts: A Personal Reflection

> *Buddhism is not the ultimate truth; it is the method that points to ultimate truth. It's the only belief system where you do it yourself.*
>
> UNKNOWN AUTHOR

Tantra

The Sanskrit word *Tantra* means "to continue without a break"—an unbroken continuity, a continuity over time, as in a succession of moments like in a movie rather than a continuity through space. It is a succession of a "thinginess," like an ephemeral ether that changes in and out of shape, form, and function over time and is never created or ever fully destroyed. Instead, it is a continuous thread of something with no beginning or end, that pervades *all life*, *all existence*, and *all phenomena*. It is a constantly changing, unceasing primordial essence that persists even as it changes, like ice changes into water, water into vapor, vapor into clouds, clouds back to water, and so on. It is the sole source and fundamental grounding of everything, also called the magical matrix of interconnected being.

There are clear parallels to Tantra in the discoveries of modern physics. An interesting aspect of quantum mechanics is that particles, which were once regarded as little pieces of matter, are now regarded as processes consisting of continuously evolving and changing energetic wave functions—energetic threads or continuums. These processes only give the appearance of a discrete, localized, and concrete form whereas, in fact, they are forever changing and lack any inherent existence. Everything so composed is impermanent, continually changing, with no static, stable basis. In this way, *becoming is more basic than being, and existence is really just a thread of impermanence in slow motion.*

Our mind stream is such a continuum and is no exception. The constantly changing sensations, feelings, thoughts, and so on of life manifest from an underlying, unfabricated, primordially pure continuum called our Buddha nature. Although mind streams, and thus we as individual beings, lack innate souls that go beyond personal identities, nevertheless there are certain aspects, qualities, or karmic imprints on this continuum of our inherent Buddha nature which may appear as a soul that flows through the cycle of existence known as Samsara. This energetic thread recycles after death again and again until the obscurations of the karmic imprints accumulated on it from our habit of ego-clinging are cleansed through practice. With sustained effort, this practice reveals the nondual, unending, timeless, stainless, wisdom awareness of this Buddha nature, our tantric thread of being, often manifesting as rainbow light at the end of a cycle of life. This realization is called full enlightenment or Nirvana.

There are, for example, countless remarkable and well-documented stories of people who have recognized previous lives that provide us evidence of Tantra and this process. The Buddhist tradition of *Tulkus*, for instance, recognizes reincarnations of former enlightened beings. Their selection is based in part on their memory of their previous life.

The fascinating story of the Karmapa's recognition of the reincarnation of Tenga Rinpoche not so long ago is just one such instance. I witnessed Tenga Rinpoche's cremation. As is the tradition, his body was held untouched for almost sixty days before the cremation. It had not decayed and had shrunk to a small fraction of its original size. It was evaporating into light, similar to the occurance of the broad daylight rainbows encircling Penor Rinpoche's residence on the day of his passing which can be found on Youtube.

Reincarnation has also been documented in the West by psychiatrists who interviewed young children who claimed to remember a past life. Each of thousands of cases documented a child's statements and testimony from family members and others that correlated with a deceased person who matched the child's memory. Unfortunately, these recollections tend to fade with age. With the exceptions of Christianity and Islam, most other spiritual traditions hold some basic belief in reincarnation.

The Preciousness of Human Life Applied

Given the above, my life seems not only special but indeed precious, as my circumstances are inconceivably fortunate for practicing dharma. My life has blessed me with

Good health, complete faculties, and decent attractiveness that have opened many doors and led to relationships;

A good and sensitive nature; an avid faith, and above-average capacity for discipline and practice—I aspire to virtue;

A location that is vibrant, peaceful, and progressive;

Many opportunities to leave my homeland and learn different languages, cultures, and perspectives for expanding my world;

Family and friends who have inspired me with pure intention and upon whom I have depended, and who have opened my heart and the door to my spirit;

A natural unfolding of the different sequential stages of the path, from my first Vipassana course in my youth to Shambala at a time of personal crisis and to the Mahayana-Vajrayana at a point of wanting to serve;

Access to teachers, all of whom appeared at the right time and for the right stage of the path;

The proximity of multiple spiritual centers nearby, all within a single lineage;

Work that provided me with meaning and enabled me to be in service to others as a support to their growth;

An incredible series of dreams and auspicious and synchronistic events that have showed me and guided me on the path;

An invisible hand, guide, unconscious urge, and unexplained karmic momentum that I have relied on for showing me the way;

Enough accumulation of merit to edit important teachings and allow me to finally teach dharma.

According to the tradition, there are indisputable signs of good karma and a protective sphere of good merit accumulated in previous lives. I have been blessed with them plus an incredible set of circumstances with many freedoms and advantages. This awesome blessing stems from a good karma that I have recognized and counted upon to not only help me but to guide me to a wholesome way. This makes me inexpressibly fortunate, as it is as if I were destined for this path.

This merit, though, from both past and present, is dependent upon others, as is made clear in all the above. I am not alone on this journey. I have leaned on others for a full range of things, both large and small and in direct and indirect ways. We are all linked and connected through a web of interdependence, an *interbeing*, where we are made of the same stuff, want the same thing, and only awaken through each other. In my work alone, I realize that I am at my best in giving to others, especially one on one. It brings out the best in me. I would not have access to "me" without connection to "them."

Impermanence Applied

> *Of all the footprints, the elephant's is the largest*
> *Of all the considerations, the foremost is impermanence*
>
> THE BUDDHA

The opportunity of this life, like all things, is just temporary. Everything is interdependent and constantly changing—family, friends, phenomena, time—nothing ever lasts. I could go at any time. Yet if I could live forever, would I ever be inspired to practice dharma? Probably not, and so, having found this moment of reprieve, I need to take advantage of it. Many circumstances have come together to provide me with this precious birth and give me an opportunity to find release.

This forces me to consider not only how I want to live and die in this life but also what it may mean for my next. I want to lead a life that is both awake and benefits others. I know the tendencies I cultivate now are the only things that will matter when I go, and my end is closer than my beginning.

Yet what have I done so far to prevent myself from dying ignorant? I have studied and called myself a Buddhist for decades but at the same time wasted so much effort in distraction and self-deception. I have been guilty of simply wanting to live more comfortably instead of being motivated to do for others. Buddhism is not a badge. My lifelong theme of *learning to love* has often just strengthened my ego and is not always reflected in my conduct. Have I really wasted my opportunity? Have I come on this journey only to return emptyhanded?

Whatever my missteps, they have still led me to this moment, to this realization. Now I know that my time is now. I would rather die than let these freedoms and advantages go to waste. I don't want the shadow of my negative karmic actions to follow me to the next life. The end is unpredictable, and each action could be my last. Thus I dedicate the remainder of my life to the most meaningful thing I can imagine—helping others along the way.

In the end, I want to love so that my heart aches, not just for the ones closest to me but for everyone. I want to weep to the depths of my soul in joyful sadness for everyone—yet let them go and simply hang in space at the same time. I want out of myself. I want a universal, infinitely vast connection with everything, where I take a breath so deep that it passes through me and where I exhale an infinite white cloud of goodness that brings everyone to the same place.

The Pervasiveness of Suffering Applied

> Disgust because there is no one to be trusted;
> Sadness because there is no meaning in anything;
> Determination because there is never time to get everything
> you want;
> If you keep these things in mind, some good will come of it.
>
> PATRUL RINPOCHE

I can't help but have at least some doubt. Can I live this life so fully without having complete faith in a better way?

Whether we fully realize it or not, suffering permeates every aspect of our lives—even when we think we are happy, the truth of impermanence pervades everything. When in love, we are afraid of losing it; when we achieve something great, we soon feel empty; when we are finally able to retire, we are quickly bored.

We are never, ever satisfied with anything. Always focused on looking good, not looking bad, we are consumed by an inherent insecurity of not being enough, trying to satisfy an ego that sways back and forth between hope and fear. We have insatiable hungry spirits. No matter our acquisitions, successes, and attachments in life, they are never, ever enough. So we heedlessly run round and round like a potter's wheel, trapped in a spin of clinging.

This is the world of Samsara.

So often in my life, for example, I have felt weary, suffocated, and claustrophobic by being swept along by this incessant, searching urge, driven compulsively by desire (nice things), abandonment (from "I am not good enough" to "No one is good enough"), weight (to deflect shame and to attract), addiction (to numb and dull), anger (quick to blame and judge), arrogance (always know better), money (to be secure), success (to be somebody), and, most recently, aging (to lose identity). It's all reactive and seemingly endless. Obsession with these things has not benefited me. What good are they now, especially at this time in life?

One of my problems is that life has been very good to me. In a way, I have been in the "God" realm, enjoying travel, career success, wealth, romance, teachings, and so on. I have played at spirituality, materialized it by making it part of my identity, but not really internalized it. Spiritually, I can be lazy and go through the motions without really doing the essential work, like an ignorant cow eating grass. But the end is near, and it is time to wake up.

I am not alone in this. This kind of suffering pervades all human existence. Our good fortune is that we have an awareness that gives us the potential to know we are stuck and inspire us to wake up. We can see the fruitlessness of our pursuits in a way that opens our hearts and minds, and we can turn our hungry spirit to serve our evolutionary urge.

The Law of Cause and Effect Applied

> Water the seed of awakening with the cool ambrosia of renunciation and compassion
>
> DILGO KHYENTSE RINPOCHE

What justification is there for having even an iota of faith in making this situation better? Our great fortune is that we are subject to the law of cause and effect, where karma can accumulate and dissolve based on thought and action.

Karma is a Sanskrit term that means "action," and it is used to explain the reciprocal connection between our actions—the cause—and the resulting consequences of those actions—the effect. You reap what you sow. It is another aspect of interdependence.

It works like this: wholesome thoughts and actions lead to wholesome states and the possibility of liberation, while unwholesome and neutral ones lead to unwholesome states and continued suffering. As such, what we are now is what we have been, what we will be is what we do now. What we are is largely what we thought, said, and did in the past, while what we are thinking, saying, and doing now forms our future.

For example, if I eat too much and don't exercise, I gain weight; if I don't brush my teeth, I lose them; if I don't water a plant, it does not grow; if I don't prepare, I perform poorly. It is cause and effect. All my actions and thoughts are fertile seeds for the mind—what we feed it and how we nurture it is how we shape it.

If I have a fear of being criticized, that self-doubt invites doubt from others. Like a cosmic mirror, my attitude becomes a self-fulfilling prophecy. If my mind is motivated by greed, hatred, or delusion, I plant the seed for receiving strife, suffering, and negativity in return. If my mind is motivated by generosity, love, or wisdom, then I plant the karmic conditions for abundance and happiness. No matter how small the seed—good, bad, or neutral—the ultimate result can amplify, like a small spark igniting a forest conflagration or a single act of protest by a lone teenager reigniting a global movement for sustainability.

Thus, every cause has an effect. The subsequent chain of reactions creates karmic imprints, both good and bad, on our psyche. The effects of these imprints can come to fruition immediately, sometime in the future, or even in the next life. They accumulate and recycle over lifetimes and predispose us to certain patterns and attributes.

This makes our karma of the past, present, and future of this life,
as well as that of our past, present, and future lives, interdependent.
Further, it pervades all life, all existence, all phenomena.

Karma arises out of a habit of ego clinging that is rooted in the lesser needs of our hungry spirit. So we cling to an identity and phenomena as being real, solid, and concrete to help us feel safe, and we develop defensive patterns of attachment, anger, and ignorance to protect ourselves. These patterns accumulate over past and present lives, obscure our essential nature, and make up our personal quirks, tendencies, and attitudes.

Stuck in this pattern, suffering prevails.

The Possibility of Liberation

> What is more meaningful than to breathe this fresh air of luminosity?
>
> UNKNOWN

The good news is that the law of cause and effect also provides us with a path to and an opportunity for freedom. We can work this karmic chain to our benefit. It is as though we are artists and our lives are the materials for our creative expressions. If we practice the dharma, the law of cause and effect unerringly leads to growth, development, and even realization—Nirvana—that it is possible to make a break from this cycle.

To reverse the chain of events, we retrain the mind. Instead of spinning in our defensive ego-clinging emotions, we train our mind to open to the positive qualities of our intrinsic nature. We do this by practicing awareness and compassion—the fundamental aspects of our nature. These two are the true slayers of the ego. In exercising them, we gradually open to the deeper truth.

As discussed previously, there are components of Bodhicitta or basic goodness, and they are featured in every single developmental method and technique of the Buddhist path. Why? Because these are not only the slayers of ego but also the fundamental and inseparable aspects of our intrinsic, true nature.

Training the mind in basic goodness pacifies the negative thoughts and emotions of ego clinging, gradually purifies the obscurations of accumulated karma, and eventually allows your inherent Buddha nature to shine through. Like two wings of a bird, you practice the awareness and compassionate aspects of your nature to fully realize and manifest that same nature.

The path models the result. In retraining the mind in this way, we replace our useless and confused thought processes with our inherent merit-generating ones that open us to blessing and good fortune. Not fully internalizing this is one of the reasons I became so stuck in my practice. My mind was constantly clinging to a method and materializing my practice. My effort always came from attachment and from a place of deficiency trying to fill a void with something that I felt was missing. Thus, I attracted the same—a consequence of cause and effect—and round and round I went.

EXERCISE

Practice Assignment

To engage your spirit of awakening, reflect on these four thoughts for twenty minutes a day for seven days. For what it's worth, I have found that journaling deepens the experience and appreciation. I have been a big fan of the journalling technique offered by Natalie Goldberg in her book *Writing Down the Bones*. Then later, occasionally take a few moments before sitting and reflect on why you care to practice. The following are some guiding ideas to help in your reflection.

The preciousness of this human birth

You have a fully functioning human body.

You aspire to virtue and to have faith.

You have access to the dharma.

You are fortunate, as most have no interest in the dharma.

Your livelihood and life conditions allow you to practice.

The impermanence of life

The universe, our planet, and all beings are subject to decay and impermanence.

The time of death is uncertain.

How you might live a short-lived life meaningfully.

Everything is interdependent and never stands on its own.

Each action you take could be your last.

The pervasiveness of suffering

The suffering of suffering.

The suffering of change.

The suffering of old age, sickness, and death.

The suffering of what you do not want.

The suffering of not getting what you want.

The law of cause and effect

Everything is the manifestation of karma.

Virtuous actions beget positive results and negative beget negative.

Speaking harshly results in quarrels.

Ill will results in anxiety.

Truthfulness results in harmony with others.

I started with these as prompts, taking notes as I reflected on them, then I put them in narrative form in my journal, and I revised that narrative periodically based on my study of the dharma and further insights that arose.

It galvanized everything. There is no turning back now, even if I wanted to.

◄o►

7

Meditation Benefits and Myths

Shamata Instruction I

Learn to calm the mind and you will always be happy.

PARAMAHANSA YOGANANDA

How Shamata Vipassana Works

The clinging habit of our hungry spirit chases one thought after another and turns petty things, even random things, into big things and obsessions. This is where a perceived little slight, for example, turns into days of dwelling in anger, or a flickering desire erupts into a budding fixation of the mind. We get stuck in these habits of the mind as we heedlessly go down one cow path after another, chasing and fortifying thoughts and emotions into patterns of likes, dislikes, traits, quirks, and personal tendencies that not only cause stress but also obscure the deeper truth of our being.

Shamata means "calm abiding," and *Vipassana* means "insight," seeing things as they truly are. Shamata cuts the spinning and quiets the mind, and Vipassana brings awareness to the impermanence of the mind's patterns and pursuits. Together their opening, releasing, and calming effect creates gaps in the habitual patterns of thought and emotion, allowing a more awake, compassionate, fundamentally innate nature of your being to shine through. You feel a little of this each time you get up from your meditation, and it strengthens over time with the routine of practice. That nature is your basic goodness, your Buddha nature, and Shamata and Vipassana work together in this process.

In the beginning, you emphasize Shamata, and then as your mind settles, you move more and more into Vipassana. As your practice matures, Shamata and Vipassana seem to merge, but they have not been separate from the beginning. In essence they are two different aspects of awareness, which is what we cultivate in meditation. Shamata is more localized and structured and calms the mind, while Vipassana is more expansive and open and provides insight into the nature of existence.

With the calm abiding of Shamata, you practice a gentle *concentration* on an object—breath, thoughts, emotions, body sensations, sounds or feelings—with a mindful *awareness* of the experience, as it is, without accepting or rejecting, just letting be and letting go with equanimity in whatever is happening. This settles and calms the mind. With the insight of Vipassana, you see the constant change, interdependence, impermanence, and even emptiness of our thoughts, emotions, and sensations. This loosens your attachment to them as well as to your grosser habitual patterns, traits, and tendencies.

Like peeling the layers of an onion, a regular practice of Shamata Vipassana gradually reveals a deeper awake and compassionate inner essence that results in greater clarity, creativity, and loving-kindness and overall greater physical and mental health.

The practice of Shamata Vipassana is one of just letting go and letting be. You do not impose anything on your mind too forcefully, nor do you let it just wander. There is no ambition to stir up thoughts nor any effort to suppress them. It is simply training your mind to relax in the awareness of Vipassana, and when it strays to thoughts, feelings, and sensations, you gently note it and return again and again to the calm abiding of Shamata.

With that, an awake and compassionate presence begins to arise naturally, which you also nurture along the way with other practices. With a steady discipline, it shines through more and more, and you begin to relate to the world just as it is with an open and aware warmth. You become more relaxed, happier, and more fulfilled.

From Shamata to Vipassana

As mentioned in the introduction, over the course of this guided instruction we cover four progressive methods of Shamata Vipassana. The presentation is modeled after the eight-week Shamata Vipassana online course offered at Namgyal, with each model presented in two parts to allow time for practice, reflection, and development before moving on to the next. We begin with the structured meditation of Shamata and then gradually move to more open, formless ones, emphasizing Vipassana.

Each method is also coupled with a condensed philosophical background of how and why meditation works, as well as tips, suggestions, and exercises for refining and fully incorporating the practice into your life and lifestyle. Together, they offer a distilled introduction to a contemplative and practical program for promoting sanity, well-being, and basic goodness in yourselves and its resulting expression in your world. The more and the longer you practice, the more impact it has on your life.

Practicing These Techniques

If you have not received Vipassana instruction before or have not attended a meditation retreat previously, then I recommend you do so before attempting a regular practice on your own. For first-time meditators, a weekend or weeklong immersion experience with an instructor is necessary for developing the full taste of what meditation has to offer. You are working with a lifetime of habitual patterns of thoughts and emotions, so it takes an immersion for the mind to settle enough to experience the deeper benefits. I remember exiting my first retreat with

Goenka, feeling in such a good place that I vowed to always maintain it in my life.

There is nothing secret or very existential in the technique itself, but without some guidance in an immersion experience it is easy to become frustrated and lose interest and discipline.

Meditation Benefits

The benefits of a regular practice are well-known and researched, and they include greater self-awareness, happiness, well-being, productivity, creativity, physical health, and spiritual insight, as well as reduced stress and negativity. No one really refutes the evidence. Emma Sepala, author and a lecturer at Yale, devoted her Stanford Ph.D. research to the benefits and found twenty scientifically validated reasons you might want to try meditation, including boosting your health, happiness, compassion, sociability, self-control, brain function, productivity, and perspective.

Moreover, the evidence shows that a regular meditation practice increases levels of serotonin and dopamine, the two biochemicals of happiness. Single events like falling in love or winning the lottery increase them too but only temporarily, whereas a steady meditation practice raises your sense of happiness and well-being consistently.

Meditation Myths

I am so busy today . . . I am going to meditate for two hours instead of one.

MAHATMA GANDHI

Even so, most people still find ways to rationalize why it is not for them. Even those who have tried it and think meditation is a magical moment of transformation still find it difficult to maintain or perfect a regular practice. But meditation is not about perfection. It is about developing awareness. Being aware that your mind wanders, that you're tired, and that it's hard to sit still is the point of meditation. So you put your oar in the water, and you learn to navigate the high and the low and the fast and slow currents. That is your practice. It is to observe the mind and how it works.

Many resist because they think meditation is about . . .

Sitting in lotus position. You can sit in a chair or on the couch; just be comfortable and keep an erect spine.

Sitting for an hour a day. Small doses of ten to twenty minutes twice a day work just fine. Start with shorter periods and build up to longer ones that fit your time and comfort best.

Sitting occasionally still reaps the benefits. No, it does not. You are loosening old habitual patterns and creating greater openness in your life. That requires repetition and a steady training just like an athlete, musician, or a professional of any sort.

It's religious. No, it's an approach to life and does not conflict with other religious belief systems. In fact, every spiritual tradition offers some form of meditation, and they all ultimately point to the same goal of becoming a fully functioning human being. The fact is, you don't have to be spiritual or religious to benefit from meditation. Just noticing thoughts, feelings, and sensations makes us more fully functioning human beings because it naturally builds awareness and compassion. There are no gods, as we commonly know them, in Buddhism. It is a philosophy and way of life.

It is weird. What is so weird about sitting and breathing? Besides, politicians, athletes, and teachers are doing it, so how weird can it be?

Then there is "I can't meditate because . . ."

I can't clear my mind. For sure you will experience the noisy chaos of a wound-up mind that's unwinding, with tons of thoughts, feelings, and emotions of the monkey mind. The goal of meditation is not to eliminate them, but instead it is to be aware in observing them. As you do, they slow down. So don't worry about how you feel during meditation but notice how you feel after and throughout the rest of the day.

I can't sit still. That's OK, just sit comfortably and move if you need to. If you are finding it difficult, shorten your periods of sitting or simply learn to allow it to be difficult. In meditation, you increase the plasticity of the mind, which does the same for the body—over time. Mind and body are connected and interdependent; body affects mind, and mind affects body.

I get anxious. That's normal because the compulsive urge of your hungry spirit is constantly moving you to do something. When you try to turn it off, then you begin to worry about all the things that you are not doing, all the ways you are not being enough, and all the ways you are feeling insecure. Let the junk come up, and let the practice calm you down.

I tried and I hated it. There's always a resistance to introducing a new routine into your life. It's a gentle discipline of training your mind or body, just as an athlete, musician, writer, or any skilled professional trains their mind or body. There are so many forms of it—transcendental meditation, Vipassana, yoga, tai chi, and so on—from many different cultures across the planet, and all for good reason.

I don't have time. Think of all those minutes you waste every day on the internet or otherwise. You can definitely fit in twenty minutes here or there to give your life a boost. More interestingly, as you gain traction in your meditation, you gain perspective. The many other things you sink your time into are really just simply that— time sinks. You have a greater view. I know from personal experience that even with young children you can find time. I simply got up before they did to practice.

All these points of resistance make introducing a meditation routine challenging. It runs counter to the years of programming of your mind and body, yet its physical, emotional, and spiritual benefits are incontrovertible. The following chapters cover many traditional tips for developing and maintaining a fresh and vibrant practice.

Practice Supports

To help support a regular practice, first create a physical container. Ideally, you want to have a safe, quiet place where you can practice each time. A place that feels yours. This helps you create and maintain a discipline. It can be a chair or a cushion in your bedroom or some other place in your home where you know you will not be interrupted for about twenty minutes. In my early days of practice, I shared a small apartment, and I used a large, clean storage space as my container. Now I have my own small meditation room in my home.

Second, assume a perky posture. You want to rest quietly with an erect torso, hands on knees, chin slightly tucked, and mouth gently closed. Initially, eyes are closed to enable calm abiding, and later in the progression they are open to empower insight. An erect torso is particularly important for maintaining an alert energy throughout your practice. You can sit in a chair or on a cushion with crossed legs, but lotus position is not necessary. Either way, it is important to be comfortable so you can remain as still as possible. The more your body moves, the more your mind moves, as they are connected. If you experience an itch or some pain in your knee or back, try to resist the urge to immediately move or scratch. Instead try to make it part of your meditation. Just note the itching or the discomfort and return to the breath. If it becomes unbearable or too distracting, then go ahead and move or scratch.

Third, reflect on the four thoughts. Take a few minutes and reflect on the spirit of awakening—sacredness, faith, Bodhicitta, or the Four Thoughts That Turn the Mind. Whatever sequence or combination works for you, take a few minutes to anchor yourself in the foundation of basic goodness.

Fourth, maintain a routine. Try to sit for twenty minutes twice a day. Doing it at the same time each day helps with developing a discipline.

Sitting once in the morning brings ease and insight into your day. Sitting in the evening brings a softness and deeper sleep into your night.

After assuming the posture, begin Shamata practice by bringing a gentle concentration to the sensations associated with the natural rhythm of your breath. Choose either the upper lip or the belly as the area to follow, noticing any sensation you feel with each inhale or exhale.

With the upper lip as your area of focus, feel the warmth and coolness of the breath on your lip as you inhale and exhale or the tingling or pulsing sensations of your nervous and circulatory systems in their natural space.

With the abdomen as your area of focus, try to feel and detect the same although your area of concentration is more open and spacious. Just gently follow the sensations of your diaphragm as it rises and falls with each breath.

If you have trouble detecting sensation in either area, breathe vigorously or gently rub the area to stimulate feeling. Then return to the natural, unforced, rhythmic flow of the breath.

There are two parts to following the breath.

The first is to develop your concentration by following your breath and noting any sensation you feel around the area of focus. You want to cultivate a precision and continuity in following the rhythm closely—noting in-out-pause, in-out-pause, in-out-pause, over and over. As you do, also note any sensations in your area of focus—warmth, coolness, movement, dullness, tingling, pulsing—to maintain a continuity in your awareness. Maintain a gentle, accurate, and mindful concentration using the breath and the sensations as the object for gently concentrating and resting your focus and your awareness.

The second part is to return to the breath when your mind wanders. Your mind will wander from this gentle concentration, distracted by thoughts, emotions, sounds, sensations, itches, or pain.

As you become aware of this, gently note it and return your awareness to the breath without reaction or judgement of any kind. Maintain a calm, abiding equanimity. Do not dwell on or follow thoughts, sounds, or other sensations in the body—come back to the breath. Do not react to any thoughts, sounds, or other sensations in the body with attachment, aversion, or judgement of any kind—come back to the breath.

Repeat this action, and begin again, and again, and again. You will do this many times. This is the training.

It is helpful to be consciously aware of what you are doing in the practice. You are developing your concentration and awareness together. Focusing on your breath is concentration—Shamata. Coming back to the breath after wandering is awareness—Vipassana.

Trungpa Rinpoche said:

Learn to work with your breath and regard any thoughts and sensations—thoughts most particularly—as just your thinking process. You don't hold on to or punish your thoughts. You simply observe them and come back to the breath. When your thoughts go up, you don't go up. When your thoughts go down, you don't go down. You just watch them go up and down and come back to the breath. In doing so, you distance yourself from them. Whether your thoughts are good or bad, blissful, or miserable, you just let them be and return to your breath. You don't accept some and reject others.[1]

8

The Monkey Mind
Shamata Instruction II

Awareness is like the sun; when it shines on things, they are transformed.

THICH NHAT HANH

The Monkey Mind

The following is a common story often told by first time meditators.

I was a little down not too long ago when a friend offered to teach me meditation. It made me think about all the other, more important things I could be doing, but she explained how meditation helps clear the mind and open us up by focusing on the rhythmic inhale and exhale of the breath.

"Our thoughts are like monkeys, constantly on the move."

When you begin to meditate, your mind will jump around like a wild monkey. You will think about the overdue library books, the squeaky brakes on the car, the upcoming dental appointment, the deadline at work, the rattling the fan in the room, the squawking birds outside, and on and on.

I asked, "What if the monkey mind doesn't go away?"

"When you have a thought, just note it, let it go, and bring it back to the breath."

I was still skeptical but decided to give it a try anyway. I straightened my posture and began to focus on the inhale and exhale of my breath. Silence filled the room, and for about thirty seconds, I could feel a newfound sense of relaxation. *It is working . . . I* thought.

And then it happened.

My mind burst into wide-ranging thoughts like a tree full of monkeys suddenly jumping around. They went something like this:

> *"This is ridiculous."*
>
> *"Shut up and give it a chance."*
>
> *Inhale . . . Exhale . . . Inhale . . . Exhale . . .*
>
> *"I am so hungry. I could really go for an egg and cheese burrito right now."*
>
> *"Wait, that is thinking. Go back to the breath!"*
>
> *"Why do I have to sit in this cross-legged sitting position anyway? Why not just sit in a chair?"*
>
> *Inhale . . . Exhale . . . Inhale . . . Exhale . . .*

Back and forth, but as new thoughts popped into my head, I religiously went back to my breath and let them go. I tried to stay focused on my breathing. Gradually, that monkey mind began to settle down a little, as she had predicted. After twenty minutes I could feel a sense of calm, and after thirty minutes the calm turned into a feeling of open, relaxed refreshment. I had achieved . . . nothing, yet I felt great.

The Monkey Mind at Work: How We Suffer

> *He who binds to himself a joy*
> *Does the winged life destroy*
> *He who kisses the joy as it flies*
> *Lives in eternity's sunrise*

WILLIAM BLAKE

This monkey mind is none other than the compulsive clinging, attaching, and gripping energy of your hungry spirit, and it is never, ever satisfied, no matter the pursuit. It dwells on and flips from one thing to another, obsessing over:

> Desiring what you want
> Failing to get what you want
> Getting what you do not want
> Fearing loss of what you have
> Craving what someone else has
> Lashing out when hurt
> Feeling not enough
> Resisting the need to change

This transpires endlessly in your mind—even in a twenty-minute meditation you experience a deluge of passing thoughts and the emotions of this ego-clinging hungry spirit's gripping energy. Yet in simply releasing, letting go, and observing these urges, and then returning to your breath, you find freedom. If you allow the thoughts to arise and pass by themselves, they move through your mind like clouds floating by in the sky.

The Power of Meditation

Shamata calms this monkey mind, while Vipassana sees whatever arises as impermanent, never lasting. You realize nothing lasts or remains fixed—every thought or perception is constantly shifting and changing. This gradually releases your fixation on seeing them as permanent, concrete, and real, and making things bigger and more important than they really are.

In observing your mind in this way, you realize it does not need to control you and you do not need to be a slave to it. It throws tantrums and gets grumpy, jealous, happy, and sad, but it need not run you around heedlessly. Meditation helps you see this and anchors you in a deeper, stiller part of yourself.

You attend to your body every day, so why not attend to your mind? With a few minutes of Shamata, you feel clearer and see things with greater perspective. The deeper reality is that the quality of your life depends on the quality of your mind. You can't control what happens on the outside, but you can control how you respond to it. No matter what's going on, if your mind is OK, everything is OK. Right now.

This practice keeps you real. You become less reactive, more grounded, more authentic, and even more humble. You see the stories and soap operas that your mind puts out, and you gain greater perspective. You start to see that you, and everyone else, is caught up in the same type of mind drama, and you become more compassionate toward others.

And . . . the more you meditate, the more you seem to benefit.

Stages and Supports for Meditation Practice

Many newcomers to meditation become frustrated because the mind seems so busy that they never invest the time necessary for it to settle into a true meditative experience. You are fighting a lifetime, if not lifetimes, of a freely and widely roaming mind that is not going to stop quickly.

Like a feather in the wind, it is driven by the shifting, clinging energies of your hungry spirit. It can make a mountain out of a molehill, cause a storm in a teacup, and spin round and round like a kitten chasing its tail.

Meditation cuts this spinning process, but its benefits do not always appear immediately. With patience and persistence, the awake and compassionate essence of our true being gradually emerges. Remember, you are retraining your mind—that takes time, patience, and commitment to a steady effort.

Again, the role of Shamata is to settle your mind for this journey, and it is the precondition for the insight of Vipassana.

The Five Stages

There is a traditional Buddhist metaphor for how this journey of our meditation experience unfolds in the gradual settling of our mind.

Like a Cascading Waterfall. In the beginning, you may find that your mind wanders so much that you feel that you simply can't do it. It is easy to quickly become so discouraged that it is difficult to even see the point—"I can't meditate!" Even so, in giving it a chance, you gradually begin to see how unrestrained the mind is in jumping randomly from one thing to another like a monkey in the forest trees. You start to notice the fleeting nature of your thoughts and gain some insight into how ephemeral and impermanent our pursuits really are. Still, it can be frustrating, and it is the reason so many give up before ever really beginning.

Like a Running Valley Stream. With a little persistence, though, your thoughts eventually begin to slow down a little as the cascading waterfall turns into something more like a running valley stream. The busyness continues to go up and down, but you begin to experience some small "gaps" in your thinking and emotional responses. That gradually brings a relaxation and even a sense of peace. This is your first real taste of the power of meditation.

Like a Slow Meandering River. As you progress further, more and more gaps occur, and you may even notice a difference in your daily life. Your mind slows even more as you become familiar with those "gaps." You experience more space, relaxation, and even a little bliss. You become less reactive to the daily turmoil and more able to recognize and manage your response to events.

Like a Still, Deep Ocean. As your practice stabilizes, thoughts still occur but within the scope of your awareness. You begin to rest in those "gaps." You are aware that you are thinking, but now it seems more like an echo in your mind against a backdrop of calm. Thought becomes more of a display within the space of the mind. Like an ocean that can be calm underneath but turbulent on the top, your meditation becomes steady. You are aware of being aware.

Like a Mountain. As a mature practitioner your mind becomes unshakeable, like a mountain in the face of a storm. When thought emerges, its movement and your abiding mind mingle into one experience. Your awareness, thought, open space, and bliss become one. There is no sense of this or that; a feeling of "just as it is" prevails—an open, vibrant, spontaneously present awareness that resonates a sense of compassionate well-being, and basic goodness.

You will experience this kind of progression, even going back and forth among the stages, as you learn to observe a lifetime of the habitual patterns of your mind.

The Five Supports: Activating an Open and Mindful Heart

As discussed before, you also want support your practice with a motivational foundation that nurtures a wholesome perspective for keeping your practice not only fresh but also heartfelt.

Appreciation. Learn to appreciate the opportunity to practice this. What a special circumstance to be exposed to this ancient proven generator of human growth and evolution. Most people are not interested, and even those who say they are curious about meditation tend not to be serious. Your interest in meditation and willingness to explore your life and bring it deeper meaning means that you are already blessed compared to others. What is then needed is only to begin. *Appreciation is an antidote to laziness.*

Joyful Effort. Then, instead of doing the practice, enjoy the practice. Shift from an achievement mind to a playful mind. You are doing this not only for you but also to benefit your family, friends, and others in your life. View the chasing of thoughts, emotions, and frustrations, even your effort to meditate, as simply the play of your mind. You want to depersonalize everything. Even your deeply rooted goal-oriented behavior is simply another expression of your ego-clinging hungry spirit. Instead, sit back, relax, and enjoy the show. *Joyful effort is also an antidote to laziness.*

Mindfulness. Remember the instructions, the why, what, and how of what you are doing, and return again and again to your breath. You want to be mindful in effort while also gently applying and gaining precision in the practice. You are retraining to be mindful of your purpose so that it pulls you back when you have slipped into distraction. *Mindfulness inspires effort.*

Alertness. Maintain a clear, open, and fresh alertness to cut off a drowsy or scattered mind before either quality can take hold. You want to keep a perky crispness that detects thoughts, emotions, and obstacles as they arise and before they take root. That "on-the-spot" awareness cuts drowsiness and restlessness before they begin and energizes your effort. This is the vibrant aspect of our awareness, an energetic edginess. *Alertness keeps you on point.*

Carefulness. Follow the middle way, and remain where it is comfortable without too much ambition or too much laxity, not too tight and not too loose. Remain thoughtful and careful in all that you do in meditation and post-meditation with yourself as well as with others. You also do not want to spoil what happens on the cushion by what comes after, so maintain a careful balance. *Carefulness assures growth.*

There is an old story of a mandolin player who was one of Buddha's students. He was discouraged with his practice, so he went to the Buddha to ask for advice.

"What happens when you tune your instrument too tightly?" the Buddha asked.

"The strings break," he replied.

"And what happens when you string it too loosely?"

"No sound comes out," he answered.

"Just so," the Buddha said, "Practice your meditation not too tight and not too loose.

The Three Allies. Among the five supports, mindfulness, alertness, and carefulness are particularly important. They are like the three allies or key assistants for maintaining and deepening practice.

Moving through the Five Stages with the Five Supports

To clarify these five supports further, the first two, appreciation and joyful effort, are the special antidotes to laziness.[1] Laziness disrupts you from the beginning and stops you right up front from progressing any further. An attitude of joyful effort dispels laziness instantly.

The third and fourth supports, mindfulness and alertness, bring precision to your practice. Mindfulness means you remember and abide by the instructions. Alertness helps you ward off drowsiness and scattered thoughts, known as dull mind and wild mind. A dull mind brings a heavy, thick, stale, sleepy, foggy state, but with persistent mindfulness, you can wake up quickly. A wild mind is a restless mind, jumpy and scattered, but with alertness you can detect these thoughts quickly and maintain your practice.

The fifth support is carefulness and balance. As said before, if you remember the instructions, then in your practice you will not be too tight or too loose. You want to remain calm, peaceful, relaxed, and natural, and if you need to perk up, reflect on your appreciation for and the impermanence of this life. If your mind is too scattered, reflect on your faith, devotion, and joyfulness. This brings you back to the core, realigns you, and stops you from falling into one extreme or the other. Together, they speed the progression of your practice.

These are important to remember. They are a combination of Shamata and Vipassana. When meditating, you need to maintain your focus, as well as avoiding becoming tired, bored, or sad, or asking yourself why this is happening. You also want to remain settled, calm, and peaceful, yet alert enough to detect disturbances immediately.

Otherwise then your grasping thoughts and emotions can distract you from practice.

Among these five, mindfulness, alertness, and carefulness are particularly important, and are often called the *three allies* of the practice. You want to ground your practice on the launchpad of sacredness, faith, and basic goodness, and then rely on these three assistants to activate, support, and expand your meditation and post-meditation experience.

Mindfulness helps you remember the instructions and the teaching. That provides a powerful support and serves as a boundary and protection barrier for your practice.

Sometimes, however, that alone is not enough and you also need *alertness*, which serves as kind of a gatekeeper. The gatekeeper is the one who checks on how everything is going and what is coming in and out of the six senses. If something runs counter to your practice, then you want to recognize and take care of it right there. If you make a mess of the kitchen while making a pie, you want to clean up while it is still baking. Otherwise, the moment is spoiled when it comes time to enjoy it. Alertness—"on-the-spotness"—stops the disruptions from coming through your gate. That is being a true practitioner because you are not really indulging in distraction. In the Buddha dharma this is known as being a hero or heroine. If you serve as a guardian to your mind like that, then you are a true warrior, because right then and there there is no more mess.

Finally, you need *carefulness*, which means always being thoughtful—not too tight, not too loose. Combined with mindfulness and alertness, you care about yourself, others, and your practice. You try to be sensitive and not careless about doing the right thing in the moment. You are thoughtful, kind, and conscientious. The heart advice of the great masters is to *always be timid in your conduct and firm and courageous in your view.* Yes, timid. Timid means not overstepping your bounds. Whether in meditation or post-meditation, you want to take perfect care in your practice.

These three also serve as the foundation of ethical discipline. Carefulness is devoting your energy to grasping, maintaining, and never transgressing the discipline. Alertness is watching your thoughts, and mindfulness is judging appropriate action. So, like a drunk elephant tied to the pillar of positive actions by the rope of carefulness and the knot of alertness, you curb the mind with mindfulness.

If we abide by these three things, Jamgon Kongtrul Rinpoche said, our foremost teacher, the Buddha, is residing within us.

Meditation Instructions: Technique II Shamata, Continued

We are gradually building the foundation of our meditation practice by calming the mind through a gentle concentration on the breath. As our mind wanders from the breath, we gently note and return our awareness to the sensations of the breath. This is all that we are doing in Shamata. We calm the mind through a peaceful resting of our attention on the movement of the breath on our upper lip or abdomen.

Bring your attention, a bare, gentle awareness, to the sensations of the inhale and exhale of the breath—just what is, as it is.

Become an objective and independent observer of any sensory feelings or vibrations associated with its movement on your area of focus.

Observe it without reaction or commentary. Like the Zen haiku, "The old pond. The frog jumps in. Plop!" Back to the breath.

Maintain a concentration that is not too tight and not too loose. Keep it light and do not overconcentrate.

———————————

Too much concentration reinforces the ego, so it can go too far and cause stress or even headaches. Keep it light and gentle. On the other hand, with too little concentration, the mind wanders and never settles. It becomes dull or agitated. Try to create and maintain a balance.

Become precise. It is not difficult to be mindful; it is difficult to remember to be mindful. For those focusing on nostrils, be mindful

... of the cool air entering in
... of the warm air exhaling
... of the gap of stillness in-between
... of the heart beating
... of the blood circulating.

For those focusing on diaphragm, be mindful

... of the belly expanding
... of the belly contracting
... of the chest expanding
... of the chest contracting
... of the gap of stillness in-between.

Remember, also, that Shamata and Vipassana are not separate, so even though we are emphasizing Shamata at this point of the instruction, when you to settle the mind and begin to have the insight into the impermanence of your thoughts, feeling, and sensations, that is Vipassana.

You are training in awareness, not stillness. Do not be judgmental of thoughts. Be more concerned about tardiness in recognizing them. Learn the difference between recognizing thought and being lost in thought.

Practice Tip

If you struggle in maintaining your concentration, try counting your breaths up to twenty or thirty while breathing naturally, and then back down again to zero. If you lose count, start over again. This helps train the mind to keep focus. However, it is not Shamata but simply a temporary skillful means for training the mind. Use it occasionally to help improve your concentration, and then return to Shamata.

9

The Grip of the Lesser Spirit

Sweeping Shamata Vipassana Instruction I

> *We are such stuff as dreams are made on, and our little life*
> *is rounded with a sleep.*
>
> WILLIAM SHAKESPEARE

The Two Edges of the Sword

Again, awareness and compassion are the two inseparable aspects of our inherent nature, our basic goodness, and from this point forward our focus is to activate and bring forth these two aspects. Together they make up the aware, empty, and spacious part of our mind and of our being, as well as the warm, energetic, and radiant part. They are both the means and the end, the path and the result, and the aspiration and the truth of our intrinsic basic goodness. They are the stuff of which we are made.

With wisdom awareness, we recognize and gain insight into impermanence and the nature that underlies all of existence. With the skillful means of compassion, we benefit others in our attitudes and actions to help us overcome all self-concern. These are not two different things—they are two aspects of our inner nature. We practice awareness and compassion to reveal our inherent nature of awareness and compassion.

When they bloom, we experience their true power and benefit in our lives. Wisdom awareness helps release old habitual patterns to reveal an open and spacious nature, while the cultivation of compassion peels back the remaining layers of self-interest to activate a kind and open heart, and a genuine desire to benefit others.

They are said to be like the two wings that work together in taking flight, the two eyes that work together for seeing deeply, and the two edges of a sword for cutting and slicing away at the grasping aspects of our ego. We cannot have one without the other. The influential second-century Mahayana Buddhist master Nargajuna said that the union of wisdom awareness and the skillful means of compassion is the one and only key to enlightenment. The problem, however, is that we tend to favor one over the other, and that is why most miss the ultimate goal.[1] Wisdom awareness dissolves the solidity of the habitual patterns of the hungry spirit, while skillful means of compassion nurtures the fundamental warmth and caring of our being. Together they drive both our psycho-emotional and spiritual growth as we progress up the hierarchy of the hungry spirit.

As Dilgo Khyentse Rinpoche has said, "To go beyond samsara and Nirvana, we need the two wings of awareness and compassion. From now on let us use these two wings to fly fearlessly into the sky of life to come."[2]

In the beginning they are deliberate practices, where our meditation

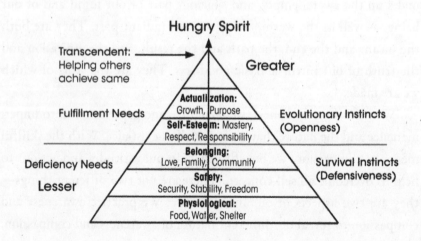

activates awareness and works from the inside out and our conduct activates compassion and works from the outside in. As practice deepens, both begin to activate naturally and eventually emerge as the two united and fundamental aspects of our nature, our Buddha nature. Compassion starts to play a greater and greater role as we feel a warmth that gives rise to opening and welcoming. In many ways, it is the ultimate ego-killer. Understanding the importance and interplay of these two aspects not only helps guide us in our practice but also deepens our commitment and growth. In growing up this hierarchy, we also gradually move from a more self-centered view of the world (benefiting self) to a more other-centered view (benefiting others).

The Practice of Awareness and Compassion

Ego-Centric ———————————————————▶ Eco-Centric

The chapters that follow first address wisdom awareness and then turn to the skillful means of compassion. Again, these are not separate but are simply two different aspects of our inherent nature. We practice wisdom awareness adorned with compassion, and the skillful means of compassion adorned with wisdom awareness. We will begin with the insight that wisdom awareness can provide, by taking a closer look at how we operate. I am putting this into my own words, drawing on my personal history and understanding. In the end, I think you will see that much of this is common sense.

We all want to be happy, but the way we go about finding happiness misses the target and brings continued suffering instead.

Why is that?

The Longing of This Hungry Spirit

There is a candle in your heart, ready to be kindled.
There is a void in your soul, ready to be filled.
You feel it, don't you?

RUMI, TRANSLATED BY SHARAM SHIVA

I have written before about how the longing of our hungry spirit takes different forms for different people at different times in our lives.[3] It drives everything that we do in the pursuit of happiness. For me, that longing has always been for freedom in one form or another. I wrote about it a long time ago just before entering a difficult time in my life.

> *Freedom has a new meaning for me. When I was younger, it meant the freedom to travel, to pursue different relationships, and to follow my deepest yearnings. It meant adventure—as in the year I studied and traveled in Europe, hitchhiking around and sleeping under the stars. I remember one special trip that captured the essence of this spirit.*
>
> *As students in Belgium, a friend and I hitchhiked down the Rhine, visiting castle ruins, across Bavaria to the Oktoberfest in Munich, down to Switzerland, and back up the Rhine through the Black Forest. We followed our every whim, looking for adventure and asking people on the way where they were headed and what might be interesting there for us. We slept in a pedestrian tunnel to avoid the rain and were awakened in the early morning by a tractor that nearly ran us over—the driver shouted something in German and laughed as he drove away. We brawled at the Oktoberfest with some others, and I spent the night in the hospital, where I received stitches for a cut from being hit over the head with a beer mug while protecting my friend. We climbed and spent the night on a Swiss mountain top, passing farmers carrying huge bales of hay on steeply sloped pastures that we scrambled on just to stay erect and exchanging greetings with a mountain hermit who was intrigued with my friend's nylon backpack and squeezed it as we climbed by. We then traveled to Freiburg in the Black Forest for a wine festival, spending the night in a residential downtown courtyard where we found ourselves locked in overnight and were forced to climb over a high wall to leave. Never before had I had such a sense of complete freedom from responsibility, worry, or direction. For the longest time, I yearned to return to that place.*
>
> *Older now, however, the meaning of freedom has changed. I still like the freedom of adventure, but it is no longer compelling. Now I seek*

freedom of a different sort—the freedom to be vulnerable and emotionally expressive and to be openly authentic about my feelings. Even more, I also want to love easily and freely without condition or inhibition. I want to feel the pain and the joy of all of life with the greatest depth but without attachment to the ebb and flow. I want to be free in the sensation and expression of feeling and emotion and to flow with them naturally, without the suffering that comes from holding or rejecting. I want to become as one with them and transcend the separation I feel in the tension and conflict of thinking I must do something about them. I want to be fully present with whatever arises and to flow with it freely, with full awareness, and without hesitation—that is total freedom, which is what I long for. To experience deeply the ups and downs, the love and anger, the compassion and fear of daily life and to not judge, hold, or control.

This longing for freedom is really about exploring my real self— finding the details of existence that bring to life the different, sometimes hidden, more authentic parts of me. I have difficulty describing it because I have not yet fully experienced it. Maybe it's a search for my soul, but I am not even sure there is such a thing as a soul. I am only sure what it is not. It is not judging myself, as when I am jealous. It is not willful behavior, as when I shut everything out and focus only on the goal or idea at hand. And it is not living in the past or in the future, as when I dwell on a painful memory or a hopeful expectation. These are attachments to the known. Freedom, however, springs from experiencing the unknown, and that only happens from moment to moment.

We all share a version of this longing of our hungry spirit. In Buddhism it is called ego clinging. It is a universal aspect of our nature to "become"—an unquenchable thirst to do whatever we are compelled to do to find meaning—and it underlies all that we do. It is a longing for success, recognition, and power and a love for finding our place in the world. It is gross, as in a drive to accomplish a big goal, and it is subtle, as in the uneasy restlessness of the mind in meditation, and it places us on a constant search.

It is the seed of creation as well as destruction. It has launched art, science, and religions, as well as wars, crusades, and nation states. It is the pulse of our very evolutionary urge to find meaning. It is palpable and energetic, but we most often don't notice it. At its most subtle level it is our monkey mind that jumps around and refuses to rest while we try to sit. That thinking, planning, worrying, and restlessness is our hungry spirit on display.

Yet despite all our efforts to find it, get it, be it—reputation, achievement, pleasure, companionship, or whatever it is—we are never, ever satisfied in its pursuit. Even when we feel we succeed, it never lasts because it keeps churning on to the next thing. Studies show that the sense of well-being brought on by achievement and acquisition is always short-lived. And when the letdown happens we can be overcome by resignation or even depression. We are the most medicated society in history, trying to cope with the dissatisfaction and disaffection showing up in our minds and bodies

We are never truly happy—even when we think we are. When deeply in love, for example, we often fear its loss, or when we get the perfect retirement situation, we get bored. In my youth I experimented with cocaine, but I found that in the peak of that high, in what felt like an exquisite bliss, I still suffered because I immediately wanted more. We are never satisfied. So we mindlessly pursue this latent urge that really has no end—spinning like a potter's wheel, round and round.

But the most interesting thing is that it is supposed to happen this way. What seems like this torment of our existence is also nature's gift. For those of us willing to take a deeper look, this hungry spirit is nature's big setup to ensure that we continue to grow and evolve to our highest potential as human beings.

As I said before, this gift is shaped, even hijacked, in our early years by the conditioning of our world and the norms of our families, our education, and our culture. We unconsciously acquire and accumulate habits based on someone else's terms, placing ourselves in a box, a Cosmic Egg, that we do not even know we are in, and it makes us smaller than we really are. This diverts us from nature's divine original intent of urging us to pursue a greater purpose and even transcendence. Instead, our longing often ensnares itself along the way, like a spider caught in its own web.

Still, it is the heartbeat of our need to become and to grow into becoming fully human, one that we need to be conscious of tapping to reveal the vaster and deepest truth of our selves—one that is awake and compassionate.

Meditation redirects this compulsive urge, this habitual pattern of the clinging ego, and opens the gate to experiencing a greater way of being and a deeper happiness. It's a method for loosening the habitual self, for finding a more authentic, genuine, and deeper self. Through it, we begin to realize the ephemeral nature of the habitual patterns of our thoughts, emotions, and sensations and that they are not as real and concrete as we automatically assume them to be. They are simply habits of the mind. Realizing this loosens the grip of our attachment to them, makes them more workable, and opens us to experience that deeper part of our self.

Like peeling away the layers of an onion, meditation gradually reveals an awake and compassionate deeper self, just as Shakespeare said—the stuff of which we are truly made. As I said before, it is often called our basic goodness—our source of worth and confidence from which we can better relate to and serve our world. Every aspect, every method, every technique of the Buddhist path is designed to tap into and nurture this awake and compassionate basic goodness.

Discovering it does not mean making radical change or doing anything weird but rather opening yourself to a deeper, more fulfilling sense of your being to reshape and reframe your life right where you are. I once considered such a change. After my first Vipassana retreat experience in the Peace Corps, I wanted to become a Theravada monk. It would have been a big mistake. It would never have been understood by my family, and, despite my inspiration, I was not adequately prepared for making such a commitment. At one of my early retreats, I had a "check-in" interview with a young Western monk. At the time, I was suffering due to the potential breakup of another romantic relationship, so I asked for advice. He responded, "I wouldn't know. I am a monk."

My first thought was "How do you grow by denying yourself such an experience? How do you learn about nonattachment if you do not know attachment?" I would have bypassed. *Meditation alone does not guarantee growth*—we need also to engage with our world, especially in the West, where there is no monastic heritage and so little opportunity to shelter in a life of reflective seclusion.

At the time, I simply did not have the psycho-emotional development to make and stick with that choice. It saved me, in retrospect. For many, such a plunge is out of reach psycho-emotionally or is otherwise impractical. I have witnessed many other Westerners take that path and later abandon it and compromise their progressive development, or even become untethered, in a way, and lost.

How do you know who you are and what you truly want if you are not first tested by life? As I said before, you must first find yourself before you can lose yourself.

We must be conscious of both our psycho-emotional as well as our spiritual growth, and the cocoon of monastic life does not always provide the best context for the former. The result can often be *bypassing* that phase of development so essential to living productively in our culture. So I urge you to keep it simple and integrate your spiritual growth into your life in a way that makes sense for you and your relationship with those around you. To change the world, just start where you are.

What we all really want is to find relevance and purpose in our life, and it is the continuous pursuit of that that gives us greater or lesser happiness. The questions "Who am I, and why am I here?" are at the root of all pursuits, the core of our deepest longing, and the source of our deepest resilience. Trying to answer those questions points to what is most innate and most powerful within us. And as we shall see, there is never a definitive answer, at least in the traditional sense.

Do materialistic pursuit and getting what you want, for instance, ever satisfy that longing and bring lasting happiness? No, because they serve no lasting purpose and only demand more of the same. Your long-ing becomes like a treadmill that spins faster and faster until it even-tually begins to feel empty. No wonder we are stressed and depressed. What we typically take to be happiness cheapens our life process.

The real problem is that you cannot possibly know what you want if you do not first know who you are. And you cannot possibly know who you are unless you challenge yourself to look inwardly to find what is most meaningful to you. Most of us, however, never do because it is not easy in this fast-paced world and not everyone has the courage for it.

But if you invest the time, I know you will gain insights into what is otherwise hidden, and slowly come to a fuller life.

The Grip of the Lesser Spirit

When we get to wishing a great deal for ourselves, whatever
we get soon turns into mere limitation and exclusion.

GEORGE ELIOT

To understand this, I want to point out a certain quality of this hungry spirit that is important to appreciate. I do not want to just give you the answer, and so, instead, I want you to listen inside as I ask you a series of questions. See if you can tell for yourself. Have you ever:

Not cried so as not to appear too sentimental?
Not made an effort so as not to risk failure?
Not shared your feelings so as not to expose your true self?
Not revealed a dream so as not to look like a fool?
Not reached out to another so as not to get involved?
Not loved for risk of not being loved in return?

If your answer is yes to any of these questions, what is it, then, that holds you back? It is your ego, or hungry spirit, as I prefer to call it.

This longing hungry spirit of yours can be traced to something deep inside you—an elemental fear of being inadequate or not being enough. You know you have it; we all have it. Many of our world traditions talk about it—we have somehow fallen from grace, possess an original sin, or have obscured our true nature, leaving us feeling incomplete. To compensate, we strive to become whole, and this explains many of our motivations.

Spurred by this basic insecurity, you try to prove to the world that you are worthy of it on its terms. You learn to achieve, to succeed, and to advance in the name of happiness. Yet your drive for wealth, power, and acquisition, as well as for position, prestige, and recognition, all stem from a desire to become greater to strive towards what you fear yourself not to be. Sadly, having more and consuming more never fills that void.

To prove yourself, you develop a self-image that either lives up to this pattern or rebels against it. Neither response, however, is authentic because you have simply defined yourself to be *just like* or *just the opposite of* the big people in your early life, and you have never gained a clear sense of who you really are. Instead, you accumulate habits and attitudes that mirror your upbringing, and you take on a socialized "you" for success that does not reflect your inner truth. You then project it and act it out in scripted patterns like, "Get a job, get married, and get a home," or, if a rebel, with some version of "Turn away, tune in, and drop out," without ever consciously questioning it.

These scripted patterns confine you and limit your capacity to be happy and successful in your careers, relationships, marriages, and parenting—every aspect of your life—and eventually cause problems because they are not the real you but the socialized you. In my professional work, for example, for every career aspirant I met wanting to succeed in what they were doing, I also often found someone longing for a different life or losing enthusiasm for their work. To not find meaning in work plucks the life out of it.

To choose not to ever awaken from this self-limiting and self-imposed frame of reference is almost unforgiveable. It allows the unconscious split between the acquired and the innate drives your entire experience and sense of who you are. You remain a prisoner of a socialized you, no matter how successful you may appear to be in your outer life.

Let's investigate this to see how it operates.

This Hungry Spirit Is Guided by Your Mental Models

I am going to say a few words, and I want you to pay attention to the image or thought that immediately comes to your mind. If I say "lawyer," for instance, what visual image comes to mind? It might be a person in a suit or in a courtroom. If I say "school," it might be a name or a building of one that you attended. If I say "mother," it might be your mom or a woman with a baby at her breast. These images are your mental models, and your hungry spirit is guided by them.

Mental models are acquired, habitual patterns of thought and feeling that guide your actions, determine what you see and perceive, and are self-reinforcing. We all have them, whether we are conscious of them or not. They are your filters and the lens through which you interpret your world and through which you project your ideas of how things should or shouldn't work. They are like the individual frames of film on an old movie projector that make your reality.

We have different mental models for different situations, literally thousands of them in our lives. They are embedded in our belief systems, our cultures, our languages, and our personal styles. They can be simple generalizations, such as "Accountants are number crunchers," or deeper, more complex ones like "Children should be seen and not heard." We accept them so completely that we live our lives by them. We construct them out of bits and pieces through our personal histories— ideas accepted from others or repeated to our self, including notions of job, race, religion, gender—and live by their dictates.

These models and frameworks are abstract simplifications of reality, and you couldn't function without them. Some of them are important and serve you well, while others don't and cause you endless grief. If I believe people to be trustworthy, for instance, I am likely to be more open, make friends easily, and take more risks with relationships. On the other hand, if I believe people to be untrustworthy, I am likely to have fewer intimate friends and be more closed and defensive and maybe even be a little depressed.

One of mine is that I view myself as independent and don't like to conform to the norms of an organization. Some might also call it "a problem with authority," but whatever it is, it is definitely the rebel mode of response to the world. A related one is that even though my coworkers don't always take me seriously because of it (my view), I know I can still "make it happen." These mental models have worked both for me and against me over the years.

Another one was about my weight. I was chunky when I was in grade school. One day, after recess my fifth-grade teacher was reading us a story that used a new word, "stout," so she tried to define it for us. She said, "Now take my friend Clint here. He is not fat, he is just stout." As my childhood friend said years later, "I was there the day your life changed!" I was so embarrassed that from that point forward I was obsessed with my weight, and I worked out and weighed myself at least once a day for the next couple of decades.

We all have these life-shaping mental modes or attitudes. Some relationship ones include "Men look only for women who are slender," or "I make most men feel intimidated," or "Men are insensitive, women are needy." Others, both good and bad, are:

People are trustworthy	People are untrustworthy
I have something to offer	I am afraid of being average
I can do it if I try hard enough	I don't have the experience
I think others are basically good	I think others are basically a pain
I know my priorities	I can't say no
I like to learn	I like to be right
I do what is right	I do what I am told
I know what I want	I can't have what I want

I feel good about me	I am not attractive
I see the good in my work	I hate my job

They Shape Your Habitual Mental Chatter

These mental models are formed and reinforced by your mental chatter, your thoughts. If you stop for a second, notice there is constant mental chatter, an ongoing monologue inside of your mind—about work, children, friends, and so on. It is an unending, discursive stream of noise about everything in your life, but this noise is rarely random. It has patterns. Each thought disappears but leaves an imprint, and that imprint develops into a pattern as it is repeated, and that can become huge over the course of decades. Thoughts accumulate and solidify and become your ideas, beliefs, fears, habits, and attitudes. They come from your parents, relatives, teachers, friends, society, and the media. Most of us pick them up and absorb them without examination, and they become the filters through which we experience life. The Buddha was known to have said, "What we are today comes from our thoughts of yesterday, and our present thoughts build our life of tomorrow—our life is a creation of the mind."[4]

Most of That Mental Chatter Is about You

Think about how everything you do is in some way concerned with you—competition, achievement, acquisition, growth, getting better, and so on. Health, wealth, and companionship seem to be our chief concerns. Also think about how much time you spend preoccupied with what others are thinking of you and how you might influence their thoughts. My bet is that like most of us, you are always concerned with your self-image and obsessed with looking good and not looking bad.

In the actions that you take, for instance, are you more concerned with doing best by others or looking good? Even in your more altruistic moments, with friends and family, you might still be thinking and doing for yourself. Do you support your family for its own sake, or do you do it because you believe this is what a good provider does and you want people to think well of you? Most of your thoughts and actions are somehow related to how you want the world to work for you and what you can get from it.

This grip of self-concern is your hungry spirit seeking to complete itself, but that drive is typically rooted in your lesser spirit—the fear and insecurity that we talked about before. As a result, it takes on self-interested ways of being and doing.

Have you ever noticed what percentage of your thoughts are based on self-doubt or not getting what you want? Or that the people with the lowest self-esteem tend to be those most easily offended? Why? Because they have the most self-doubt. Think for a moment of how

> The need to achieve can come from a feeling of inadequacy
> The need to micromanage can come from a feeling of being out of control
> The need to seek pleasure can come from a feeling of not having enough
> The need to play the victim can come from a feeling of powerlessness
> The need to be overly friendly can come from a feeling of not being accepted.

Of course, not all of your mental models are based on insecurity, but many of the more important ones driving your life are. They are your meta-mental models, also known as cocoons, issues, trips, or your Cosmic Egg. These are the places where you hang out and the ways of doing life in the world that you repeat over and over again. Again, some of these serve you well, while others get in your way. Here, however, I want to focus on the ones that cause you problems, the ones that are based in the fear and insecurity of the lesser spirit. Some typical ones include

I am better than . . .	I know better
I am worse than . . .	I can't trust anyone but myself
I must be seen as . . .	I can never do anything right
I deserve	I can't make a difference
I don't have the experience	I am afraid of being average

I have no boundaries	I don't take emotional risks
I must be in control	I must do for everyone else

These are your socialized self-images that you adopt and that you hold by constantly promoting or defending them. They are your routine ways of dealing with not being enough, and they are difficult to see. You can become so fused with them that they become your identity, and you work hard to keep up that appearance and get what you want.

The deeper ones often come from childhood events or from experiences during the first phase of life that still run our lives.

As I shared earlier, I lost two of the most prominent adults in my life at a young age. As a result, I took on an abandonment issue that for years manifested as being cautious, aloof, and reserved. I would protect myself by withdrawing, not fully engaging, and then justify it through some version of being independent or cool. It was the only way I knew how to be accepted without ever taking a risk.

Another example is of a woman who was ignored as a child and felt "not seen" or not as recognized as she felt she should be. She adopted an "I must be seen" attitude, and she constantly fought for attention and identity and was sensitive to how the world saw her.

We all somehow acquire such a wound in childhood and, as a result, early on we adopt identities or habitual patterns that serve the need of being accepted in the adult world, rather than attending to the deeper needs of our inner selves. This continues as adults as we constantly look for affirmation outside ourselves for something we imagine we lack within, and it sets us up for problems later on.

Trungpa Rinpoche used to call these wounds our "thingies." Even the most privileged of childhoods results in a thingy of some sort—no matter how subtle—and an unexamined adult life is often just a reflection of it. It is an acquired habitual defense of the child within that we unconsciously live out, even into late age.

It is also nature's way, if you choose to look, to make sure that you continue to grow. *If you have no pain, you will never long for freedom.*

They Are Self-Limiting

The sad story is that you live your life through these "thingies" and me-centered mental models but often do not know it. Have you, for instance, ever had a job that feels beneath you, or a relationship that consistently annoys you, or a pet peeve that sometimes gets the better of you? These feelings are often caused by your mental models not matching up to reality or your inner truth, and they stop you from exploring other ways of being, even though you appear to be free. As I said before, some of these mental models are useful—you can't function in life without them—but others cause you problems.

You are trapped in a habitual mental pattern, and you don't know you are in it. A friend once told me life is like being stuck inside a cereal box, where your goal is to get out but the directions on how to get out are written on the outside of the box. Being unaware that you are even in a box, you respond to your world based on your scripted notions of what you can or cannot do or what you should or should not do. They are self-imputed barriers, your Cosmic Egg—an interconnected web of beliefs, values, behaviors, and judgements that accumulate and solidify into patterns over time. And so you tend to walk down the same old path without questioning it. As Sam Walter Foss wrote:

> For men are prone to go it blind
> Along the calf-paths of the mind,
> And work away from sun to sun,
> To do what other men have done.[5]

Of course, the most common self-limiting belief is "I am not good enough," but other common ones might include "I am not creative," "That's not *my* job," and "We don't do that here." If you believe in any of that, then you will likely make it your reality. A more subtle example might be a financial manager who looks at a problem based on his specialized point of view, while a product manager looks at the same problem based on hers. They get stuck in their respective views and make themselves reactive and powerless to do anything else.

When you have a hammer, everything looks like a nail—we may also know it as tunnel vision.

I witnessed this self-limiting behavior in my professional work all the time. One of the biggest challenges, for example, was to get people to attend a workshop or a training. Many tended to resist with boxes like "Leadership can't be learned," or "That is too touchy-feely for me." Yet, without fail, when such folks *did* attend, the lightbulbs came on, their paradigms shifted, and they became huge fans.

There was a young faculty member who came to me at noon on the first day of a five-day program claiming that if she hadn't carpooled that day she would have left already. By the end, she said she would return the following day, by midweek she was thrilled at what she was learning, and by the last day she was asking how she could include leadership development for her research team in her grant proposal to the National Science Foundation.

They Cause Stress

Is there anything you relate to that does not produce a reaction of attachment (what you want), rejection (what you don't want), or indifference (you don't care)? I bet you cannot name one thing. And when the world does not line up with the first one—what you want—do you ever become anxious, irritable, or judgmental? Who, for instance, is at fault for the traffic jam you were in this morning? Was it the traffic, or was it you because you did not leave early enough? Our self-concern results in our objectifying our world, and when it departs from our script, we get upset.

In the Buddhist worldview, this is called the truth of suffering, the first four of the Four Noble Truths. We are in a constant search for happiness based on our self-centered and self-limited world view. So we avoid what we don't want and cling to what we do want, but we are never satisfied and are numb to everything else.

When the world does not conform to our view, our mental model, we tend to first sideline ourselves in judgment and irritation, and then blame the world and not take full personal responsibility. I have an issue about waiting in lines, for instance, that causes me endless suffering. Whether it is the cashier, the traffic, or the airport, any time I need to wait for someone else I become very impatient and irritable. It's the flip side to my desire for freedom—I feel contained and out of control, so I start to blame everyone else for what they are doing wrong.

These reactions are my defense mechanisms. Defense mechanisms are automatic responses that we use to project and defend what we want and believe ourselves and our world to be. We could also call them neurotic habitual patterns. They reduce our anxiety and stress by shifting the burden of responsibility and protecting us from being consciously aware of a thought or feeling that we cannot tolerate. Let's say you are angry with someone because they are overly critical of you. Here are some of the victimized defenses you might use:

Denial. You completely reject the thought or feeling: "I have no problems, you do!"

Suppression. You are vaguely aware of the thought or feeling, but try to hide it "I'm going to try to be nice."

Blaming or judgment. You shift the burden "He doesn't have a clue."

Rationalization. You come up with various explanations to justify the situation "He's so critical because he's trying to help us do our best."

Sublimation. You redirect the feeling into unproductive activity "I'm going to get a drink."

The problem is that in trying to deal with the stress, these defenses distort the truth as you automatically hide behind a variety of thoughts, feelings, attitudes, or boxes that are their cause. Your reactivity prevents from you from opening and seeing the true reality.

Worse, you project this reactivity into the world and act on it as truth, and the "reality" you experience reflects it. Your mind begins to "spin" rationalizations and your fears become self-fulfilling. One of the fundamental laws of the universe is that what you feed into the world is mirrored back to you. It's the law of cause and effect, or karma (as we have already seen). If I have doubts about something, I will not act with confidence, and others pick up on it and hesitate in return. *Negativity is reflected by more negativity, defensiveness by more defensiveness, and control by more resistance.* On the other hand, if I project openness and optimism, the world seems to respond and become more workable. Have you ever noticed, for instance, how the reactions of others toward you change if you simply smile—they become more open, even accommodating?

EXERCISE

When your "thingy" erupts—meaning stress—what are the causes and circumstances? In other words, what are some of the triggers to your stress and anger?

◄O►

They Cause Problems

I had a colleague with whom I had a disagreement. We never talked about it because our conversations were always long, and even though the issue seemed important to him, I did not really want to be bothered. He sensed my indifference and reacted as if I did not care, in spite of my half-hearted attempts to placate him. I then in return reacted by feeling justified because I just saw him as being needy and high maintenance—just as I thought to begin with. So I blamed, rationalized, and became dismissive and even began to pull others into agreeing with my view, while he was doing the same. Then the cycle repeated as we unconsciously colluded in going back and forth, reinforcing our respective points of view and blowing things out of proportion without ever revealing our real stories and learning the deeper truth. Our relationship suffered and our understanding of the truth suffered. As was said before, what we put out into the world comes back to us—our reactivity and negativity become a self-fulfilling prophecy.

My actions in treating him this way were based on an idea of what I wanted from him. There are parts of the relationship I found valuable and did not want to give up, but this need to hammer everything out in excruciating detail required way too much of my time. I put this person in a box—an object—and the result was a *cost to me* (I don't feel good about myself in the way I am handling it), *to the relationship* (it's not going well), and *to the truth* (it's difficult to understand what's really going on). As a result, we failed to deal with the issue constructively, and we both stopped learning and growing in the relationship. We didn't like suffering, but we did seem to like the innocence we found in it because we both felt right and justified. Instead of trying to understand, we were trying to avoid blame by appearing pure. So I prized my suffering and sustained it by refusing to give in or to open.

In this way of relating, we make ourselves alone and unhappy—even more so than when we began.

So just as with the world in general, we also objectify people through our mental models of how they should or should not work for us. We see them as either having what we want, being in the way of what we want, or being irrelevant to what we want (*attraction, aversion, indifference*). When you treat people like this, they unconsciously respond in kind. Even when your behavior is correct, but your intent is not, others pick up on it and feel the lack of sincerity. For instance, a compliment or an apology that feels insincere, an attempt to listen that feels as if you do not care, or a personal interest question that seems superficial. It's inauthentic, others sense it, and they close and resist. *People respond to your being, not your behavior*, because they can see through the behavior.

When you do this, you also fool yourself because you hang on to your view, do not see yourself as part of the equation, and fail to appreciate the other person's perspective. When you have a problem with someone, for instance, your me-centered boxes skew and distort because your automatic reaction is to make you right and make the other wrong without ever really listening to them. As a result, you cut yourself off from their side of the story, and from the full truth.

We also fool ourselves through stereotyping. Stereotyping is a form of bias, and our mental models are full of all sorts of different biases. Have you ever been quick to judge people based on their looks, age, style, or dress and make up your mind before ever giving them a chance? And how often are you just off? I used to for instance, stereotype all M.B.A.s as greedy and all West Pointers as "John Wayne." I would automatically dismiss their ideas, particularly around leadership, but later found I couldn't have been more wrong. Do you ever put people in a box like that and never relate to them authentically? White-Black, Christian-Muslim, Shia-Sunni—our boxes drive our beliefs and actions and we never bother to really check them out. No wonder the world is filled with conflict.

EXERCISE

Is there a typical attitude you might carry toward people you know? How do these play out for you? Is there a person who is particularly toxic for you? If so, what are the triggers?

◄o►

They Self-Alienate

There is a story of an old master who was visited by a famous philosopher.

"Master, I have no peace of mind," he said. The master replied, "Let me hear what you know already, and after hearing you, I will answer you as best as I can."

The philosopher then listed the areas of knowledge in which he was proficient. "Master, I know every science and every art in the world— metaphysics, physics, astronomy, chemistry, biology, psychology, aesthetics, ethics, culture, religion, and philosophy. There is nothing I do not know, but I have no peace of mind."

The great master replied, "All this that you have learned is a bundle of words, with no content inside. You have smeared yourself with a veneer, but you are quite different from that which you have gathered on to yourself. The shirt is not the person, and therefore your learning and your accomplishments are not what you truly are."

Underlying all our problems, then, is the fact that these mental models and habitual patterns of self-concern separate us not only from our world and other people but also from ourselves. They are conditioned responses that are self-alienating, splitting us from the real and authentic self and causing stress and even confusion.

Continuous Agitation

To conclude, I would like to share an excerpt by Yongey Mingyur Rinpoche from his book *In Love with the World*. He is the youngest son of Tulku Urgyen Rinpoche, a well-known Buddhist master of the twentieth century, and is, in his own right, now one of the world's most respected Tibetan Buddhist teachers. In this book he tells the story of his near-death experience in the first few months of his four-year wandering retreat in India and Nepal, and in this excerpt he points out the same message of self-limiting suffering conveyed above. It also telegraphs where we are headed in meditations.

> This continuous agitation we experience (hungry spirit) never ceases except for a few peak moments. We are constantly restless for the scent of something better, but it is always slightly out of reach. We remain convinced that the perfect temperature, the perfect partner, or the perfect job, is just around the corner. We imagine our compulsions and cravings will weaken, and a new friendship or new job will rescue us from our loneliness, insecurities, and disaffections. These fantasies change over the decades and some even come to fruition. But this agitation is constant and always pointed towards happiness and contentment and away from dissatisfaction.
>
> That agitation is pointing to an innate quality. Even behavior that is misguided and destructive, like stealing, sexual misconduct, or addictive substances, is motivated by the wish for happiness. The universal constancy of this is found throughout all our endeavors. However misguided at times it may be, this yearning for happiness draws on an inherent desire for care, comfort, and a sense of well-being that arises from the core of our being—a basic goodness.

It does not and could not arise from a belief, or an imposition of religious dogma or social values, because those are all concepts subject to change and whim. Instead, this orientation towards basic goodness is with us just as awareness is, recognized or not. We never live without it.[6]

For all this insight to come to fruition, our meditation needs to become a discipline and not just an occasional thing.

EXERCISE

Go back over your life and think about the events, relationships, and activities that have shaped it. What were the big turning points, good or bad? Where has the longing of your hungry spirit taken you? Where has the sense of achievement turned into a feeling of it not being enough? Where has the feeling of disappointment led to resentment and resignation?

━◦━

Meditation Instructions:
Technique II
Sweeping Shamata Vipassana I

We now move to the sweeping meditation technique, the second in the series of four as we move along the continuum of Shamata to Vipassana. Again, *Vipassana* means "insight"—insight into how we limit ourselves with concrete frames of reference that cut us off from our deeper nature and make us smaller than we are.

Always begin with Shamata. After you have settled your mind in Shamata for a few minutes, turn your awareness from your breath to the crown of your head. Dwelling there, gently notice any sensations that might arise. Don't force anything, just gently rest your attention on what is there. Note any sensations that arise—tingling, pleasure, or discomfort. As thoughts or emotions arise, simply note them here and return to the sensations.

Meet every sensation with equanimity without being pulled into any reaction of attraction, aversion, or indifference.

Be aware of how everything is constantly changing and never permanent—warmth, coolness, tingling, vibrating, or pulsing, and how every sensation is constantly changing and never remains the same from moment to moment.

This is called insight into impermanence, and it comes with maintaining equanimity. It is also called supreme seeing. Investigate this with an open interest.

Next, gradually sweep your attention across the top of your head, doing the same thing—constantly noticing the changing sensations and meeting them with a calm, abiding equanimity. As thoughts or feelings arise, gently bring your attention back to sweeping, allowing them just to be. Notice how they arise and often just fall away. Notice their impermanence.

Sometimes you will feel things and sometimes not, but do not force it. Dwell on a dull spot a little, and if you still feel nothing, then gently tap the top of your head to jump-start the sensation.

Continue to gently move your attention around the top of your head, noticing any sensations, and then slowly move it to your face, ears, sides of the head, and your neck, doing the same.

Then move down your shoulder to your arms, hands, and fingertips, one arm at a time.

Then the front of your torso, and so on, sweeping your entire body this way all the way down to your toes and slowly back up again to your crown, one appendage and section at a time.

Then repeat the sweeping, up and down the body.

As your mind wanders, gently meet your thoughts and emotions with equanimity and return to the sweeping. Notice how everything shifts and changes. As you gain comfort and familiarity, gradually increase the speed, and finally settling into a speed that is comfortable for you.

Continue until you feel the session is complete, then bring your attention back to the breath and relax there for a few minutes. Gently open your eyes, ending the session.

10

The Freedom of the Greater Spirit

Sweeping Shamata Vipassana Instruction II

We are not imprisoned by our circumstances, our setbacks,
our history, or our staggering defeats along the way. We are
freed by our choices.

JIM COLLINS

The Mutability of Habitual Patterns

Thought and Emotion Are Not Fixed or Solid

Have you ever met someone who committed some minor offense at your first meeting and then you shut them out afterwards before ever really knowing them? Or have you ever known someone who felt mistreated as a child and now does not trust others? These ideas are based on facts, but the continuing reaction is a fixed interpretation of them—a pattern, a box, and part of the Cosmic Egg. Many of your mental models do not necessarily represent your current reality, although you believe them to be your reality. In this sense, it's not necessarily the events that make you suffer, it's your continuing story about these events afterwards that make you suffer.

For me, my father didn't abandon me—he simply passed away. My pain comes from years of reaction to that event, and it affected many of my close relationships. Similarly, someone who was ignored as a child because they were the youngest of a large family may have wanted to be seen and respected. In both situations, we continued to interpret our world through an idea based on an old event. But who was continuing to do it to us? It was an old wound that was still running our lives.

If you open yourself up, however, to new life experiences, you can see that these habitual patterns can change. For instance, I used to have an odd one around cottage cheese. When I was a boy my mother would force me to eat it, and I disliked it so much that I would gag. But at one of my early meditation retreats, I moved from detesting cottage cheese to loving cottage cheese, simply by opening up, clearing my mind, and letting go of that old idea from childhood. Maybe being hungry and not having another choice had something to do with it, but in either case, it worked.

The very first time that I was conscious of breaking a mental model was when I studied abroad. I had grown up and was educated in a small town in upstate New York, and by the time I was in my early twenties I had only traveled out of the Northeast once on a spring break road trip to Florida. My world was quite small in every sense.

When I enrolled in a French-speaking exchange program in Belgium I did not know French, so I had to learn it as I went along. During my time there I traveled extensively, became fluent in the language, and made lots of diverse and interesting friends from many different cultures—Belgian, French, Scandinavian, Turkish, Mexican, Dutch, and more. It was transforming because in immersing myself a new language and new cultures, trying new things, I had this sense that I was starting all over again. There were no established roles or expectations to live by, and I felt a tremendous freedom to experiment with everything.

I found the experience of food to be more aesthetic, politics more liberal, sexuality more open, and life routines more balanced. I learned to cook, I learned to dance, I learned to be a little outrageous, but most importantly, I learned a great deal about my real interests, other ways of living, and the influence of culture and language on my perspectives. I found French, for instance, a far more emotionally expressive language, and I found myself far more expressive and less reserved too. As a result, my world expanded, my confidence grew, and my whole self-concept and demeanor began to shift.

My reality changed as my mental models changed. Look for yourself. Where have your ideas, attitudes, or mental models of things changed over the years?

Realize, then, that if any one of your mental models is not true, maybe none of them are. They are mental constructs that are void of any inherent, independent, solid existence. As my Ayahuasca experience showed, thoughts and emotions are like soap bubbles that pop upon close examination.

This is often quickly realized in meditation practice as our awareness grows. The emotional constructs are stronger and more resilient, but when brought under the microscope of awareness they eventually reveal themselves to be less solid or concrete than we treat them. They begin to flicker and fade. What does that say about your reality? The life you are living is *a* reality, but it is not *the* reality.

In Fact, They Are Empty

They lack any inherent existence other than being a temporary thought, emotional construct, or habit of your mind. We are confused about happiness, for instance, because we really don't know what brings happiness in the first place. Our old boxes can make us acquisitive, ambitious, and pleasure seeking but not necessarily happy. You may find happiness in such things, but is it enduring? Fulfilling personal desires and ambitions in the pursuit of things in your outer world does not compare to loving relationships, satisfying work, or helping someone in need. These come from attending to your inner world.

The pleasures of your outer world are short-lived and often confine your hungry spirit to an endless, and increasingly empty, loop of thoughtless, shallow activity. What a frail premise to lean on for your happiness. As said before, you cannot possibly know what you want if you do not first know who you are beyond the pursuits of the lesser spirit.

Your greater spirit will not give you peace until you begin to understand this—you get stuck because the self-centered ways of the lesser spirit develop into an acquired self-image that you want to project and protect, but this is not who you really are; *this is just the idea of who you are.* This confusion builds up over time and results in stress. Your idea of yourself is itself just an accumulated habitual thought pattern that has no solid reality and skews the truth. It is as fleeting as a flying bird's footprints in the sky.

Your happiness comes less from acquiring anything at all and more from a deeper understanding of yourself.

Again, I use myself as an example. I arrived at midlife believing I had an ideal marriage, a successful and reputable career, and a great family life. But deeper understanding came rushing to the surface as the marriage began to unravel. Suddenly the veneer of who I thought I was pulled away, leaving me painfully revealed and with many, many unanswered questions. I felt insecure and lost. I began to doubt, and my world began to doubt me in return. I started to make poor choices— and those choices led to even greater doubt.

Everything spiraled down. I began to feel abandoned in every aspect of my life—my marriage dissolved, my work was not going well, and my friends, family, and even children distanced themselves. My self-doubt had become a self-fulfilling prophecy; I felt abandoned, so the world did the same in return. Yes, this was my midlife crisis, and it was brought on by the collapse of who I thought I was. My life issue was raging out of control as I had no place to hide from it anymore. It was like the universe had taken me by the shoulders and shaken me, saying, "Deal with this!"

As Dante said, "In the middle of the journey of our life I came to myself within a dark wood where the straight way was lost."[1] Every little mental model I had of myself seemed to pop like a soap bubble, and I felt tremendously raw, abandoned, and afraid.

So, They Can Change

The thing you need to know is that your hungry spirit can adapt— you can mount and ride it to gain your freedom. Its pursuits are mutable, and it works based on the information you selectively feed it—thoughts, beliefs, and attitudes. It serves you poorly when it is grounded in the lesser, in thoughts, feelings, and activities that *defend* or *protect* you. It serves you best when it is grounded in the greater, in feelings that *open* and *project* you, and is directed toward things that reach and serve something beyond you, that make you more open, even vulnerable.

This means that once you become aware of your life-limiting habitual patterns and mental models, you can begin to change them. They are problems only if you are unaware of them. There are certain external conditions in life that are out of your control, but you can still choose how you respond to them, and therein lies your growth and your freedom. Instead of feeling victimized and automatically defaulting to the belief that the problem is always "out there," you can choose first to look inward, adapt, and respond in a different way. For example, instead of complaining about the problems you have or about such and such a person who is not doing their job right, you can step back, choose to stop blaming and defaulting to your defensive patterns, and work to see other possibilities. Everything then becomes more workable.

There is an old Zen story of a master who has a stick and says to the student, "If you say this is a stick, I will hit you. If you say this is not a stick, I will hit you. If you say nothing about the stick, I will hit you." The student comes many days in a row and says the wrong thing and is hit with the stick every time. He becomes so frustrated and angry that one day he finally takes the stick away from the master. The master bows and says, "The next lesson begins tomorrow." You can change your mental model.

You can consciously choose how you respond by dropping your old frames of references and giving yourself the freedom to adopt a new way. Your mental models—habitual patterns of thought and emotion—are mutable because they are empty constructs to begin with. Marcus Aurelius said "If you are pained by external things, it is not that they disturb you, but your own judgment of them. And it is in your power to wipe out that judgment now."

Following are examples of how reframing and behavior change can help liberate you from old patterns. The reason? They are impermanent illusions to begin with.

Strategies for Change

These basic strategies work with your habitual patterns in a healthy, constructive way. They bring growth, self-esteem, and some actualization of the greater spirit, but they are still in the realm of the psycho-emotional and not of the spirit necessarily. What they do is move us up the hierarchy to a level of maturity for genuinely and authentically approaching a path of spiritual awakening—in the middle to upper end, still looking up, not at the place of deficiency but in one of worth and even abundance.

Turn Fear into an Ally

When I was a boy, I was so terrified of heights that I would panic simply being around a ladder. This panic was beyond being a healthy fear of heights—I would freeze. Then as a young man I had an opportunity to go rock climbing in a wilderness adventure program. I was determined to face my fear, so I was the first one to go up. The climb was about eight feet with an 80 percent pitch. I had cottonmouth, I was gripped by fear, and I slipped a couple of times, but I muscled my way up it. Even though I was on the end of a rope, I was still terrified. Then the instructor said, "Now I want you to do it again, blindfolded." Again, panic set in, but, not to be outdone by my peers, who I knew would do it, I did it again, blindfolded. The result was amazing. I felt more in control and able to turn my vision inward to feel my way. I realized how my fear was just a habit of sight, a projection, and very workable.

Not only was that breakthrough invigorating, but it also emboldened me to tackle other fears, like speaking up in a group and working through conflicts with others. It proved to be an extremely helpful guide for dealing with the many other fears that arose in midlife, and I would draw on this experience again and again in facing other insecurities.

As Ralph Waldo Emerson said, "Always do what you are afraid to do." Traveling your own path requires learning to work with fear. We all have fears, many of them rooted in self-doubt. But there are healthy fears, like a fear of heights, which even avid rock climbers have. And then there are unhealthy fears (the intensity of my fears made it unhealthy). The unhealthy fears are the ones that signal the way to personal growth—our hang-ups contain our wealth, and our neuroses our wisdom.

Unhealthy fear shapes the boundaries of what we know and feel is possible in our lives. These fears are different for each of us. For some, it may be a fear of public speaking: "I freeze in front of groups, so I can't do that"; for others, a feeling of being out of control: "I can't let them do that—they would do it wrong"; for still others it is losing our job, going to parties, or saying something stupid. I even knew a person who was afraid of Claymation, of all things! These unhealthy fears make us small.

Whatever that boundary is for you, cross it. I had a fear of heights— I crossed it; I had a fear of being exposed in groups—I crossed it; I had a fear of public speaking—I crossed it; I had a fear of being vulnerable in relationship, and I crossed it. There is so much growth in crossing the threshold of your fears.

To cross them requires awareness, courage, and action. It requires awareness because when you are aware you see the world more accurately, and this helps diffuse your emotional reactions. Fear often comes from what you don't know. You may not order something new off the menu, for instance, for fear of not liking it, or you don't address a conflict for fear of a bad outcome. More poignantly, fear comes from not wanting to know what you don't know. You may not ask for feedback, for instance, for fear of it being bad, or you don't ask someone out on a date for fear of rejection. When you are aware of these fears, however, and examine their habitual causes, their grip loosens.

My fear of rejection comes from my abandonment wound, but who is abandoning me now? No one. I am just asking for a date. What are the consequences of rejection? Not much—just pride—so why not? It is just an old habit that I can discard like a worn-out shoe.

It requires courage even to ask these questions, but we often confuse courage with fearlessness. Courage is not the absence of fear but is transcending fear by deciding that something else is more important. True courage is learning to work through your fear, and when you do, it feels like a breakthrough. Have you ever noticed, for instance, that when you work through your fear, it creates an uplifting, exhilarating energy? Just like the feeling I had in working with my fear of heights. You have broken through a self-imposed limitation, and that instills a confidence you can ride for further change.

And, of course, when you choose not to, you feel anxious, embarrassed, guilty, or fearful. These feelings are often your boxes, trips, patterns, or Cosmic Egg under attack, and a sign to wake up. Carl Jung said, "Whatever shadows we don't want to see in ourselves, life will bring to us as destiny," over and over again. This is like Bill Murray in *Groundhog Day*, whose life repeats a pattern over and over until he finally "gets it" and chooses to respond in a different way.

I used to be invisible in groups and would even freeze when asked to speak because I was afraid of saying something stupid. At times I would have something to say but would wait, unsure, until someone else would finally say it. Then I would feel embarrassed. My life kept putting me into these situations, and this went on for years without resolution. Eventually I chose to stretch myself by taking active roles in groups, and I attended several intensive small-group workshops that forced me to fully engage—and the pattern broke. Group participation and presentation then became central to my work.

When you see a repeated pattern like this, it is like you are unconsciously calling forth a certain reality to seek its resolution. Your habitual mental pattern is causing you to suffer. This suffering is a vehicle for your growth, and it becomes a stepping stone to freedom if you choose. Anthropologist Joseph Campbell said, "Where you stumble, there lies your treasure." Your triggered habitual fears are clues pointing the way to your freedom. So pay attention to them and use them as signs to wake up and do your life differently. My friend who kept losing her job, for instance, learned that she was self-sabotaging through her version of the "I can't make a difference" habitual pattern of insecurity.

Challenge the patterns that make you small.

Finally, it requires action. Have you ever felt nervous, for instance, before confronting a difficult conversation or making a big presentation, and then seen your nervousness disappear soon after you start? It was the same with me in athletic events and doing presentations—nervous, but relaxed soon after the action began. The best remedy for dealing with fear is to act; it dissolves the fear.

EXERCISE

Where might there be repeated insecure patterns like this in your life? How might you address them?

◄◦►

Flip Problems into Opportunities

There is a famous quote by anthropologist, author, and mystic Carlos Castaneda, who said, "The difference between an ordinary person and a warrior is that an ordinary person takes every problem as a burden and a curse, whereas a warrior takes it on as a challenge and opportunity."[2] So flip problems into opportunities. Every day we are faced with a number of adversities. Usually we see them as problems, burdens, because the world is not conforming to our view—our box. As we have seen, these problems cause us enormous stress, frustration, and anxiety. Yet we can reframe them by again changing our attitude and treating them as opportunities to learn and grow as a person.

For example, let's say that someone said something to you that is rude or offensive. Instead of seeing this as a problem, you could view this situation as an opportunity to practice patience and forgiveness and to work skillfully with the other person. You could take the anger and redirect it in a positive way to resolve the problem. You could also take it as an opportunity to practice assertiveness. The person is actually a gift—a teacher—to help you grow.

If you are only looking at what is wrong, then you will only see problems. The more you focus on your issues, the more you will attract them and feel angry, victimized, and bitter. On the other hand, if you look for solutions, the lessons to be learned, and the changes to be made, then you will begin to attract opportunities. If you are out of work, for instance, you might desperately start looking for another job. Alternatively, you might change your mental model by looking upon this as the opportunity to now do anything you want, to get the *right* job, or to start your own business.

This is the difference between being a victim and a victor. "My boss doesn't respect me," "I am not paid enough to do that," "I just do what I am told" are the responses of a victim. You get into the blame game—you blame the bureaucracy, the boss, the weather, the food. You can blame an infinite number of things, but when you do this, things get complicated. People start to blame back, and we are back to playing ping-pong again.

Instead of being a *victim*, where you remove yourself from any part of the explanation of the situation, you could choose to be a *victor* by taking on some of the responsibility for the situation yourself and responding and working with it more constructively. Being a victor does not always mean that you win, but it does mean choosing to play the game by seeing it in a different way. Being a victim happens to all of us from time to time. The important point is to become aware of it so you can flip it around.

Victim	Victor
Nothing I can do	I look at alternatives
It's the way I am	I choose another way
They make me mad	I control my feelings
They won't allow it	I can change it
I can't	I will
I have to	I prefer to
If only	What if

EXERCISE

Look at some of the common problems you face—how might you reframe them as opportunities? Ask, what are the lessons to be learned? What might be the solutions? What opportunities are there? Ask, if not, then what is next?

◄○►

Reframe Perspective

A friend of mine told me a story of a man who planned a peaceful, solitary meditation retreat in a cabin in the woods. On starting his practice, he heard the gurgling of the brook nearby. As time went on, this gurgling seemed to grow louder and louder, and it began to disturb his peace of mind. He found his thoughts constantly following the sound of the brook, and soon he started to crave the silence he believed he was missing. At one point the sound became so unbearable for him that he went into the water and started moving the rocks around. So instead of looking within to find peace of mind or changing his mental frame, he tried manipulating his world. The forest was not conforming to his box.

This story may seem absurd, but how often do you do something like this? When you do not get what you want, don't you become frustrated, irritated, stressed? It's not by moving rocks that you find happiness, it's by transforming your relationship to them.

Contrast that with a very old tale about a woodcutter. Every day the woodcutter would take a break from his work to refresh and renew with a walk through the forest. One day on his walk, he came upon a man crushing a pile of stones with a heavy sledgehammer. The man was sweating and working hard but was not very happy—he cursed under his breath as he worked. The woodcutter stopped and asked, "What are you doing, my friend?" Angrily, the man replied, "Can't you see? I have to crush this pile of stone in order to get paid today!" Feeling sorry for him, the woodcutter continued his walk and soon came across another man doing the same thing as the first. He was working just as hard, but in contrast he was the personification of contentment—whistling and genuinely happy in his work. "And what are you doing my friend?" the woodcutter asked. "I am building the foundation of our new cathedral," came the reply.

It was the same work but a different frame. It's often *not what you do, but how you do it*. You can switch your mental frame, and the change can be life-changing. Instead of fixating on what you want or are not getting from the world and trying to manipulate it, first find out who you are and what is most important, and consider a change to your mental frame.

The interesting thing is that we are most unhappy when we selfishly make ourselves the center of our world and most happy when we do not. The self-centered cravings we adopt in the pursuit of happiness are the very same thing that cause us endless suffering when we don't achieve it. A healthier strategy is simply finding a cause or purpose to serve that brings meaning and self-worth.

Behave into New Ways of Being
Just like our thoughts, feelings, attitudes, and intentions, our actions too are causes and have consequences. If you cannot muster a feeling of confidence, then act confidently until the feeling comes. In other words, when all else fails, just do it—fake it till you make it. Acting with confidence can build confidence. Daniel Goleman says we do not

think our way into new behaviors, we behave our way into new ways of thinking. We can rewire ourselves through our actions, and those actions can lead to changes in our being. This is exactly what poet John Dryden meant when he said, "We first make our habits, then our habits make us."

American philosopher William James once said, "I don't sing because I'm happy; I'm happy because I sing"[3] Singing evokes happiness, even when we are feeling down. Instead of the power of positive thinking, it is the power of positive action. Similarly, acting with kindness evokes feelings of kindness, acting with confidence brings a feeling of confidence, and expressing gratitude evokes a feeling of gratitude. It is the same principle. If you want to be interesting, be interested; to be appreciated, appreciate; in giving you receive; to get a smile, give one away. Your sense of well-being grows, and that gives you strength to cope with whatever comes.

A while ago, I was standing on a crowded bus. At a stop, a women entered on crutches. A pale, frowning man seemingly absorbed in his own thoughts and troubles, saw her predicament and spontaneously offered her his seat. She was delighted at the favor, and he glowed with the small positive difference he had just made.

The mistake many make is to believe that simple awareness is enough to break out of the cocoon of self-absorption. It is not; you also must act. It's the same with building self-esteem at work. You don't just think your way into new behavior; you also behave your way into new ways of thinking.

I have often heard from those who wanted to shy away from a challenge because they didn't feel fully prepared. This is usually their self-doubt talking. Do not wait until you feel good enough or confident enough before taking on a big challenge—jump in and try it. It's not actually about feeling good or prepared, it's about the quality of your effort. Do it, muddle through, experience failure, and learn on the way. Eventually you will begin to have success. Act, and the self-esteem will come. Try it and see what happens.

Give Generously

A few years ago, I arranged for students to do volunteer cleanup work for a local land trust. We spent the day cleaning up garbage on recently acquired property near family homes in a poor rural community. The day was wet, but we had fun in the muck, mire, and stench of the cleanup, growing tired and dirty by the end of the day. In our closing circle, I asked everyone for their personal reflections. As we went around the circle, everyone was expressing their gratitude and appreciation for the opportunity to help. Then we came to a student who was in tears. She said that the highlight of her day was when she went up to say hello to one of the families. They thanked her from the bottom of their hearts for cleaning up their "backyard." Now the children could play again in the forest without fear of getting hurt. We were then all in tears—when we are giving to others, we are nourishing our hearts.

In giving, you receive. When you give something to someone else, you are often the one who feels best. It nurtures your basic goodness and allows it to shine through. Have you ever given your time to help someone with a flat tire, given directions to someone who is lost, given up your seat to someone who needs it more, or simply given support to someone having a bad day? What happens to you inside? I'll bet that those small acts of generosity are often the highlight of your day. Everyone is better off, and you get a "helper's high".

As Emerson explains, "It is one of the beautiful compensations of this life that no man can sincerely help another without helping himself."[4]

One Christmas season, I decided to cash in a basket of coins I had accumulated. Every day when returning home, I would empty whatever change I had in my pocket into this basket. In the past, this change would disappear, as my children would pick through it for extra spending money. Now, in an empty nest, it was overflowing. So I threw the change in a bag and headed to the local grocery store where there was an automatic coin sorter. As I was entering the store, an old friend was ringing the bell for a Salvation Army donation stop. I spontaneously handed him the bag of coins, and we instantly broke into laughter and appreciation for what we were both doing. That moment stuck with me and continued to serve as a source of joy and comfort for days.

Many of our world traditions point to the value of generosity for our happiness as well as our success. Research agrees that volunteer activity induces a sense of well-being and that giving is an essential component of good mental health. The whole field of servant leadership emerged from the notion that it is in our own self-interest to consider the self-interest of others. Even the grandfather of capitalism, Adam Smith, would say that. Servant leaders succeed because the needs of followers are so looked after that they reach their full potential and perform at their best.

Generosity takes many forms—you can give money, you can give time, or you can give a piece of yourself. These are all important, but I think what is most important to our happiness is our attitude. Does your generosity feel like single acts of giving, as in donating to your favorite cause each year, or is it more a way of life? I don't mean giving everything away, but rather I mean giving in different ways and within your means, wherever the opportunities arise. Who is more generous, for instance—Bill Gates, who makes a one-time gift of half of his fortune to create a foundation in his name, or the mother in Darfur who gives up meals each and every day so her children can eat? Again, both are important, but I argue the benefits to your happiness are greater if it is more a way of life and you do not expect recognition in return.

There is an ancient Buddhist metaphor about this. It asks, *do you give as a king* who magnanimously shares his wealth with his people after it is gained, *do you give as a boatman* who ferries himself and others across the river safely together, or *do you give as a shepherd* who makes sure his flock is always in front and arrives safely first? Which do you think induces a greater sense of well-being? Give a piece of yourself, too—that is where the greatest sense of well-being resides.

I did not always give of myself, but *I learned to behave into a new way of being.* I remember debating with a friend, for instance, about my wanting to be more generous in my feelings with others but that I couldn't. Since I didn't *feel* generous, I argued how I could I *be* generous? Finally one day, I just tried complimenting a friend, even though it didn't feel quite natural to me at the time. Surprisingly, not only was he moved but so was I. It allowed me to connect with him, and I felt better about myself. My acting generously aroused feelings of generosity.

Later, at one of my support team meetings, this issue of giving of myself came up again. The team still wanted more of me, so they challenged me with an exercise—to go around the circle taking turns to sit in front of each of them, look into their eyes, and express what I saw and what I felt. To my amazement, pressed in this way, my intuition and my heart came rushing forth. Somehow, on a gut level, I knew both the gifts and the challenges each person had in this life and pointed to them accurately. In expressing this in words, I also felt my appreciation and compassion for them and was soon in tears. In those few moments, I gave myself over totally to each one of my friends and discovered a gift that I had always thought was missing but that was there all along.

This way of giving is now an integral part of my life, as a friend, as a mentor, and as a professional coach. I spend much of my day in this role, and over the years, I have found that I am being transformed by it. My listening skills have improved, my compassion is deeper, and my emotions are expressed more. I also have a stronger sense of confidence and self-worth. In fact, I am happier than I have ever been, and I spend little of my time worrying about *me*. As Winston Churchill said, "We make a living by what we get; we make a life by what we give."[5]

Nine Helpful Metaphors

The point of all of the above is to reveal in detail how our self-centered thoughts and emotions are not as solid, concrete, and immutable as we treat them. Our so-called reality is changeable, and that realization opens us to growth, freedom, and greater happiness.

Just as Ayahuasca showed, we are not our thoughts, our roles, or our status. Whatever emotions, thoughts, sensations, or perceptions we have, these manifest, repeat, and accumulate into an identity and sense of who we think we are, but not truly who we are.

They are insubstantial and transitory, and upon investigation they dissolve and disappear like the illusion. Buddhism has nine famous metaphors for describing this.

Like a Shooting Star. When you see a shooting star, you only see it for a few seconds before it disappears. Similarly, your experience of a thought or emotion is as ephemeral as a flash of light shooting across the sky.

Like a Fire Ring. When you spin a ball of fire around in a circle, it looks like a solid ring of fire. In the same way, your perception of what is real is just an illusory pattern.

Like a Butter Lamp. When a butter lamp is lit, the flame looks solid and permanent, but this is another illusion, because when the oil is exhausted, the flame disappears without a trace.

Like a Magic Show. When a magician performs, the magic looks real, but it is a combination of many interdependent parts that make it seem so. Similarly, your thoughts and emotions combine to make an experience look real, but they are subject to change the more or less that you hold onto them.

Like Dew. In the morning, dew looks strong, thick, and stable, but as soon as the warm sun rises, it evaporates and disappears. Similarly, your thoughts and emotions are only a temporary effect waiting for their causes and conditions to change.

Like Bubbles. Your perceptions and impressions are like soap bubbles. They look real and exist with rainbow colors, yet they are very fragile. As soon as the wind blows or something changes, they pop. Everything is constantly changing and so too are your thoughts and impressions.

Like a Dream. Dreams seem very real because what you experience in the daytime also happens in a dream. You experience hope, fear, acceptance, and rejection. But the moment you wake up, it is all gone. It is just a memory that quickly fades.

Like Lightning. When you see lightning, it looks so strong and powerful, but as soon as it comes, it goes. It is just a flash. All your thoughts and perceptions are like this. Nothing lasts forever, and when it goes, you cannot even find a trace of where it has been.

Like Clouds. Clouds appear in the sky, move in the sky, and dissolve in the sky. You cannot see where they come from or where they go. Just so, your thoughts and emotions arise, reside temporarily, and then fade away.

All these phenomena appear but are not real, in the sense of being solid and permanent. Yet we tend to treat our perceptions so and to subconsciously presume that things last forever, but it is not the case. When we are in our routine of daily life, everything feels solid and strong, and we rarely think it will change. Yet eventually something shifts, and our experience becomes a memory that then fades away. Our minds—our thoughts and emotions—are like this.

We begin to see this in our meditations. There is nothing ever solid and substantive about them to hold onto. We have an unending stream of thoughts, emotions, and perceptions constantly arising that seem real and concrete. Yet as we bring our awareness to them, they begin to shift, change, dissolve, and arise again in an endless display of changing forms. This permits us to see just how vast and open our being really is.

Meditation Instructions: Technique II Sweeping Shamata Vipassana, Continued

I was introduced to sweeping meditation at a ten-day silent retreat led by S. N. Goenka at his center in Igatpuri, India. It was also my first deep dive into meditation, and I later recorded the following reflections in my journal.

Journal Entry

I brought my awareness to my head and tried to feel any sensation there, perhaps heat, tingling, or vibration.

I couldn't at first, so I brought my hand to the top of my head and kept my palm about a quarter of an inch from it, without touching. The sensations gradually arose. Then I brought my hand down, keeping my awareness there, and vibrating, tingling and pulsing sensations grew.

I stayed aware of these sensations as Goenka reminded us to recognize their anicca—*their impermanence. Like everything else, they were constantly changing. So let them go, let them be within equanimity. However pleasant or unpleasant, do not hold on to or reject them, but instead rest in the experience of steady awareness.*

Then I moved my attention to the sides of my head, my forehead, and my face, just noticing any sensations and meeting them without any reaction. As my mind wandered, I noted it, and gently brought it back to the sweeping. I felt the tingling of my nerves, the tightness of my muscles, and the pain in my knees as I moved my awareness gradually and methodically down each section of my body. My mind wandered at times, roaming between the past and the future, but as I became aware again, I gently returned to the sensations. If I could not feel anything, then I tried to stay with the awareness of no sensation.

I just wanted to remain with whatever was happening, trying to notice any changes, both in the sensation and in my reaction. Eventually I found that every speck of my body—my skin, my pores, my blood vessels—constantly vibrating, pulsing, and changing.

Experiencing this constant change helped me let go of a fixed state of mind—the ground of anxiety, stress, and mental obscuration. In recognizing anicca and meeting it with equanimity, fixation faded and allowed me to relax in my being. Every thought or impulse to grasp or reject dissolved of its own course, leaving gaps utterly free of any conception and memory.

Freedom.

As I began to speak again at the end of this retreat, I felt vertigo as the vibrations my vocal cords reverberated on the inside of my ear

*drums. That was how silent my world had become. I was also so blissed
out that I felt for sure I only needed another day or two to experience full
enlightenment, which eventually served as a cruel reminder not to cling
to the bliss, either.*

As you sweep, visualize your awareness as water flowing over a creek
bed, covering every nook and cranny of your body. Nothing is left out,
nothing uncovered.

Imagine your awareness penetrating deeper into your body, feeling
the pulsing, movements, and vibrations.

As thoughts, emotions, and sensations arise and fall away, notice
how they are like the metaphors described above.

In sweeping painful spots, maintain equanimity without rejecting,
and just be attentively present with each experience. Experiment with
this in two ways:

Without dwelling or hovering over it, just pass on by without hesi-
tating or reacting as you continue sweeping.

Stop and rest your awareness on it, again without reacting. Relax into
the pain and just be there with it. Notice any changes in it as you
do. After maintaining equanimity for a while, continue sweeping.

Remember, in this method you are developing your awareness by
being mindful of your bodily sensations as well as thoughts that arise
and distract you from the practice. Always note and meet them with
equanimity and return to the sweeping.

Coda: A Text Exchange with My Friend Tom

ToM: Sitting quietly, doing nothing, not knowing what is next and
not concerned with what was or what may be next, a new mind is
operating that is not connected with the conditioned past and yet
perceives and understands that whole mechanism of conditioning.

It is the unmasking of the self that is nothing but masks—images, memories of past experiences, fears, hopes, and the ceaseless demand to be something or somebody. This new mind seems better, more peaceful—there is no doer in it and nothing to be done.

CLINT: Yes, it's a truly raw, open, and beautifully vulnerable place. This is where genuine spiritual paths coach us to be. That is the meditation. You created a set of external conditions that led you there, a literal homelessness. I attempt to do the same, but more from a cushion.

So interesting to be lifelong friends and still share these things at this stage in life.

11

The Cosmic Joke: Peering into Transcendence and Who Am I?

Open Shamata Vipassana I

*If you search for the origin or root cause of anything—
whether a plant or a thought—you will find it has a
continuity stretching back to beginningless time.*

HH DALAI LAMA

Menander's Questions

If thoughts and emotions are ephemeral and empty in essence, meaning
empty of any inherent, fixed, and substantial identity of their own, then
what is their source? Who is thinking and feeling? Where in the mind
does that sense of self come from? There are no answers to these questions. When you ask, you always arrive at a speechless state, one that is
spacious, open, and awake. That is the source of all being, from which our
sense of "I" and everything else arises and to which it dissolves back again.
Whether it is a thought, emotion, or sense, or the perception of any phenomena at all, it is the same. When you look for the source, it is like writ-

ing letters in water—they fade as soon as they appear. There is nothing to find other than awareness itself. That open ultimate source is called Tantra, meaning the continuous conscious state of our being—awake and expressive—that pervades all perception, experience, and existence.

A story adapted from an early Buddhist text called *Menander's Questions* is often used to introduce this key point.

About one hundred fifty years after the Buddha died, a king named Menander encountered the venerated Buddhist monk Nagasena. The king did not know this monk, so he asked for his name. The monk gave it to him and added, "This is only a name, an appellation, a matter of conventional usage. There is no individual person to be found in here," he explained to the king. "Nagasena is only a label, a designation."

King Menander then asked, "Who is wearing the robes, who enjoys them, who meditates, who practices?"

The monk answered, "The designation Nagasena."

Pushing him further, the king asked, "Could it be that the hairs on your head are Nagasena?"

The monk said, "No."

The king then asked if his true identity could be found in other parts of his body, such as his nails, teeth, skin, sinews, heart, liver, lungs, stomach, excrement, blood, sweat, tears, or urine? "Your brain, perhaps?"

The monk told the king his identity could not be found in any of those body parts.

The king then asked if the monk was " . . . a feeling of pleasure or pain, a perception, an impulse, or a state of consciousness?"

It is easier to be sure that "I" is not a body part than to be sure "I" is not a perception or state of consciousness. We could bet our lives that "I" was not our embarrassments, our pride, our failure, our panic. Nonetheless, these feelings still hold a grip on us.

The king then accused the monk of lying to him, "You said that you are Nagasena, when no such person exists."

When the king and Nagasena looked for "I," there was no one to be found. Just like thoughts and emotions, the notion of self crumbles. If we are not our thoughts, our roles, or our status, nor our embarrassments or our fears, then what are we? And where do these arise and reside upon investigation?

We have been moving gradually up to this point, but now we take a deeper dive into our investigation of who we really are and how we operate through a series of customary inquiries of the Buddhist tradition. I received this teaching several times from different teachers, and the following section is based on a talk given by Khenpo Tsewang Dongyal Rinpoche during the annual spring retreat 2014.

All is Empty: An Intellectual Analysis

The teeth, the hair, the nails are not "I"
And "I" is not the bones or eye
The mucus, the nose, and phlegm, are not the "I"
And neither is it made from lymph or thigh
The "I" is not the body's grease or sweat
Nor the lungs and liver make it set
The stomach and inner organs, are not "I"
Nor does the body's excrement apply.
If such a thing as "I" exists indeed
Then the grip of hope and fear would seed.
But since no self or "I" exists at all,
Then what place exists for hope and fear at all?

SHANTIDEVA

The Hidden Flaw of the Mind

When we think of "I" or the sense of "I," we generally think of three principal things—our body, our senses, and our mind. In the Buddhist tradition these are known as body (our form), speech (our sensory reaction to form), and mind (our interpretive response). Most of the time we lump the three together and identify completely with them as our self—"I"—without further thought. We automatically think *I am my body, I am my senses, I am my mind*, and that's it.

Let's take a closer look at what the truth really is.

We start by asking, where does your body come from? It starts with our parents, arrives at birth, develops as we grow up, and does not last for a long time. It is impermanent. Looking closely, we find no independently and inherently existing thing that we call a body. It is made of interdependent parts of arms, legs, bones, flesh, blood, molecules, and so on that we simply label as "body." No single piece stands on its own. There is no inherently and permanently existing body at all. It's made up of interdependent parts that are infinitely divisible into finer things like cells, molecules, particles, quarks, and so on.

Next ask, where do the senses come from—the sense of touch, sound, smell, taste, and sight? Here again we see each is made up of interdependent and impermanent parts. Let's take speech as our example. Speech first manifests at birth when we begin to cry and develops into language and other sounds as we grow up. These sounds are made up from different elements of your body—your vocal cords, your breath, and the mind (your intention). These three things bring about your voice, which can be further subdivided into interdependent parts just like the body. There is no single independently existing voice; it comes from a combination of things.

Then we move to the mind, which also begins at conception and develops into the thinking mind we now have. The composite of three things—body, senses, and mind—we think constitute an "I," but which one is most important? We all know the mind rules everything. Every impression we have or activity we undertake we label as positive, negative, or neutral, without exception, and through them we make ourselves happy, sad, or indifferent. But who makes this designation? It is not our body or our senses; it is our mind quietly doing this.

The mind rules the actions of our body and the interpretation of our senses. Body and speech are incapable of any independent thought and action, yet we blame them because we lump them together with the sense of "I" and fail to see that it is the mind that truly rules everything we think, say, or do.

Someone may make you angry, but the cause of that anger is your mind, not your body or speech. The mind recollects the anger and then reflects it outwardly in body and speech. Even if you beat someone out of anger it is still not addressing the fundamental cause, because body and speech are activated by the mind.

This is true of all the senses. So if body and senses are ruled by mind, then we continue our search for "I" in the mind.

Who Am I?

I remember one day when I was ten to twelve years old, I was at home in the bathroom taking a pee. As I did, I would often gaze at the wall, just zoning out. That day, out of the blue, I spontaneously asked myself, who am I? My mind went into a void, searching for a response, and my body started to shiver and shake, spraying pee all over the toilet and the floor. I was stunned. There was no answer to the question—my mind went into a speechless void and my body made a mess to clean up.

So ask yourself this question, and investigate it thoroughly. Look for the looker. Am I my body? No, we already answered that. Am I my senses? We answered that too—we are not. Then maybe "I" is my mind or is in my mind. I look there and ask, who am I? Am I a father, a son, a husband, a friend, a leadership guru? Investigate every identity you have, and the answer is always yes, but still partial and not It. It is still not the universal source, still not the fundamental, concrete "I." The answers are always partial—"I am not just that." It was the same message as in one of my early Ayahuasca ceremonies.

Yet the more you inspect "I," the more questions you create. The more you analyze, quantify, and qualify, the more unknowable it becomes. With intimate inspection, everything seems to fall apart—just like your habitual thoughts and emotions, your sense of "I" has no base. It crumbles upon investigation.

Investigating in this way, you realize these identities are just another habitual thought pattern of the mind that fades as you bring your awareness to them. You are not who you think you are. Your sense of self is none other than another illusion, just like all your other thought patterns. You move into a speechless state, you crack the Cosmic Egg.

EXERCISE

Take a few minutes and ask yourself, who am I? Try to identify any single concrete thing that identifies "I."

If "I" is just like thought, another ephemeral and empty construct and illusion of the mind, then let's investigate the mind itself.

◄○►

Where Is the Mind?

You should know, because it manipulates and turns the wheel of your existence in every activity, every feeling, and every instance.

But when you look quickly and directly at the mind itself without thinking, you cannot really find it. You may see a flickering and shimmering intelligence that is vague and constantly moving. If you try to hold it, it disappears. If you try to make it stay still, it flies around like a bee caught in a jar. You cannot say if it is this or that because you cannot put your finger on it. You cannot identify it in any way, yet it makes you feel happy, sad, or indifferent. If you try to catch it, you won't; if you try to make it stay put, you can't; if you try to name it, you don't. There is nothing else and no one else experiencing this except your mind, yet you can't handle it intellectually. Work this analysis on your own and discover this for yourself.

Methodically ask, where is the mind, where is it coming from, and where is it going? These three analytical questions are like a powerful koan of the mind,

> Where is mind coming from?
> Where is mind staying or dwelling?
> Where is mind going or ending?

Reflect on these three questions and see where they lead. If there is any even slight doubt, think about it again.

You look for your mind by focusing the radar of your awareness on you. Where is mind, where does come from, and where does it go? Who is the comer, who is the stayer, and who is the goer? Reflect and investigate in these three ways. This also means looking into the past, looking into the present, and looking into the future. Trace the mind across all three times and see where it goes.

In posing these questions, you cannot really find anything. There is nothing that you can say. There is no place from where mind is coming from, no place where the mind is now, and no place where the mind is going. So try changing the questions.

What is mind abiding, how is it abiding, and where is it abiding?
What is the shape, form, or color of the mind?
What is the nature of thought and its destination?
What is mind and mind's nature?
What is this thing that is aware from moment to moment?

Investigating in this way, you end up in the same place. There is never anything to find, no definitive answer. Again, it is like letters written on water—whatever appears soon folds back into the water. So instead of being trapped in your feelings, let them disappear like the letters.

Extending this metaphor then, what is that water? You eventually discover that it is none other than the awake reflective quality of consciousness itself, what the Buddhists call wisdom awareness—that is, the sole source of everything you know. Wisdom awareness is insight into the impermanent and ephemeral nature of all perception and seeing everything just as it is without an interpretive mental frame.

That wisdom awareness is like a mirror—whatever appears is reflected in it. That reflection doesn't react with "Oh, what wonderful qualities I have," when something pleasing is placed in front of it. It just reflects what is. That interpretive response is the function of your ego—the "I." It is the one that decides whether something is good or bad. It comes from the programming of your acquired mental models. Your interpretations are not based on fact. Instead, they are mentally distorted stories, projections, and illusions, just as we have seen.

So there are no answers to these questions. Most of what we consider reality is simply concepts and labels that we attribute to things that are not solid or real. Take away the subject—the looker—and the object—the looked at—and what we perceive simply becomes like a reflection in the mirror. As you come face to face with this ultimate truth, you realize that whatever appears in the mind arises from emptiness, abides in emptiness, and fades back into emptiness.

To know ourselves is to know this reality. All we have is this wisdom awareness, which is itself devoid of any inherently solid existence. Yet it is the source of everything we know.

What does the understanding of this do? This points to the truth of emptiness of the self or of the idea of self. We are not free of these ideas, but now we have insight into the truth. This loosens our attachment to self and to phenomena and opens us to the deeper truth embedded in the awareness itself. Thus the Cosmic Joke is that we believe in all these thoughts that float through our minds, rather than in the inherent and vast wakefulness within from which they spring. That awareness is the ultimate truth; without it, nothing else exists.

We are programmed to believe that we are defined by our mental constructs, those habitual patterns we talked about, rather than in the infinite presence of awareness. But by investigating "I" and your mind in this way, you begin to discover its qualities to be the source of all that is. There is nothing real beyond your awareness, as everything you perceive appears within it, as it is.

In this way, the mind is like a crystal ball. When a crystal ball comes into contact with something red, it turns red, or with blue, it turns blue. But even if it turns red or blue, the crystal remains unchanged. The crystal may change colors, but its essence does not change into something else.

In the same way, the reflective wisdom awareness of our mind may stray into thoughts and emotions, but it has not even for a moment changed in essence and turned into something else.

We are vast, formless, and aware in essence, and that is the source and substance of all our reality. Yet as we have seen, we continue to look outside when the source of what we are really looking for resides within. The more we search outside, the more lost we become. The truth is in the here and now of our awareness and not back then or over there.

What Are Phenomena?

Just to be clear, like the "I" and the mind, phenomena are empty too. How is that? We return to the story of Nagasena and the monk.

> The monk then reversed their roles and asked the king how he arrived at that spot. He said, "By chariot." Then the monk asked, "Is the chariot the axle, the wheels, the yoke, the reins?" The king said the chariot was not one of those particular parts.
>
> The monk asked if there was a chariot separate from these things. The king answered, "No."
>
> Nagasena suggested it was now the king who was lying. "You say you arrived by chariot, but you cannot say what a chariot is." To this the king said, "I am not lying, for it is because of these parts that a chariot exists as a name, a label, a matter of conventional usage."
>
> "Exactly," agreed the monk. "Because of my body, feeling, perception, and so forth does Nagasena exist as a name, as a label, as conventional usage, and so too a label does not a chariot make. There is no essence of person or chariot at all to be found in a name."

There is no one thing that stands on its own as inherently existing, not governed by the laws of cause and effect, and not in constant flow. Everything is interdependent and divisible. There is no single thing that cannot be broken into its component parts ad infinitum.

Instead, everything is made up of a constantly fluctuating matrix of interdependent and changeable parts ruled by the laws of cause and effect. Change and impermanence are the only constant. We have already found this to be true internally in the self and the mind, and it is also true of phenomena.

To test this, investigate for yourself. Take anything—any phenomena, any "thing," and explore it from any of the following perspectives, which are themselves interconnected and not discrete.

Impermanence: Nothing lasts. All phenomena, from the biggest to the smallest, or from a mountain to a molecule or even smaller, are subject to constant change—growth and decay, sickness and health, youth and old age. This is true even at microscopic levels. Every advance in research on the origin of matter points to smaller and more ephemeral elementary particles, like quarks and vibrating wavelengths, which are in constant flux and change, appearing and disappearing.

Interdependence. It is impossible for anything to exist inherently on its own because everything arises interdependently through cause and condition—a plant cannot grow without a seed, fertile soil, sunshine, and water, nor can a cloud exist without water mixed with a cooling temperature. Anything dependent on another thing has no independently existing self-nature, and everything—everything— is interdependent with something else. Test this, analyze it for yourself.

Divisibility. There are no phenomena we cannot atomize to the point of finding nothing—not even a beginning, a present, or an end—just like the universe itself. What we consider as being a chair, for example, is a label, an illusion. When you look at it, you see it as solid, made of wood, and brown in color. Yet if you break it down into its components, wood is composed of atoms of hydrogen, carbon, and oxygen, and the brown color is simply a radiating wavelength of radiation that we see. Physicists would say the chair is 99.99 percent the space within the atoms that make it up, which in turn cannot be located in any specific place as they are moving at incredible speeds and flying off all the time. There is never a single unity of anything.

Relativity. As we saw before, two people may see the same thing but very have different interpretations of it. No one has the same perception as they view or examine things because people base their perceptions on their different perspectives and experiences in life. One may see a pile of cord on the floor and see a rope, while another sees a snake. The English love their bland fish and chips and shepherd's pie, while Indians love their hot curry and sour chutney. It is all socialized and relative to the culture in which we grow up.

What This Means

We have now investigated body, speech, and mind, and looked at thoughts, emotions, "I," and mind, and found them all empty of any inherent solid existence. We even found our perception of phenomena to be the same. This is a wisdom awareness that gives us insight into the true nature of this truth. This insight tells us that the self, the mind, and the phenomena that we take for granted as fixed and concrete are no more than the labels that we affix to them. When we see or experience something—anything—we attach a judgment of like, dislike, or indifference—and that grasping solidifies our perception. But when we investigate the source of that perception, as we did above, we find it is truly open, fluid, and empty. That insight loosens our attachment to it as mere projections of the mind. This aids our meditation as it de-objectifies our thoughts and emotions, releases the grip of the hungry spirit, and opens us to a more sustainable, healthy, self-fulfilling, and adaptive truth.

Empty Is Not Empty

There is one more essential point, and to explain it I borrow a story from Mingyur Rinpoche's book *In Love with the World*:

I like these teachings, but there is just one problem. I really like making art for a living, but after listening to your talk today, I see that even my art is emptiness. Now maybe I need to let go of my artwork, but if I do that, I will have no income.

Emptiness does not mean nothing. Everything comes from emptiness. It is still full of lively potential, full of possibility.

So, tell me, what is your happy dream?

To have a house on the beach.

Ok, let's say that one day you have a nice dream in which you have a house on the beach. And you are happy, right?

Yes, of course.

Then suddenly a fire burns your house down, without dream insurance. How do you feel?

It breaks my heart.

Is that house real or not?

Of course it is not real, it is a dream!

If you have a big problem like your beach house burning down, what is the best solution?

Maybe wake up from the dream.

When we lose a burning beach house in a dream, we wake up and it vanishes.[1]

If you know you are dreaming, then the fire cannot burn you and the house is still there. Similarly, you can practice this way—"everything is like a dream"—without denying yourself a career either. These are simply perceptions that are dreamlike and empty in essence. When you lose a burning beach house in a dream, you wake up and it vanishes. When the king and Nagasena looked for "I," there was no one to be found. If you recognize both as a dream, then you can enjoy them without attachment.

We are like the dreamt-of beach house. Not real but not not real either—*real but not real.*[2] Our essence is not empty-empty (meaning completely void). When you recognize the dream house in the dream, you know that it is not real but it is still there, too. Real and not real together. This is our reality. Understanding this, we become less attached—less fixated on dos and don'ts, thises and thats, and here not there, making everything more open, flexible, and workable.

And, although empty, this reality is not inert or a nothingness. Your essence is still open, awake, and vibrating a warmth of loving-kindness. In being still and fully present in the current moment, it begins to shine through all the obscurations of your old habitual patterns. Hopefully you feel this at least a bit as you arise from the cushion, and with a steady practice, it grows more and more. That is the raw stuff of which you are truly made, the source of everything.

Discover This for Yourself

You must find this out for yourself—that is the practice. Someone else's word is not enough. In the Buddhist tradition, this is called *the lion's roar*—a fearless, open statement to challenge yourself to explore. So examine it for yourself, as a jeweler would examine a diamond. Reflect on this truth, then examine it in your meditation, and finally you will begin to approach it on your own.

There is an old story that says if you are afraid of tigers and someone says there are no tigers around, but it's a place where tigers are typically found, you would doubt whether there is a tiger or not. You may want to go there, but you wonder whether it is safe, so it is best to find out for yourself. You then search everywhere from the top of the valley to the bottom searching for any sign of a tiger. You go everywhere, and if there is no sign of a tiger, then you can take the word of others who said there are none. It is always best to find out for yourself.

Likewise, if someone says the mind is empty and another says the mind is real, you must find out for yourself. This is why we search, look, and investigate, because we need to know the answer to loosen the habitual grip of our hungry spirit, our ego, our Cosmic Egg, and cultivate a true spirit of awakening.

EXERCISE

Put these three questions to yourself. Where does mind come from, where does it dwell, and where does it go or fade to? Do the same investigation for thoughts, emotions, perceptions. You can't do that with a lot of people around, so go to your room, shut your door, turn off your cell phone, and ask the questions. Do it periodically to remind and deepen your understanding. A revelation about yourself may emanate that is contrary to what you have thought.

—◄o►—

Place That Understanding on the Launchpad of the Spirit of Awakening

To bring this insight to greater realization, empower your practice by placing it on the launchpad of the spirit of awakening with sacredness, faith, and basic goodness, as discussed in chapter 6. Now you feel this discovery to be so precious, so special that it brings a confidence for moving forward and a desire to explore more and to share it with others. As you do, it starts to shine through, transforming your world as you progress on the path.

Meditation Instructions: Open Shamata Vipassana I

What We Are Doing

As you bring this attitude of letting go and letting be—equanimity—you start to depersonalize and to experience all your senses as constantly changing—arising, falling away, appearing, and disappearing. If you follow them, they strengthen and stay; if you let them go, they weaken and fade. As you do, you begin to discover the truth of their ephemeral and impermanent nature. You gradually become lighter, happier, and more caring as your true nature begins to shine through. Eventually you see there is no inherent identity behind the experience except thoughts and emotions that come and go.

This opens you to a fuller spectrum of life beyond your personal drama and brings a feeling of spaciousness and even a loving-kindness.

Open Vipassana Instruction

Now we move beyond sweeping and expand our meditation experience to all our sensory perceptions, not just of the body and mind, beginning with hearing, feeling, and thinking (later we will add specific practices for taste and sight). Again, start with Shamata to settle and rest your mind.

Move your awareness to the most dominant sensory experience and rest it there instead—thought, emotion, sound, bodily sensation—and simply note any changes and experience it all without any reaction. As it fades, return to the breath and repeat.

Meet each experience with equanimity. Equanimity neutralizes the clinging of the hungry spirit and gradually opens you to an inner being, as discussed above. This means meeting each experience without acceptance, rejection, or indifference. Just meet it with bare, open awareness, also known as wise attention, and move on.

Note how thoughts and emotion arise about the past but are now present; those of the present arise but are not constant; and those of the future arise but have not yet occurred. All are ephemeral and subject to change.

Become a neutral observer of you. Notice the difference between having thoughts or emotions and becoming lost in them. Notice that the only constant is change, and notice how it applies to you and your practice.

Sometimes it helps to make a mental note of what you are perceiving to help maintain your attention—so in hearing or feeling something, note "hearing, hearing, hearing," or "feeling, feeling, feeling." This helps with precision of awareness; however, try not to make it a habit as it is only a temporary mental construct to help you maintain focus and equanimity.

Commentary

Here we begin to combine the concentration of Shamata as relating precisely to situations and concepts with the awareness of Vipassana as a backdrop for opening and accepting whatever is perceived. The awareness of Vipassana is the ability to not cling to the discoveries of Shamata, and concentration is the vanguard of awareness. It flashes onto a situation and then diffuses the one-pointedness to a broader awareness. In this case, concentration goes beyond simple fixation—an object for the ego to grab onto, a goal, an orientation—it is just being mindful of what is happening.

In making this subtle shift, you take away the notion of achievement, but then boredom inevitably sets in. Boredom is the result of nonexpectation. You must develop a comfort with boredom, or otherwise you never progress. This means you must destroy the ego's game of achieving something.

Instead, observe the transparency of your thoughts and emotions, their suchness, their "is-ness," but also observe the looker, the observer. There is an old Buddhist metaphor about the difference between a lion and a dog. When you throw a stick at a dog, the dog chases the stick, but when you throw a stick at a lion, the lion chases you. So the lion's roar is to dissolve whatever arises by simply observing it and resting in place without chasing. Unfortunately, the mind's usual response in meditation is to save face by putting a rationalizing, self-justifying patch on top of the current response. This causes it to spin in thought and create negativity. Instead, just observe and release those concepts too.

The following are some bits of advice from the Facebook page of the cofounder of the Insight Meditation Society, Sharon Salzberg.[3]

"Don't push thoughts away, let them float by."
"Returning to breath is returning to resting the mind."
"Can you feel the whole breath?"
"Observe without judgement."
"Meditation is 95 percent being and 5 percent doing."

"It's a practice, not a commandment. You won't go to hell if you don't do it perfectly."

"An unpleasant sound made contact with your ear, see if you can leave it at that."

"Stop meditating and just be."

"The essence of meditation is awareness."

"You can always begin again."

"The moment you notice your mind has wandered is a moment of awakening. Something you can celebrate."

"Observe your thoughts, sensations, and breath, and occasionally look at the observer. In time there is no experience, just the experience."

"Begin again."

"Let the body guide the breath, not the mind."

"Dissolve into your outbreath."

"You don't meditate to get good at it, you meditate to get good at life."

"You will begin again, one hundred times, that is the practice."

"Notice the gap between thoughts."

"See 'you' in the gap."

"Begin again, again, and again."

Working with Physical Pain

As your sitting practice develops and you try to maintain your posture, you will be confronted with pain in your body—your back, your knees, your hips, or wherever. The most important thing for dealing with pain is to be nonreactive and meet it with equanimity. Also remember that you are trying not to move too much because the more you move the more your mind moves. They are connected. This makes stillness important in both cases.

I have found two effective strategies for dealing with pain, and maintaining equanimity in both is important. In fact, working with physical pain is a wonderful way to develop both concentration and equanimity. First you zero in on the pain and use it as your focal point of concentration, while maintaining your equanimity. Dwell on it. I once experienced a pain in my knee from remaining still for so long that it throbbed. I relaxed without reacting and just rested my concentration on it. I found, just like everything else, that it would rise and fall away, come in and come out, and after a while it went away altogether. The second strategy, again not reacting to it at all, is to note it with equanimity and return to your breath, just as you would with a thought or emotion. You are not ignoring it, but you are not reacting either. Both work, so experiment to see what works best for you.

12

Bodhicitta and
The Six Paramitas
Open Shamata Vipassana II

*Suchness, once it has been seen, becomes the ground for
arising compassion.*

LONGCHENPA

When you leave your self-centered habitual patterns, you open and give
others a different person to respond to, and in doing so, you change
your world as well as theirs. Their attitudes begin to mirror yours. You
enter a space where your understanding of one another expands and
creates new possibilities for action. In *The Different Drum: Community
Making and Peace* by M. Scott Peck, there is an old tale called "The
Rabbi's Gift" that makes this point.[1]

*There was an old monastery that had fallen upon awfully hard times.
Once a great order, over time it had dwindled down to only five monks—
the abbot and four others—all well into their seventies. The order was
dying.*

*Deep in the forest surrounding the monastery, there was a little hut
that a rabbi from a nearby town used occasionally for personal retreats.*

The old monks had developed a sixth sense about the presence of the rabbi, and they always could tell when he was there in the forest. On one such occasion, the abbot, who had been agonizing over the demise of his order, decided to visit the hut to ask the rabbi if he could offer any advice.

The rabbi welcomed the abbot into his hut, but when the abbot explained the purpose of his visit, the rabbi could only empathize with his plight and commiserate with him. "Yes, the spirit seems to have gone out of the people. It is the same in my town. Almost no one comes to the synagogue anymore."

So it was that the abbot and the rabbi spent time that day talking of deep things. Finally, it came time for the abbot to leave. The men hugged and the abbot said, "It is wonderful that we could meet and talk after all these years, but I have failed in my purpose for coming here. Is there no advice at all you can give me that would help me to save my dying order?"

"I'm sorry," said the rabbi. "I'm afraid I have no advice to give. All I can tell you, though, is that the messiah is among you."

Upon his return to the monastery, the abbot was joined by the other monks who asked, "Well, what did the rabbi say?"

"He couldn't help," the abbot replied. "We just sat and talked. And as I was leaving, he said that the messiah is among us. I have no idea what he meant."

In the days, weeks, and months that followed, the old monks pondered this and wondered if there could be any possible significance to the rabbi's words: "The messiah is among us. Do you think he meant one of us monks here at the monastery?

If he meant one of us, he surely must have been referring to Father Abbot. He has been our leader for more than a generation.

On the other hand, he could have meant Brother Thomas; he is a holy man. Everyone knows that Thomas is a man of light.

Certainly, he could not have meant Brother Eldred! Eldred gets crotchety at times . . . but even though he can be a nuisance, when you look back on it, Eldred virtually always has a valid point to make. Perhaps the rabbi did mean Brother Eldred.

But surely not Brother Phillip; he's so passive, a real nobody . . . but then, almost magically, Philip has this knack of appearing at your side just when you need him the most. Maybe Phillip is the messiah.

But of course, the rabbi wasn't referring to me. I am just an ordinary person. Yet what if he was? What if I am the messiah? Please, God, not me; I could not mean that much to you, could I?"

As they reflected in this manner, the old monks began to treat each other with extraordinary respect on the off chance that one among them might be the messiah. And on the remote chance that each monk himself might be the messiah, they each began to treat themselves with extraordinary respect as well.

Because the forest was so beautiful, people still occasionally came to visit the monastery, to picnic on its tiny lawn, walk along its paths, and sit quietly in the chapel. As they did so, without even being conscious of it, they sensed this aura of extraordinary respect that seemed to surround each of the elderly monks and that permeated the atmosphere of the whole place. There was something compelling, empowering about it. Without knowing exactly why, they began to come back to the monastery more frequently to visit, to play, to pray. They began to bring their friends to share this special place. And their friends brought their friends.

In time, some of the younger men who came to visit began to talk more and more with the elderly monks. After a while one asked if he could join the order. Then another. Then another. Soon the monastery once again housed a thriving order and, thanks to the rabbi's gift, became a beacon of peace, love, and hope.

I have always found this story inspiring and thought it a wonderful way to reintroduce the power of compassion, which is the second principal aspect of our path, our practice, our nature, our basic goodness.

Compassion in the Buddhist sense is not the sappy, enabling, and conflict-avoidant variety, sometimes called idiot compassion. That compassion is a form of ego clinging based on giving people what they want as opposed to what they need and letting them walk over you to avoid discomfort or even conflict. Often it comes from a desire to be nice and liked. It is selfish because we would rather tend to their feelings than address the real issue.

What you want to nurture is a wakeful compassion, one that sees the right thing to do and acts for the benefit of all. It is a compassion adorned with *wisdom awareness* (again, seeing things just as they are without the obscurations of the ego clinging of our hungry spirit), and it is courageous. This is true Bodhicitta or basic goodness, and it is aimed at awakening it not just in oneself but for all sentient beings. These two, then—awareness and compassion—are, again, the two primary aspects of your inherent nature as well as what you practice on your path. As said before, *you practice what you are.*

Thus far we have focused on developing *wisdom awareness* and *the truth of emptiness*, but those alone are not enough to transcend the ego. Now we begin to focus on *the skillful means of compassion*—meaning to benefit self and others in the world. It is to think, speak, and act skillfully in ways that are both true and beneficial, that combine both wisdom and compassion.

Without compassion, the emptiness of wisdom awareness can lead to a cynical pessimism, whereas without wisdom awareness, compassion can degenerate into an idealistic sentimentality. Compassion without emptiness can make us a sucker, while emptiness without compassion can make us a manipulator. They must work together; otherwise, our deepest potential never fully manifests.

However, as I learned in my Ayahuasca experience, compassion is not necessarily an automatic outcome of increasing awareness. The more we invest in developing the skillful means of compassion, the more likely its full expression will manifest spontaneously in realization. If we do not, a residual ego lingers, and we fail to realize our fullest potential. It is the ultimate ego killer. This can make the practice of compassion an article of faith on the path, as it only arises

spontaneously coincident with the full realization of genuine emptiness. It is an automatic function of the ultimate experience of primordial awareness, but we need to practice it along the way to avoid any
shortcomings when that goal is near.

As said before, this makes compassion both an effect and a cause. In
the beginning we learn to become friends with ourselves through practice, and that leads to an openness or a compassion. It is a basic warmth
that serves as a bridge to the outside world. As it grows, it brings a feeling of wealth and abundance that gives trust and confidence, allowing
authentic practice and authentic presence to truly dawn. It arises naturally and gradually with the suspension of the aggression of the ego. It
manifests fully as a universal Cosmic Love, where we relate to "what is,"
and accept it "as it is."

The Six Paramitas

To nurture wisdom awareness and the skillful means of compassion
together on the path, the Buddhist tradition practices the Six *Paramitas*,
also called the Six Perfections. Their origin lies in the Theravada teachings and the early Pali canon, and they developed more through the
Mahayana tradition. In addition to sacredness, faith, and the spirit
of awakening discussed in chapter 6, they are the means for bringing
Bodhicitta to life on the path. Also known as application Bodhicitta,
they provide a framework for applying Bodhicitta in our daily life.

Traleg Rinpoche introduces them with the following:

If we want to obtain enlightenment, it is necessary to actualize wisdom and compassion. This is done by the practice of what are called
the six paramitas, or "transcendental actions." Para in Sanskrit
means the "other shore." Here it means going beyond our own
notion of the self.

From the Buddhist point of view in general, and from the
Mahayana in particular, if we want to progress properly on the

path, we need to go beyond our conventional understanding of the self. So, when we say that paramita means "transcendental action," we mean that our actions and attitudes are performed in a non-egocentric manner. *Transcendental* does not refer to some external reality, but rather to the way in which we perceive our world and conduct our lives—in an egocentric or a non-egocentric way. The six paramitas are concerned with the effort to step out of that ego-centric mentality.[2]

In this way, the Six Paramitas build on and bring to fruition both wisdom awareness and the skillful means of compassion. The healing practice of the Six Paramitas aligns principle with action by providing a path not only for spiritual growth but also the psycho-emotional development necessary for it. Thus they address the lack of developmental means I found in my Ayahuasca experience by providing both the means as well as the ends to spiritual growth. It is a behave-your-way-into-a-new-way-of-being or a fake-it-until-you-make-it approach, where the path models the desired outcome. It is as if by magic, in aligning your intentions and actions skillfully with the paramitas, you create your own psycho-emotional healing and spiritual opening. In practicing them, you leverage the aspects of your greater spirit to inspire and hopefully propel you into transcendence.

The Six Paramitas are the following:

Generosity
Cultivate an attitude of giving to open the heart and mind.

Material—to give what you can with pure motivation
Emotional—to care for and support the well-being of others
Service—to help foster the awakening of others

As discussed before, an act of generosity provides a powerful way to reveal our inner qualities. A gift of material things or of ourselves in support of another frees us from attachment, from stress, and from self-ishness and can spark a sense of abundance and well-being. It can take the form of material support with money, food, and shelter for those without, of emotional support for those fearful, insecure, and stressed, or of perspective for those struggling with life's meaning, purpose, and higher purpose.

In whatever form, the most effective generosity is to give without any expectation in return. It is to open and offer without any motive other than to do the right thing in the moment and without being afraid of letting anything in. Something as simple as giving feedback, for example, can be an act of generosity, even courage, whether it be appreciative or constructive. In either case, it is difficult to neutralize the pull of ego because it makes you vulnerable. Yet in not holding back, you discover you really do have something to give and it begins to stop you from demanding and grasping all the time. In learning to give, you do not judge or evaluate but instead you open, assess, and give what is needed, naked of ego, and that brings a wholesome sanity.

Thus in giving we receive. It nurtures the heart and uncovers our good qualities. This is one reason why making offerings is so important to Buddhist ritual.

There are many parallels to generosity in the happiness, emotional intelligence, and personal effectiveness literature of today. There is, for example, the powerful concept of the servant leader, where you lead by serving a purpose or a cause beyond your own personal self-interest and by serving those who also serve that purpose or cause. You function as the steward of both. It brings not only success but also self-worth. The interesting thing is the evidence also shows that the more you make your leadership role about yourself and serving you—or even just your roles in life generally—the more likely you are to get into trouble. Across the board, self-centeredness brings stress and stagnation, while an other-centeredness brings success and self-fulfillment.

I have a personal story that demonstrates the point about generosity and how we can behave our way into new ways of being. Years ago, I started an intentional community inspired by M. Scott Peck's story of "The Rabbi's Gift". I invited friends, acquaintances, and others whom I did not know but was told might be interested in joining an ongoing conversation about life. We were a group of about twelve or so, as the group changed a little over the three and a half years that we met together. We convened every other week in my home and took turns picking the topic of personal or spiritual investigation and facilitating the session. After about a year of lurking on the edge, the group picked me as the protagonist, saying they wanted to hear more from me. They said I had insight but was holding back, and they wanted me to be more generous in sharing it with the group. I responded, "I don't feel like giving that way, and if I don't feel it, then it would be inauthentic." "Try it anyway," they urged. So one by one, they had me sit in front of each of them, look into their eyes and share the strengths I saw. I made it to the third person before we all broke into tears but continued. I learned so much, but most of all how giving of your special talents not only nurtures the heart but also self-worth. As Shantideva said:

> *May I be an isle for those who yearn for landfall*
> *And a lamp for those who long for light*
> *For those who need a resting place a bed*
> *For all who need a servant, their slave*[3]

Moral Discipline

Settle the mind to work with a situation as it is:

> Refrain from negative actions.
> Gather positive actions.
> Avoid slipping into neutral ones.
> Act on behalf of others.

Initially, discipline is about binding oneself to certain precepts, as is the case in most of the world's spiritual traditions. Ultimately, however, discipline is not a matter of tethering oneself to rules like that, but rather it is to act according to what is best for the moment and the situation as it is, irrespective of ego. You remain open, not watching yourself with conceptual ties that bind at all, but rather communicating with the situation just as it is. It is not an attempt to be pure or right, which is just another object of clinging for the ego. There is no rigidity; you just remain present and act according to what is right from the broadest, highest, most egoless perspective. In this way, you find temptations less relevant and guidelines less necessary because you flow naturally with the rightness of the moment.

The reason for this is that if you remain stuck in the biased, narrow-minded thinking of clinging to certain rules or codes of ethics, true virtue eludes you. Why? Because there are no silver bullets in life. *Everything is situational.* Every time you are faced with a decision, you are dealing with you as the decider, the situation compelling it, and the others affected by it. Those three are in constant flux, so everything "depends" and requires judgment. If you are caught up in fixed concepts of right and wrong, good and bad—instead of just remaining true to your basic goodness—you will spin around the potter's wheel of the ego trying to find ways to rationalize and justify your view for each situation. So keep it simple. What ultimately frees you is to stop reifying the rules, and instead connect to your nature to see what is right for the moment.

What if there is no clear direction or action to take? When in doubt, be transparent. Say you don't know, and invite the perspective of others. Don't hide behind the rules, and instead seek the higher cause collaboratively. That vulnerability builds trust and confidence.

The discipline of mindfulness arising from meditation helps provide such clarity. It tames the mind of distractions and opens the way for seeing things clearly so you can act appropriately for the moment. Without that support, emotional upheavals continue to mug you and distract from a deeper truth. A steady discipline of mindfulness allows the dust to settle and the virtuous qualities—kindness, relaxation, steadiness—to arise naturally. Thus until you train mind to be present and relaxed, the paramitas alone will not liberate you because of the constant lurching of self-clinging.

Mindfulness arising from meditation is the root antidote to many ills. We cannot eliminate every outer cause of our suffering, but we can manage our response by learning to discipline our mind with regular practice.

Patience; Remain in Equanimity
Refrain from retribution.
Avoid playing victim.
Be grateful for the lessons.
Remember basic goodness—like discovering gold buried
in a poverty-stricken house.

No emotion is more perilous to our basic goodness than anger; even a flash can have a long-term impact. We have been known to hold onto it for lifetimes in family feuds, ethnic rivalries, and so on. We love the addictions to anger, gossip, and overwork that feed our critical mind. We are so accustomed to these that, strangely, we associate them with comfort, satisfaction, and well-being. It is the type of anger we condone, cling to, and remain unwilling to examine. It can destroy superficial good works in an instant. It always rises because we are not getting what we want or we are getting what we do not want because we are so heavily invested in our likes and dislikes.

Why don't we get angry at ourselves for causing our own distress? There are people in my life, for example, who are so talkative and opinionated that there is rarely an opportunity to express another point of view. Over time I have just tuned out and approached everything they say under an "attitude" where I lack any patience at all for listening. Nothing resolves, and it's a situation where I cannot really walk away, so I just stew in resentment, and it compounds and infiltrates every interaction.

We'd rather travel around the world and help the homeless than deal with a troublesome mother or spouse. How can say we want to benefit others when we can't even give another a compliment? Worse, how often do we find ourselves delighting in another's misfortune? This is like being stung by a scorpion as you throw it at another out of anger. So much of this self-defeating hypocrisy comes from our fixed views of good and bad and our distorted views of our impeccable self that quickly devolve into knee-jerk reactivity and uptightness.

Instead, pause and relax. Don't let your ego hijack you. Seek another way of relating to your world. These troublemakers of your fixed view are also fodder for your freedom. They are an opportunity to practice, so treat them like a treasure. When they bother you, you learn patience; when others strike out in suffering, you learn compassion; when you buy into aversion, you learn tolerance. Instead of being stuck in self-ishness, you become helpful. Instead of being jealous, you rejoice in appreciation. Instead of being angry, you seek another way. All these troublemakers then become a treasure or like a doctor's medicine. Learn to respond in a way that connects to your basic goodness, your inherent nature, rather than with the aggression that obscures and worsens the situation.

In the end, working with anger is not about trying to control one-self. Instead, true patience is about adapting to a situation because we don't have a solid, immutable expectation from the beginning. I have had occasional blowups with my daughter since she was a teen-ager, but they never stick. Why? We listen and don't personalize our differences—we don't hang on, we open (eventually). Generally, we get trapped and swept up in anger by fixating on and personalizing ideas, especially about our self. Instead, we want to have a flowing relation-ship with others and the world and not automatically resist. Free from the compulsive concerns of fixation, we abide patiently without feeling that we are just waiting for something to happen.

When we learn to do so, we no longer seek enlightenment for ego's benefit. We have no need for our territory at all, just open space.

Joyful Effort: Find Joy in What Is Positive,
Virtuous, and Wholesome

Nurture Bodhicitta to inspire and maintain diligence

Maintain zeal by always doing good and never doing bad—always on, never off

Pacify the enemies of practice—fatigue, laziness, doubt—again and again

Our life is opened by generosity, activated by discipline, strengthened by patience, and now filled with joyful effort because we are completely interested in and learning about its creative patterns, never tiring of working with them. We take ourselves less seriously. We delight in polarities but do not side with any extreme. We accept that there is a message and explore it further and further with a peaceful, intrinsic interest. We adopt some traditions but do not accept all on blind faith. We explore when to accept and when to reject.

Having tamed your mind without losing your sense of humor, you have learned not to take yourself too seriously. When things go wrong, you become curious, wondering where the experiment will lead. When things go right, you rejoice in the success and the good acts of others. When things go wrong, you step in to help move it along. When all is said and done, delight in your basic goodness and reach out in kindness and support of another.

This cultivates an enthusiasm that derails any despondency or the laziness of playing deaf and dumb. In midlife I remembered how fortunate I was in many ways. That feeling of appreciation seemed to invite blessings as many more positive things happened—my dream job, an expanding circle of relationships, and extensive travel abroad. So be proactive in taking charge and playing to the positive in your life—you are never too young, too busy, or too old. Like a heroic act of perseverance, take heart in your basic goodness and become a beacon for yourself and others.

The power of positive thinking is well documented in the happiness and personal effectiveness literature. In my work, I often shared the case of "Jell-O at Lunch" where researchers asked two groups of four-year-olds to complete a series of learning tasks. The first group was given neutral instructions, "Just do it as quickly as possible." The second group were given the same instruction but were first asked to think about something that made them happy, like having Jell-O at lunch. The second group, the one primed with a happy thought, was consistently faster and had fewer errors than the group that had not been.

That research has been replicated again and again. Separate studies involving roughly 275,000 people concluded that a positive attitude and affect led to higher salaries and greater success in work, marriage, health, sociability, friendships, and creativity.

Think about that. It just makes sense. Positive emotions broaden your intellectual, emotional, physical, and social resources and build resilience and confidence. When you are in a positive mood, people respond better, and your relationships are more likely to cement. You are more sociable, energetic, charitable, cooperative, and liked. You also learn more because you are more open to new experiences and more tolerant, creative, and nondefensive.

Why is this so? It is a virtuous cycle of building and reinforcing your basic goodness. You are aligned with your heart essence. Without the wind of this joyful effort, your inner fire does not grow.

Concentration; Remain Mindful
Maintain the precise, calm abiding of Shamata
Develop the panoramic insight of Vipassana
Apply both to the other paramitas and in post-meditation

Concentration is about developing and maintaining a continuity of wakefulness as much as possible in all life situations. Initially we train the mind to concentrate with Shamata, but not in a fixed, trance-like way. This frees the mind from wandering, dullness, and stress. Eventually we learn to gently anchor our self in that mindfulness of Shamata, while balancing it with a panoramic awareness of Vipassana that carries on throughout post-meditation life. This helps us stay on the "spot" without constantly being mindlessly swept away by impulsive thoughts and emotions.

Although often included under the paramita discipline, concentration is also about maintaining the allies discussed in chapter 8; *carefulness*, *alertness*, and *mindfulness*. With carefulness, you consciously devote and focus your energy on maintaining your practice. With alertness, you observe your thoughts and sensations while remaining in equanimity. And with mindfulness, you assess whether you are acting consciously in a good way. You then become like a drunk elephant tied to a pillar of positive actions by the rope of mindfulness and tamed by the hook of alertness.

Until you train the mind in this way, the paramitas cannot liberate you because the paramitas and the discipline of letting go of self-clinging by the hungry spirit are one and the same. The three allies of concentration pacify the enemies of practice—attachment, fatigue, laziness, and doubt—so that you can maintain a state of wakefulness. It is the active awareness and precision of concentration as well as the panoramic awareness of space and openness that free you and helps you maintain focus in the other paramitas.

The best way to begin developing this continuity of awareness is by applying it to your daily life routines. In my early Vipassana retreats, for example, I learned how to eat mindfully. Now when alone, I automatically use that memory as a trigger to eat mindfully. You can also do this when brushing your teeth, getting dressed, taking a walk, preparing a meal, and even going to the toilet. These are all helpful ways to create a habit of tuning in its all that you do. I share some of these applications in the last chapter.

Wisdom. Remember, "It Is There and Not There"

Relative truth—seeing and analyzing things as we know them in daily life.

Absolute truth—seeing things as they truly are.

Balancing and applying both to the other paramitas.

Wisdom awareness is to perceive everything as if it is an illusion—real, as in a dream, but not real, as in solid and concrete. It is a lens of perception into which each of the other virtuous activities should lead and dissolve. Without it, all the other perfections are still ego burdened and subject to righteousness and weaponizing your virtue in its service. The ultimate Bodhicitta is without attachment. As such, wisdom releases any attachment to the activities and even to the teachings, the methods, and the path in general. Each of the actions of the Six Paramitas is thus adorned with wisdom awareness.

Here it is important to point out the difference between relative truth and absolute truth. This is a key concept in Buddhism. Relative truth is our conventional subject-object, "me-it" dualistic truth of what we know and experience in everyday mind. Absolute truth is the nondualistic truth of how things really are, absent the filter of that everyday ego mind. It is inexpressible, and empty of any convention. Relative truth is deceptive and an illusion, like seeing a rope and mistaking it for a snake. Absolute truth is like seeing the rope for what it really is—empty in nature and absent any conceptual label pasted on it. Known as the two truths, relative and absolute truth are not separate realities but two ways of seeing a single reality.

Dzongchar Rinpoche characterizes relative truth as "it is there," and absolute truth as "it is not there"—it is empty.[4] As discussed earlier, the mental frames affixed to perception are an illusion, a projection—they are *there but not there*—like the reflection of a face in the mirror. You see your face, but you know it is just a reflection and not really your face. Or like a rainbow—it is *there but not there* at the same time because as you approach it, it disappears. Still, we get involved with it as if it were real, like watching a movie. Everything in life is like this. However, knowing it is *there but not there* helps release us from the pain of holding on to either or both, even in the methods of the path and the paramitas, which themselves are empty of any solidity.

These two need to balance each other in working with ourselves and our world. Returning to the leading quote of chapter 2, "Let your view be as vast as the sky, and your conduct as fine as barley flour," if you are hung up on your view of emptiness without the balance of good conduct, nothing matters, and you do whatever you want and become *nihilistic*. On the other hand, if you are fixated on good conduct without the balance of the view, everything matters—you get wrapped up in the rules of good deeds and become *idealistic*. Yet always in Buddhism the truth is in the middle, and so you need both—*there but not there*—to progress on the path.

On the path, then, you conduct the first five paramitas within the frame of the *there not there* wisdom of the sixth. For example, generosity shows cause and effect, such as when an act of generosity effects a feeling of generosity, whereas in absolute truth, where subject (the giver) and object (the receiver) are both empty, there is no such connection. It's more like a dream; it's *there but not there*. So in practicing each of the first five, you don't objectify them, or otherwise you solidify them and they become just another projection of the hungry spirit. Instead, you want to bring them into the sphere of absolute truth like a dream. As you do, you begin to internalize what is temporal and a product of projection and the habitual pattern of relative truth and what is the real, pervasive, and inherent nature of absolute truth.

In this way, you practice six paramitas at the relative level as a dream on the path until they unite in the end at the absolute level. You practice the relative while emulating the absolute until you realize the absolute without holding any aspiration or attachment. Your path models the desired result.

In practical terms, the paramita of wisdom is knowing that your actions and intentions are your projections, and that helps you release all grasping toward the other five. You practice them as if they were a dream—*there but not there*. These two truths, relative and absolute, are what is called a provisional teaching in Buddhism—helpful for where we are on our path but not the final truth. The ultimate truth is that there is only one reality where the relative and absolute unite. Absolute truth is the true nature of the relative. Relative truth is the manifestation of the absolute.

As students, we need to come to grips with this because wisdom and the skillful means of the six paramitas are only effective if relative truth and absolute truth are united—meaning *there but not there*. As alluded to above, we don't cling to the cultivation of our good deeds because that is idealism and it confounds the path to complete liberation. Clinging to virtue still binds. On the other hand, we do not ignore unwholesome acts either because that is nihilism, which discounts the virtues of our nature as the path to liberation.

Thus what are known as the two paths of wisdom awareness and the skillful means of virtue (skillful means of the five other paramitas) must work together. They are also known as the two accumulations—the merit of wisdom accumulated from *there but not there* and the merit accumulated from the virtuous activity of doing good deeds. Here, merit means the positive momentum created by progressing along the path.

You may ask, if empty from the beginning, why cultivate these other five at all? Returning to my Ayahuasca experience, compassion does not necessarily arise fully from the practice of emptiness alone. It is an equal aspect of our nature along with wisdom awareness and needs to be nurtured with it through our attitudes and behaviors along the way. Otherwise we miss the ultimate mark. So we work with the paramitas at the relative level on the lower ends of the hierarchy of our hungry spirit until it is realized and united with the absolute level in transcendence.

How to practice the Six Paramitas through the union of relative and absolute truth has been captured many times poetically and metaphorically by many Buddhist masters. The following are a few examples.

Generosity without expectation
Discipline without aspiration
Patience with all, in every respect
Diligence in gathering all good qualities
Concentration without absorption

Wisdom possessed of skillful means
Being without fixation is generosity
Being without abiding is discipline
Being unguarded is patience
Being without effort is diligence
Being without focus is concentration
Being without conceptualization is transcendent knowledge
Not grasping is generosity
Not remaining is discipline
Not guarding is patience
Not trying is diligence
Not thinking is samadhi
Not aiming is wisdom

Applying the Six Paramitas

To promote the right view and conduct for your progress on the path, you apply the Six Paramitas in your daily life. You simply frame your daily activities around them as a way of practice. In this way you take it beyond intellectual understanding and begin to actualize it in your practice and in your being.

I use the cleaning of my house as an example. I have long had an attitude of "tidy house, tidy mind." It is my version of feng shui, where I want my living space arranged in a way that helps me create and maintain a sense of peace and harmony in my mind. Of course this drove my children nuts when they were young, but it had real import to me and even to some others. Visitors often comment on how comfortable and relaxing my home feels to them.

When it is pleasing to others too, that is an act of *generosity*. When I do it peacefully and with a pleasant and steady conduct for keeping a calming atmosphere and everything right, that is an aspect of *discipline*. When I experience hardship and difficulty in trying to maintain that atmosphere but am not overcome by frustration, that is an aspect of *patience*. When I do this with appreciation and purpose, and without a sense of drudgery and obligation, that is an aspect of *joyful effort*. When I do this consistently without being too distracted, that is an aspect of *concentration*. Finally, when I try to bring clarity and depth to my understanding of why I am conducting myself this way, that is an aspect of *wisdom*.

Another example is that when I feel uncomfortable with the action of another but stop to ask and listen to their point of view, it is an act of *generosity*. When I do this with equanimity and listen carefully, that is an aspect of *discipline*. When I disagree but manage to remain calm and somewhat open, that is an aspect of *patience*. When I try to appreciate their point of view, that is an aspect of *joyful effort*. When I persist with openness and determination to resolve the issue, that is an aspect of *concentration*. Finally, when I feel it is resolved, or maybe not, and walk away without pride or emotional residue, that is an aspect of *wisdom*.

A final illustration is when I am together with others at a group event, I help organize the space we share, and that is an aspect of *generosity*. When I do this with respect for working with the different views of others, that is an aspect of *discipline*. When I experience hardship or inconvenience but don't complain, that is an aspect of *patience*. When I join others with appreciation and excitement because I see the purpose, that is an aspect of *joyful effort*. When I take my time to do this carefully and mindfully without becoming distracted, that is an aspect of *concentration*. Finally, when I reflect on the reasons and meaning for doing so, that is an aspect of *wisdom*.

EXERCISE

When faced with an activity or challenge, in your mind reflect on how you might skillfully apply each paramita. I do so in my initial practice each day as part of my Bodhicitta practice.

◄o►

Meditation Instructions:
Open Shamata Vipassana, Continued

We are progressing on a continuum of Shamata and Vipassana techniques, from pure Shamata to Sweeping Shamata Vipassana, and now continuing with Open Shamata Vipassana meditation.

To review, in this method we gather the distracted mind by placing our awareness on whatever sensory experience is most dominant in the moment—touch, taste, sound, sight, smell, and thought—just being with it in equanimity. Instead of just thoughts, and senses associated with the breath and body, the other sensory modes also become an object of awareness. This expands the field of awareness in your practice. Even though thoughts arise with respect to the forms you see, the sounds you hear, the odors you smell, the flavors you taste, and the sensations you feel, you remain in equanimity while using these senses as supports for your awareness.

In this way, awareness then becomes the backdrop of all your activities. For now, however, since your eyes are still closed, the objects of awareness are just the sensations of the body along with sound and thought.

For example, as you rest in Shamata, a sound may arise that dominates or is more pronounced than any perception coming from the other two senses, like the sound of a train in the background. Direct your awareness to that sound. The following is a description from Myingyur Rinpoche.

> Be with the sound.
> No commentary.
> Befriend this sound by staying close to it.
> Let your thoughts and emotions drain into this sound.
> Use just this sound to gather and rest your mind (as opposed to breath)

> *If thoughts come, that's OK. Just let them go. They are like clouds passing through. Return to the object of sound.*
>
> *Relax in equanimity.*
>
> *As the sound of the train fades, allow your awareness to remain open to other sounds, but alighting on none of them. This is open awareness, Shamata without object.*
>
> *Let it be.*
>
> *Whatever arises, let it be.*
>
> *Stay with the awareness.*
>
> *Do not go towards the sound. Do not withdraw from it.*
>
> *Do not pick and choose.*
>
> *Stay aware.*
>
> *Relax.*[5]

Soon sounds that may have been disturbing become soothing as you meet them continually with equanimity.

As another dominant sensory experiences arises in your mind (thought or emotion) or your body (pleasant or painful), shift your awareness there and do the same. Whatever arises, let it be. Remain in equanimity by neither pulling it toward you nor pushing it away.

If there is no dominant experience, return to Shamata and rest your awareness there. Gradually, the mindfulness of Shamata becomes less localized and Vipassana awareness more panoramic.

Recap of Instruction Thus Far

To recap the technique to this point, in sharpening Shamata,

> Maintain awareness of any sensation for entirety of breath, beginning, middle, end—try to stay with the entire movement.
>
> Don't try to penetrate or over focus—just stay gently with the movement.
>
> To assist, note the rising and falling of the breaths or counting of the breaths.

In expanding Vipassana,

> Widen the sphere of awareness beyond breath, thought, and emotion to encompass the other senses—sound, smell, taste, and touch sensations.
>
> Whatever the predominant sensation, direct your awareness to it, noting or labeling it (optional).
>
> Stay with and meet it neutrally, objectively, and with equanimity— the key point.
>
> Note how whatever your experience is it never stays and always moves.
>
> As it fades or is no longer predominant, return to the breath.
>
> If nothing predominates, rest in the breath and the openness of the mind.

That is the practice, that is the training. To help with precision, note these three things:

> Past, present, and future thoughts
>
> Positive, negative, and neutral thoughts
>
> Attraction, rejection, and indifferent thoughts

Be aware of them while maintaining equanimity, and as they fade, return to the breath. But eventually let this go too—it is thinking of thinking and just a temporary aid.

What does all this do?

> It relaxes us
>
> Gives insight into our sense patterns and their impermanence and
>
> Releases their grip and our attachment to them
>
> Reveals an open and fullhearted awareness

Working with Different States of Mind

There are three particularly challenging states of mind that you are confronted with in meditation. These are *desire*, also known as the Vipassana romance; *anger*, also called the Vipassana grudge; and *dullness* or sleepiness, often regarded as ignorance. These are called the three root poisons to our nature, and in the Hinayana version of Shamata Vipassana there are specific antidotes for each of them. With an object of romantic desire, for instance, you might visualize that person's skeleton, or with anger you might imagine placing yourself in that person's shoes.

While I might argue these are good strategies off of the cushion, I would not recommend them as a practice while on the cushion. The reason is that they stimulate thinking instead of supporting simple awareness and recognition. Better to learn to neutralize them by recognizing and being aware of them without reacting or feeding the impulse in any way. Instead, learn to stay with desire or anger in wakeful equanimity until it fades, and then return to the breath. It is the same strategy as with any of our other sensations.

With dullness and sleepiness, the general strategy is to reenergize Shamata by cranking up your concentration. However, my favorite method is the sweeping technique. Focusing on the sensations of the body fires them up and brings energy. If that doesn't work, then, especially while in retreat, take a walk and do walking meditation, for which there are instructions in the last chapter.

The sweeping technique also works for an agitated, busy mind. Concentration possesses a cutting-through power and can be used for both dullness and agitation.

13

The Bodhisattva's Way of Life
Open Space Vipassana I

*All the happiness there is in this world comes from
thinking about others, and all the suffering comes from
preoccupation with yourself.*

SHANTIDEVA

Let's begin with an old tale called "The Bridge," from an unknown
source and told many times by many authors.

*There were once two brothers living on adjoining farms who had a falling
out. It was the first serious rift in forty years of farming side by side,
sharing tools, and trading labor and goods as needed without any issues.*

*But then the long partnership fell apart. It began with a small
misunderstanding and grew into a major difference, and finally it
exploded into an exchange of bitter words followed by months of silence.*

*One morning there was a knock on the older brother's door. He
opened it to find a man looking for work. "I'm looking for a few days of
work," he said. "Would you have a few small jobs here and there that I
could help you with?"*

*"Yes," said the older brother. "I do have a job for you. Look across
the creek at that farm. That's my neighbor. In fact, it's my younger*

brother. A few months ago, there was a meadow between us, and then he dug a trench, so now there is a creek between us. He did this to spite me, but I don't want to leave it at that. You see that pile of lumber curing by the barn? I want you to build a fence—an eight foot fence—so I don't have to see his place anymore. That will cool him down."

The man said, "I think I understand the situation. If you show me the nails and the other tools, I'll be able to do a job that pleases you."

The older brother had to go to town for supplies, so he helped the man get the materials ready and then he was off for the day.

The man worked hard all that day measuring, sawing, and nailing.

It was about sunset when the farmer returned, and the man had just finished the job. The farmer's eyes opened wide, and his jaw dropped.

There was no fence there at all. Instead, there was a bridge . . . a bridge stretching from one side of the creek to the other. It was a well-done piece of work with handrails and all—and his younger brother was running across, beaming, with tears in his eyes and his hand outstretched.

"That is quite something for you build this bridge after all that's gone down between us."

The two brothers met in the middle, taking each other's hand and hugging one another. They turned to see the man hoist his belongings on his shoulder. "No, wait! Stay a few days. I've a lot of other projects for you," said the older brother.

"I'd love to stay on," the man said, "but I have many more bridges to build."

When you leave your self-centered habitual patterns, you give others a different person to respond to, and in doing so you change your world as well as theirs. Their attitudes begin to mirror yours. You enter a space where your understanding of one another opens and creates new possibilities for mutual growth and action.

This is the way of the *Bodhisattva*.

The Bodhisattva

A Bodhisattva is one who practices and brings the Six Paramitas to life. *Bodhisattva* means "Awakened Warrior" (*Bodhi* = "awakened" and *Sattva* = "warrior")—one who takes a vow to seek enlightenment to eliminate suffering for all beings. Like a heroic person, a Bodhisattva heeds an inner call, the greatest of all in life—the call to wake up and become fully human and to inspire, support, and model the way for others to do the same.

In the early Buddhist texts, the Bodhisattva is portrayed as flying with two wings, because the Bodhisattva has no place to stand, as there is no turf, no views no possessions they call their own. There is no solid self, unchanging identity, or any security as we would know it. But a Bodhisattva does not need such space, because it soars like *Garuda*, the mythical bird that flies across the universe in an instant on its two wings of wisdom and compassion. Instead of looking for a safe harbor, for a place of security and comfort, a Bodhisattva places full trust in these two wings.[1]

Both are necessary for our journey because one alone is not enough. We want the wisdom that sets us free to be who we are authentically meant to be while also having the compassion that recognizes, connects, and supports the interwoven web of life. Like two sides of a coin, these two aspects are inseparable and inherent in our nature. They are the genuine expression of our natural humanness that is awake, clear, and compassionate—unadulterated by the habits of self-concern.

The sanity of this tradition is powerful. As aspiring Bodhisattvas, we take on a great responsibility. Instead of doing nothing, we choose to step out of our comfort zone and wake up to who we are and help others with their muddled lives.

No longer content to just work alone, we work for others. This has a quality of selflessness, but not exclusively so. His Holiness the Dalai Lama calls it "selfish selflessness." In support of others, we support our own awakening and compassionate growth too. In a way, we become the property of others. We take a risk. We work with ourselves and others to bring sense, growth, and meaning to all our lives.

We begin by discovering some little authentic truth about this in ourselves, a powerful inner one, a passion, a skill, a positive outlook rooted in our basic goodness that we can use as a vision and a voice to make positive change in the world. Inspired so, we are willing to give up our privacy, our comfort zone, to contribute to a greater vision.

You can start right where you are with your projects and embrace the world with it. You do something that helps you drop your self-centeredness and draws on your passion and compassion to contribute to the lives of others. It need not to be grandiose, but it does mean taking steps, something you can do that is manageable and in which you can achieve success that brings a self-confidence from having made a positive difference in some way. Then, like a flywheel, build on the momentum of that experience.

This way of life then becomes part of your practice and your practice part of your way. As a teacher, an artist, a business professional, a homemaker, or whatever—just shape whatever activity you do in a way that gives you meaning in serving the greater good. Apply it in a practical way and not just as an "everything is love and light" Bodhisattva. Simply learn to lean into your talents in an enlightened way right where you are, right now, and let it lead you wherever.

Years ago, I was moved by the novel *Siddhartha* by Hermann Hesse, a classic portrayal of a heroic journey. Siddhartha, the privileged son of a Brahmin, unsatisfied with life, sets off to find a new way. We follow him through the different stages of a journey where he gradually discovers how happiness is attained learning that it is not through scholastic methods, achievement, or pursuing the carnal pleasures of the world, but only through self-understanding.

Early in the novel, Siddhartha meets Vasudeva, a ferryman who has attained enlightenment by listening to the river. He is a deeply peaceful and happy man. *Vasudeva* means "one who dwells and shines in all things," a basic goodness. Siddhartha asks him for transport across the river, but says he has no money. Vasudeva takes him across for free, saying that "Everything comes back."

Many years later Siddhartha returns after much exploration, seeking to cross the river again but this time offering Vasudeva the rich clothes off his back for passage. Vasudeva refuses and again takes him across for free. At first, they do not recognize each other, but on the way, they realize they had met once before. Siddhartha decides to stay, and he becomes a ferryman himself.

Time passes, and the two men grow old together, but with the guidance of Vasudeva, things change for Siddhartha as he learns to listen to the river. The river, like himself, is unchanging and yet always changing within, bringing deeper and deeper understanding. He begins to feel himself a part of a greater whole and gradually realizes his own enlightenment.

His work with Siddhartha now complete, Vasudeva retreats to hermitage in the forest.

From the first reading of *Siddhartha*, I knew I wanted to be some type of ferryman—one who guides people to the other side . . . from an old to a new sense of self . . . and inspire others to do the same, just as Vasudeva did for Siddhartha and as Siddhartha later did for his old friend and spiritual companion Govinda, who had for a long time tried a traditional path to no avail.

That inspiration has been my North Star ever since. It was authentic, as it was not based on someone else's terms. Yet I never knew what form it would take. I thought I wanted to be a teacher but not in any subject for which my degrees qualified me. So I put it on the back burner to keep warm, an aspiration that I followed in incremental steps, and it eventually led me to where I am now.

We can be Bodhisattvas right now, right where we are, and let our heartfelt aspirations guide us in the choices we make in whatever we do, just by

Being of service, doing what we can, when we can, to make positive contributions in the lives of others

Noticing when we get caught up in our own stories, so we can
return to openness, appreciation, and the support of others

Welcoming opportunities to learn and grow, even though they may
be difficult or painful

Affirming and honoring the reality of interdependence and that
even the little things we do, good or bad, matter to our world

Remembering that we are enough and have something to offer in
support of our loved ones and others

Constantly nurturing the clarity of our mind and turning toward a
fully awakened life

These are little things that add up to big things in your heroic journey to the authentic you.

The Bodhisattva's Way of Life: The Paramita of Wisdom

*Wisdom is the recognition during meditation that all
phenomena are empty and during post-meditation that all
phenomena are unreal, like a dream or a magical illusion.*

PATRUL RINPOCHE

Within the sixth paramita of wisdom are four additional ones that drive
the full realization of a Bodhisattva. They are called different things
depending on the level and lineage of the teaching, but all hold similar
meaning. Most often known as *aspiration*, *strength*, *loving-kindness*, and
equanimity, they offer practical ways for developing wisdom in everyday
life.

Like the other paramitas, we contemplate and apply each as if
a dream, *real but not real* and *there but not there*. This way we cling
to them less as a panacea and open more to internalizing their true
meaning.

An Aspiration to Follow Your Bliss

A Bodhisattva aspires to adapt in different ways to benefit themselves and others, and here it is framed around igniting the desire to pursue or shape work to their natural talents in a way that makes a difference.

Comparative mythologist Joseph Campbell first coined the now well-known phrase *follow your bliss*. He saw the pursuits of our hungry spirit as a spontaneous production of the psyche and archetypal process expressed in the myths and traditions of ancient world cultures. They are a universal truth that portrays humanity's search for meaning in a common tale of separation, initiation, transformation, and return that he called "the Hero's Journey." The examples he used included Odysseus's return to save his family in the Homeric tales, Percival's quest for the Holy Grail to save the kingdom, King Gesar's fight with the spirits of the four directions to unite the Tibetan people, and Arjuna facing his doubts before entering battle in the Bhagavad Gita.

He used the journey to convey the profound lesson of tapping into the energy and passion that bring transformational change. He compared myth after myth where the hero or heroine took a leap of faith in crossing a threshold into the unknown to forge a new way. The outcome was never clear, yet it always resulted in new knowledge, strength, and insight. The hero never attached to a specific outcome; instead, they muddled through a pathless journey of questioning and discovery, letting inspiration guide them and unfold naturally in facing the unknown.

Like the protagonists in each tale, Campbell knew that the one common thing we all possess and share is the desire to make a difference in the lives of others, as a businessperson, an artist, a therapist, a homemaker, or whatever. Whether conscious of it or not, we all seek a purpose or a vision to satisfy the constant urge and longing of that hungry spirit inside.

In my professional life, I guided others in developing a personal mission statement to help them zero in on what was most important, and then challenged them to frame personal and professional life choices around it. Over the years, I guided thousands and heard and collected many statements, and without exception or exaggeration, people, in a reflective moment, want to do good in the world. We all want to make a positive difference in the lives of others—it is our nature—but are often stumped about how to go about it from where we stand. We tend to default to playing someone else's game rather that looking inward where the deeper inspirational truth is more often found.

Yet, as the woodcutter story showed, the interesting thing is that *it is not the work that you do, it's how you do it*. If you shape your work to you—to your values, your sense of mission or purpose—and not you to your work, you are on the road to finding meaning in it and creating a more rewarding future and way of life. The formula I used in coaching others was:

Play to your strengths,
Model your values, and
Serve your purpose (mission)
In shaping your work to you and not you to your work.

You play to what makes you tick, the real, the authentic, and the empowered you—your basic goodness. When you do, you naturally perform at a higher level, create more meaning, and kick up more opportunities for yourself. Then with each new opportunity, you just follow your bliss. You learn to *love the work you do until you find the work you love*; that strategy always ends with giving and serving in some way. Never, in working with M.B.A.s, academics, or other professionals over many years, was it ever in the end about money; in a reflective moment, it was always about making a positive difference in the world. It was about playing to their talents in a way that gave them meaning by serving others.

Always.

I discovered this for myself in making my early career choices. I started in financial management because that was what I was trained to do, but not inspired to do. It was a mismatch from the beginning, as I was horrible at math and reported to a comptroller who could smell a mathematical error as it walked in to the room with me. However, I was creative and was an early adopter of spreadsheet technology for doing the calculations, so I did well. I was then inspired to show others how to do the same, so I became involved in training them in desktop systems design and development, which was a step closer to my true strengths. That created another opportunity in planning full systems rollouts and eventually strategic planning, which were more strengths of mine. This in turn led to facilitating systems development teams and organizational change efforts, where I learned about leadership and how to build and lead teams—my sweet spot. Finally, a major donor funded the creation of a leadership program, and I was in the right place at the right time. I had positioned myself for my dream job just by following my bliss—my interests, my strengths, and what gave me meaning.

This little formula for success has since been validated by research.[2] In following your bliss, you naturally gravitate toward applying your talents in a way that makes a positive difference in your life and the lives of others—a Bodhisattva's way of life. You may not find it early in your career, but just follow your bliss until you are led or come close to it.

Whether you realize it or not, the reason this works is you are playing to your greater spirit and the need for self-actualization, even transcendence. As you do, you shift your focus from what the world can offer you to what you can offer to the world, and you move from that early passion to a genuine service mindset, and from a place of pointless activity to a place of genuine meaning.

But it takes courage.

Begin by simply reframing what you want in what you do now. Like the woodcutter, ask, *Do you have a job, a career, or a calling?* If you are a teacher, for example, do you teach history, or do you have a career in education, or do you have a passion for shaping the minds of future leaders? Do you craft you to your work, or your work to you? It makes a difference in your attitude, your performance, and your future. It is not the work that you do, it's how you do it, how you shape it. With a different frame, you create different possibilities and different outcomes. In following the thread of your bliss, you eventually discover what is authentic to you, where you are supposed to be.

This means being vigilant in asking questions and paying attention to what gives you meaning. Be a conscious learner of what does and does not give you fulfillment in work. I ask people not only to write a mission statement but also to pull it out occasionally and ask how they are doing in modeling it and playing to their strengths. This stimulates some to either make changes or change their statement. By homing in like this, you are in a position to take advantage of new opportunities as they arise. As a highly effective person, you get the most out of any situation because you constantly seek, adapt, and reinvent your ideal. Thus you launch yourself into a place of influence while grounding yourself in basic goodness.

EXERCISE

Developing a mission statement

We all have something we do well and feel good about. Often these things feel natural to us, but it's important to see them as being special. It takes asking yourself, what are you passionate about, what makes you feel great when you do it, or what do I stand for? It can feel awkward, but in taking the step, you may find something important.

A mission statement typically has three elements: the value you create, who you're creating it for, and the expected outcome. It answers the questions "Who am I?" and "What difference do I make?" It has been proven to provide powerful insight in just twenty minutes.

List some personal characteristics you feel great about. List three to five personal strengths expressed as nouns. If you are having problems thinking about what they are, reflect on feedback you have received, activities you excel at and enjoy, and personal assessments you may have taken. Express them as nouns. Here is an example:

Personal Characteristics
You May Feel Great About

technical expertise	energy	courage
strength	enthusiasm	creativity
sense of humor	insight	patience

I am _____

(For instance, coach, facilitator, servant, challenger, or creator.)

List ways you successfully interact with people. Again, list personal strengths
that you feel great about, but now expressed as verbs. For example:

Ways You Successfully Interact

teach	serve	lead
support	inspire	motivate
collaborate	produce	plan

I _____

(For instance, inspire, motivate, awaken, serve, or challenge.)

Describe your perfect world. This is the out-of-the-box step. Just try it and
go with it! Visualize what your perfect world looks like. What are
people doing and saying? Write a description of this perfect world.

My perfect world: _____

(For instance, "Everyone feels empowered to be fully who they are,
they model it in the world, and they help others do the same.")

Draft your mission statement. Combine two of your nouns, two of your
verbs, and your definition of your perfect world.

My life purpose is: _____

Here, as an example, is my own personal mission: *My life purpose is
to use my coaching and facilitation skills to help others become fully alive, to
develop skillful ways to pursue what gives them meaning, and to inspire them
to do the same for others.*

—◁o▷—

The Strength to Take the Heroic Path

This is about a person having the resolve of a Bodhisattva to advance to fulfill their potential, and the courage to pursue the call of their longing. There is obviously an aspect of strength and daring in this, even heroism. It is the drive and the longing to awaken to your fullest potential and share the boons to create what Trungpa Rinpoche called "enlightened society." It is about breaking away from conditioned ways of being, entering the world of the unknown to rediscover lost parts of yourself, and returning to share what you have learned in order to make the world a better place. Instead of serving self-interest, you serve self-discovery and the pursuit of wisdom. Having discovered it, you return to inspire the pursuit of the same in others.

Being heroic is not about being bigger than life—it is about all of us who take on the challenges and frustrations of life to find another way. It is about anyone able to step out of their comfort zone, their cocoon, to stretch themselves in taking on something new and face the risks and challenges of personal change despite fears, uncertainties, or circumstances. We have all faced change and the fears that come with doing something new or different. For some, it may be launching a career, getting married, or traveling abroad. For others, it may be trying to resolve a conflict that you have been avoiding or taking a stand on an issue that you believe in. And for others, it may be the strength to pick yourself up and reinspire yourself to approach a recurring challenge or the loss of a job, or loved one.

Any time you fail to cope with a challenging life situation like one of these, it is a refusal to face a doubt or a fear or to transcend your self-imposed habitual frame. Instead you feel your life does not provide you with enough, so you hold on to what you have and defend it tightly, and you rarely open yourself to new possibilities or even to get a breath of fresh air. In selling yourself short like this, you restrict your being, succumb to your doubt and fears, and allow your deepest desires and needs to go unmet.

Trapped in that fear, you make yourself small. Marianne Williamson famously said, "Our deepest fear is not that we are inadequate. Our deepest fear is that we are powerful beyond measure. It is our light, not our darkness, that most frightens us."[3]

Taking a heroic path is to respond to the call to wake up from this and make a difference in your life. Campbell said, "You must be willing to rid yourself of the life you have planned, so that you can have the life that is waiting for you."[4] You can live life through the scripts and expectations handed to you by others—or you can live one of your own design by making conscious and courageous choices.

This is not as far out of reach as you might think. Rather, it is often a process that begins right where you are, in the here and now of your everyday life. Any time you are faced with a challenge, it is an opportunity to break through the boxes of doubt and fear to achieve more than you believe possible by speaking up, addressing a conflict, stretching yourself. Then you just do this over and over again.

When you face a challenge, you have a choice. You can slip into malaise and lackluster effort or heed the heroic call and choose a new way of life. There is nothing more ennobling of the human spirit. But this is not easy. It takes courage to go against the grain. To live a full life, you need the strength to find your own way. So take some risks— take a chance in speaking in front of a group, ask someone for a date, stretch for a job you want but don't yet feel fully qualified to do, say "I love you" first, admit a mistake, be transparent when in doubt—do any of these things that make you feel vulnerable, and the growth follows. Soon you develop a comfort with vulnerability, on the edge of your seat, being at the raw edge of life in general, fully alive.

Start with taking some simple steps right where you are. *Lean into your fear* and *do some things that scare you*. Stretch yourself. Push the edges of your comfort zone, which are often defined by your fear and not knowing. *Don't try to escape discomfort*. Pema Chodron says, "You can leave your marriage, you can quit your job, you can only go where people are going to praise you, you can manipulate your world until you're blue in the face . . . but the same old demons will always come up until finally you have learned your lesson, the lesson they came to teach you" by looking within[5]. Finally, *learn to turn problems into opportunities*. Instead of playing the victim of circumstance, turn it around and play the master of circumstance by finding another way. Instead of sidelining yourself in blame and judgment, be proactive in creating new possibilities.

Taken together, these first two wisdom paramitas of aspiration and strength provide a simple and compelling truth for personal growth—*follow your bliss and lean into your fear*. Framing your life choices this way breaks the defensive pattern of your self-concerned monkey mind and opens you to new possibilities and your basic goodness.

Loving-Kindness in Treating People as People

Goodwill and kindness are what most distinguish rich, trusting, and effective relationships, and they are paramount to feelings of happiness and well-being. We are wired to connect. Abraham Maslow argued that the feeling of belonging arising from loving-kindness must be satisfied before self-esteem and self-actualization can be realized. As such, Bodhisattvas never part from the loving-kindness of Bodhicitta in their service to others.

Yet we often struggle to make and maintain positive supporting relationships. Why? The reason is *your relationships with others are only as good as the relationship we have with ourselves.* When we are unaware of our trips, issues, or whatever neuroses we have, we project them onto others, and we relate to others from a me-centered world. We unconsciously objectify them. We have our view, which is partial, and we project that view onto them without ever opening to theirs. Then we try to persuade them to our view, and if that doesn't work, then we either cope or leave.

It's tricky, even if you think you are skilled. If you are trained in effective communication skills, you are still likely only to "weaponize" them in trying to validate your view. When there is a difference, for example, are you trying to make the person wrong, or are you simply disagreeing with them? There is a subtle yet significant difference. Remember, there are always two sides to a story. Despite your skills, you still see others in terms of their relationship to your view. You objectify them, and that is inauthentic—"They are not as busy as I am" or "This person doesn't help me."

It is important to be honest, but being honest is sometimes a hard thing to do. Reflect on the last time a close one asked what was wrong and the difficulty you had in being truthful about it. Most likely you would rather make nice, not say anything, and just continue to feel hurt, guilty, or fearful. When you don't say what you are feeling, you create disharmony. Philosopher Martin Buber said that the origin of all conflict is that "I do not say what I mean and I don't do what I say."[6] On the other hand, if you do say what you mean, it often comes across as disrespectful. So you are damned if you do and damned if you don't.

The question, then, is how can you be authentic without being a jerk? How can you be both firm and kind? Being authentic is not just saying what is on your mind; it is about expressing your truth in a way that honors both yourself and the other. It requires opening to others, genuinely, and in doing that you learn to empathize and touch your basic goodness.

There was a time when Buber was in his office in prayer and was interrupted by a knock on the door from a troubled graduate student, who asked, "May I see you?" Buber said, "Come back later." The student, who was depressed and struggling to find meaning in life, never returned. A little later, Buber learned that the student had taken his life. This troubled him deeply and put Buber in a deep reflective mode as he wondered how he might have worked with this situation differently. "Here I had a chance to be with God, and I lost God in prayer." His reflections resulted in his most famous work, *I and Thou*. In it he argued that he had treated this student as an *It*—an object he wanted to go away, as opposed to a *Thou*—another child of God.[7] The difference is profound.

Everyone has Buddha nature. Thus the key in instilling a kindness in relationships, whether harmonious or conflicted, is to *honor the thou,* and just *treat people as people.* When we objectify others, we always treat them as either having what we want, being in the way of what we want, or as irrelevant to what we want. When they have what we want or are in the way of what we want, we make them blameworthy and become resistant to them. They sense it and respond in kind. Whatever underlying attitude you have, no matter how subtle, your partner picks up on it and mirrors it in return, and you never end up understanding each other.

The hard truth is that when it comes to relating effectively to people, it is your attitude that matters most. As William James said, "Whenever you're in conflict with someone, there is one factor that can make the difference between damaging your relationship and deepening it. That factor is attitude."[8] So instead of leading with a statement asserting your point of view, you lead with a question. *Seek first to understand, then to be understood.*

In that way, you just treat the other as a thou, a person, and you unhook yourself from a judgmental or adversarial dynamic by seeing them as equal to yourself. It is authentic because it is coming from a place of inquisitiveness and not from your self-centered universe. The irony is, "If you want to be interesting, be interested." Interest invites openness. You cannot be intimate with others unless you drop your self-absorption long enough to be open and take genuine interest in them. It is an act of kindness. The resistance drops, and you connect and communicate. They sense it and mirror it in return.

Learning to Learn with Equanimity

The wisdom of equanimity permeates and completes all of the other paramitas. For a Bodhisattva, this means learning to be generous without being a patron, to be patient without having a territory, to be morally disciplined without needing a precept, to be joyful in effort without exertion, and to be concentrated without fixation. Thus we need to be conscious of how we grow and develop, and the Buddhists do this with equanimity through an approach called *hearing, studying, and practicing.*

I prefer to call it "learning to learn"; to not only learn but to learn how to learn—to be a conscious learner. As a conscious learner you think not only about how to apply the teachings of the Buddha but also about how to adapt them to changing contexts while still abiding by them in principle. As a conscious learner, you learn how to get to the core of the purposes, principles, and values that guide you in all your choices. You learn to learn without getting caught up in materializing, concretizing, or holding onto the rituals, methods, and teachings themselves, because you want to *avoid the trap of convention or unconsciously turning doctrine into dogma.*

Within this frame of learning to learn, then, hearing and studying mean listening and making sure you understand the teaching. It's not enough just to read it once over or listen to it while you are half distracted by responding to text messages. Instead, you intently study and reflect on the meaning. I often take notes as I read or listen to the dharma and then later reorganize and outline them as a way of study to make sure I understand. I literally have volumes of dharma notes I have taken over the years, organized in three-ring binders, and I go back to refer to them and revise them from time to time. I have drawn on those notes a lot for this book. Then I try to apply them in my life and reflect on them again, and even more insights come. When I am in a writing mode, for example, I keep a journal next to me in my sitting practice because insights often pop through that I don't want to forget. This happens in both my writing and my practice.

Let's take another example of trying to incorporate a regular meditation practice in your life. You have all heard and learned of the value of meditation, so you now have an interest and you research different ways, receive some teachings, and make a plan to sit regularly. As you do, you have completed the *hearing and studying* and are now benefiting from them through *practicing.* You know what you are doing and why you are doing it and can easily adapt it because you have learned and integrated. Further, you know your motivation for maintaining a regular practice is going to be constantly challenged. So to maintain your motivation and continue to learn, you periodically attend teachings, read and learn more about the dharma, and connect with other practitioners for support and further learning. You now are consciously managing both your motivation and your learning. You are learning to learn. Your neighbor, on the other hand, may try to practice every day out of some sense of obligation but has lost appreciation for what they are doing or why. It becomes part of a checklist, and eventually the motivation wanes and the practice stops. They cut themselves short because they lack full appreciation of the why and how.

As practitioners, we want to be conscious learners. We have been asleep long enough, and now it is time to wake up. In learning how to learn, you appreciate, respect, and treasure yourself and this path. The treasure of this way of life is right in your lap, and you want to glorify it by learning to learn.

Most importantly, you also want to learn to learn while abiding in equanimity—wisdom awareness—as we have spoken about before. You do not want to be like the spider caught in its own web, attached to and hung up on the methods and techniques of the path. That is spiritual materialism. Instead, you maintain equanimity without holding onto the learning, the meditation, or any expected outcome. You want everything to appear as a dream and to remain in equanimity as a neutral observer with each step along the way. Otherwise, you still hold, concretize, and materialize the teaching and the path itself. You want to appreciate, respect, and honor this path by conducting and taking every action within the light of wisdom.

So from the start, you want to work from the equanimity of wisdom awareness that knows both the relative and absolute truth of *there but not there*. If you study from the perspective of the wisdom level, study and contemplate at wisdom level, and meditate and apply them at the wisdom level, then all is good, and you begin to internalize. So even here in the learning process, the path to realization models the result of realization.

In this way you also avoid derailing yourself through the spiritual materialism spoken about in the very beginning. You do not want to cling to the path itself. All is empty, even method. So again, take every action, learn, and apply every method within the light of wisdom, and make it a habit.

Tonglen:
The Heart Practice of a Bodhisattva

To strengthen feelings of loving-kindness and compassion, a Bodhisattva practices Tonglen. Tonglen is a mind-training technique that reverses ordinary states of mind from selfishly seeking happiness and pleasure for ourselves to willingly opening ourselves to taking on and relieving the suffering of others. It is often translated as "taking and giving."[9] The practice of Tonglen is the wish to benefit others and is known as *aspiration Bodhicitta*, where, as said before, the launchpad and Six Paramitas are applied and known as *application Bodhicitta*.

Tonglen synchronizes the breath with a visualization of breathing in the bad and breathing out the good. You take on and relieve the suffering of others while giving back a feeling of warmth and loving-kindness. This may seem self-defeating but as Trungpa Rinpoche said, "The more negativity we take in with a sense of openness and compassion, the more goodness there is to breathe out. So there is nothing to lose."[10] There is nothing to lose because if you conduct your practice within a compassion adorned with wisdom awareness, then your reservoir of basic goodness is limitless. You cannot use it up.

The practice of Tonglen begins by first reflecting on the virtues of *loving-kindness, compassion, sympathetic joy,* and *equanimity* known as the Four Immeasureables or the Four Boundless Thoughts. They are so called because our inherent capacity for love and compassion is limitless by our very nature. So we wish that:

All beings know happiness and the cause of happiness
They be free from suffering and the cause of suffering
They never be separated from supreme happiness without suffering
They rest in equanimity, free attachment, and resentment of others

I adapted this for a wedding ceremony I was asked to contribute to:

Through *loving-kindness* you learn to relate to another in an open
and tolerant way that reveals a vulnerable heart.
Through *compassion* you learn to put yourself in the shoes of
another, to see and appreciate them for who they genuinely are,
and to care for them as you would yourself.
Through *sympathetic joy* you learn to delight in another's happiness
in a way that brings abundance and generosity to your own being.
Through *equanimity* you learn to love without making a bond of
love and to sing and dance together while still being alone.

This reflection helps cultivate connection and bring forth compassion. Whereas Shamata and Vipassana practice helps us to see reality, the Four Immeasurables help us feel and relate to our interconnected reality. They complement one another in cultivating both awareness and compassion and help provide the balance I found lacking in Ayahuasca.
The practice has four stages.

Begin with Touching Your Stillness and Equanimity
Without equanimity, the other immeasureables would not be boundless. The more you relax in equanimity, the more balance and openness comes into your being.

*You start by breathing in the rumbling qualities of emotions, the dark
and heavy, and breathing out the qualities of spaciousness, light, and
the loving-kindness of Bodhicitta. Synchronize these thoughts with
your breath for a while.*

Then in this calm and open state, reflect on how beings are the same as you, possess the same potential, and want the same thing—to be happy.

Remember the kindness of others and how friends have been kind and then mean, and mean and then kind—just like you.

Reflect on how the interdependence of different life situations and confusion leads to different life outcomes beyond one's control, yet everyone is still suffused with the same nature of basic goodness. We are all equal, wanting the same thing.

Appreciating this, a genuine sense of appreciative loving-kindness arises, a boundless one that wishes everyone to know happiness and its causes. This brings you to an open space where there are no blocks from attachment, aversion, and indifference.

Then Focus on a Personal Situation

After a few moments, move to the main part of compassion. Bring to your mind someone you love. Often this is a parent or child, but if not, then someone for whom you have felt genuine affection and think of naturally with loving-kindness. Then visualize breathing in the darkness of their suffering and breathing out the light of wisdom, happiness, and compassion. Continue coordinating with each breath until your heart opens fully and you feel a genuine, even expanded feeling of loving-kindness as a feeling of sympathetic joy blooms—you want, appreciate, and rejoice in their happiness and well-being. As if in a dream, breathe in all their suffering and breathe out a feeling of loving-kindness and sympathetic joy.

Expand Outward

As you connect, gradually expand this practice to other family, friends, and loved ones, breathing in their suffering and breathing out the wish for their happiness and well-being. As your practice strengthens, continue to expand outward to acquaintances, others in your community, and all those suffering from war, poverty, sickness and so on. Imagine all beings having been your mother at one time, and breathe in the darkness of their suffering, breathe out the light of your loving-kindness. You take in with great compassion and give out with great love. As you do, *you feel increasingly connected to all and everyone*. All sentient beings are equal and wanting the same—to be happy.

Go as far as you can feel it. You want the practice to be authentic, so go as far as you can, and as your practice deepens, expand out further.

Conclude

Always end with a reflection on how even the concepts of this practice only manifest through interdependence. You have temporarily employed mental constructs to tap into a deeper continuum of basic goodness. Then dissolve it into light and try to maintain this appreciation post meditation.

EXERCISE

Practice on your own for ten minutes or so, and then incorporate it into the start of your regular sitting practice for a few moments. I begin each meditation with eliciting Bodhicitta in this way, and it sets the stage for my meditation.

◄○►

Meditation Instructions: Open Space Vipassana Meditation

Again, we are progressing in our meditation techniques from a structured form to a more formless one where our object of concentration gradually becomes more open and less concrete. In this section, we learn the fourth and final technique, as taught by Chogyam Trungpa Rinpoche.

With this technique, we open our eyes for the first time. In opening the eyes, we once again expand our realm awareness and learn to practice and work with the most powerful of our five physical senses.

Eyes open, gaze slightly downward in space, and focus about a foot in front of you.

Relax your eyes and soften your gaze. Instead of looking narrowly in a pinpointed way, just broaden your focus and rest your gaze in a space several feet in front of you without any object or particular focus.

Breathe gently and normally. Then begin to follow your breath out only, and feel how it diffuses into space. With each outbreath, dissolve and become more open, tender, and vulnerable right in the moment, naked and raw.

Pause briefly in the gap between the exhale and the inhale resting in its openess.

Let the inbreath occur naturally, but do not follow it in; just stay with the openness of the outbreath. This is how you anchor in Shamata with this technique. It is far more expansive and subtle. You are gradually letting go of any object as a focus for your concentration. It will seem confusing at first, as your mind will search for something to hold onto. But just meet that too with equanimity.

Then, finally, follow the same Vipassana technique as before— as thoughts occur, notice them and come back to the outbreath. Just recognize them as thoughts—regardless of whether they are good, bad, or neutral—and return to the breath. Do the same for any dominant sensation in your experience—sight, sound, or bodily sensation.

Overall, become a warrior of being in the moment of nowness, on the spot and beyond any reference point—open, spacious, and vivid.

———————————

Chogyam Trungpa describes this technique in the *Sacred Path of the Warrior.*

In meditation practice, as you sit with a good posture, you pay attention to your breath. When you breathe, you are utterly there, properly there. You go out with the outbreath, your breath dissolves, and the inbreath happens naturally. Then you go out again. So there is a constant going out with the outbreath. As you breathe out, you dissolve, you diffuse. Then your inbreath occurs naturally; you don't have to follow it in. You simply come back to your posture, and you are ready for another outbreath. Go out and dissolve—*tshoo*, then come back to your posture, then *tshoo*, and come back to your posture.

Then there will be the inevitable *bing!*—a thought. At that point you note your thinking. Noting your thoughts gives you tremendous leverage to come back to your breath. When one thought takes you away completely from what you are actually doing—when you do not even realize you are on the cushion, but in your mind, you are in San Francisco or New York—you note "thinking" and bring yourself back to your breath.

It doesn't really matter what thoughts you have. In meditation, whether you have monstrous thoughts or benevolent thoughts, all of them are regarded purely as thinking. They are neither virtuous nor sinful. You might have a thought of assassinating your father, or you might want to make lemonade or cookies. Please don't be shocked by your thoughts, any thought is just thinking. No thought deserves a gold medal or a reprimand. Just note your thoughts and go back to your breath.

The practice of meditation is very precise. It must be on the dot, right on the dot.[11]

14

Karma and Taking Everything as Path

Open Space Vipassana II

Meditation practice isn't about trying to throw ourselves away and become something better. It's about befriending who we are already.

PEMA CHODRON

Revisiting the Law of Cause and Effect

In your life, can you think of anything that exists independently of everything else? Is there ever a thing that was not created by or interdependent with something else? A tree grows from a seed, a puddle from drops of water, and a fire from a spark, This is the rhythm of nature. Every single object or event is created *only* by its interdependent relationship to other objects or events and is constantly changing.

In a similar way, have you ever had the feeling that there are no accidents? That everything is connected and happens for a reason? Success or failure is not purely accidental or just the result of good or bad luck. It is directly or indirectly the result of a series of choices and steps you have taken that have brought you to where you are, and they could not have brought you to any other place. Does any of the following surprise you?

A volunteer donates to a local charity event and returns home to discover extra money they had forgotten they had.

A teacher goes out of her way to provide extra credit for a student, and that student later recommends her for her dream job.

A driver aggressively tailgates someone traveling the speed limit on the highway, eventually passes, and is then pulled over and given a ticket.

What this describes is the law of cause and effect. We touched on this earlier, but how do we work with it on our path? Plato was the first in the West to describe this law, and it was the foundation for much of the philosophy and science that followed. In the East it is known as karma, and it operates as the universal law governing the cosmos.

The law holds that every event or action is the result of interdependent causes and does not exist independently of those causes, which are themselves the cause of other events or actions. In other words, everything is interdependent, so there is no such thing as randomness in the universe. For every effect you experience, there is a contributing cause, or a series of identifiable causes. For example:

If you don't eat properly, you gain weight
If you don't brush your teeth, you get cavities
If you plant a seed, it grows
If you don't water it, it dies
If you love, you are loved
If you are angry, others avoid or resist
If you are generous, others open
If you are interested, you become interesting
If you nurture basic goodness, you gather basic goodness

There are several interrelated and overlapping aspects to this law. First, not only your actions but also your thoughts and feelings have causes and effects. The mind is a powerful force; it shapes your reality even to the point of becoming what you selectively think and feel most of the time. Have you ever noticed, for instance, that a habit of aggression is reflected in the body and demeanor of a person, while others who are more open and accepting reflect just the opposite? Our mind affects our body and vice versa.

Second, for every action there is a reaction. If you churn milk, it turns to butter. Likewise, all your thoughts and actions are interdependent and have consequences. This is how successful people are proactive, while those who are less mindful get stuck. Are you looking for a job, a career, or a calling? You get what you look for. A friend once asked me, what does a frog's eye see? Flies! It is narrowly stuck on one thing. Your outlook shapes your outcome. If you act with awareness and a plan, you likely move toward what you desire. A more passive and reactive approach is mirrored in kind. It is basic cause and effect.

Third, what you sow is what you reap. If you plant an apple seed, you get an apple, and not something else. If you sow a good cause, you will reap a good result; if you sow anger, you reap negativity—what you put into the world, you get back. If you are experiencing a repeated pattern in your life, you are doing something to cause it. Even at a subconscious level, what you reap today is the result of what you have sown in the past, and what you sow today you reap in the future. Einstein said, "The most important decision we make is whether we believe we live in a friendly or hostile universe." Your frame of reference makes a difference. The results are not always immediate, but in time they appear. Buddhists say the result may even take more than one lifetime, but eventually it comes.

Finally, there are no accidents—the uncanny coincidence, the unlikely conjunction of events, or the startling serendipity. Who hasn't had this kind of thing happen in their life? You think of someone for the first time in years and run into them a few hours later. You hear an unusual phrase, and then hear it three times in the same day. You are on a back street in a foreign country, and you bump into a college roommate. When writing, you hear something on the radio, and it's exactly what you need to clarify a point. Each day you encounter meaningful coincidences. Carl Jung called these synchronicities "God's breath." In some way you have sown a cause, directly or indirectly, that has attracted them to you.

Simply knowing this law of cause and effect does not produce any change in your life. Like any other principle, it proves useless unless you are mindful and apply it. The more awake and in tune you are with your environment, the more likely it is that a karmic chain appears to help guide your way, even to your freedom. That wakefulness is the self-actualizing aspect of your hungry spirit. Happy, healthy, successful people have learned to access it and work it to their benefit.

This is why Einstein famously said, "God does not play dice with the universe." Whatever you put into the universe—thoughts, emotions, energy, actions—comes back—good or bad. There is a cause and an effect. Everything is interdependent and connected; for every action there is a reaction, no matter how subtle. This law pervades all science, all relationships, and all mind. Positive begets positive, negative begets negative. What we nurture is what we become. What we sow is what we reap. What you were in the past is what you are now. What you are now is what you will be in the future. Maybe not immediately, nor how minor, eventually it ripens.

Over time, cause and effect shape our thoughts and actions and accumulate into habits of style, traits, and personal routines that make up what is called our karma, or our personal propensities that have a momentum of their own and become self-reinforcing.

This is, once again, the *cosmic mirror*, in which we see what we are programed to see, and what we put into the world is what we receive in return. This interdependence can manifest immediately, as in how we respond to a disagreement, over time in how we invest in our personal development, and according to Buddhism, over lifetimes as we carry it from one lifetime to the next.

This makes our karma of past, present, and future of this life,
as well as our past, present, and future lives, interdependent.
Further, it pervades all life, all existence, all phenomena.

Leveraging Cause and Effect on the Path

The good news is you can leverage this karmic chain of events and ride it for personal growth and even liberation. What you nurture and gather is what you become. If you nurture basic goodness, you reap basic goodness. In practicing selfish selflessness, your world responds in kind because everything is interconnected and changeable. It is as if we were artists painting our own palette.

This means we want to be conscious of nurturing our noble qualities and ride that karmic momentum to freedom. In fact, if you don't actively nurture your virtue, your meditation will not go well; it won't take root. Why? Because it goes against the grain of who you innately are, your inherent nature, the very thing that meditation is revealing.

Thus the path becomes doing anything that cultivates your basic goodness on and off the cushion. *You take everything on as path*, just as the six paramitas encourage you to do. In daily life, you exercise the skillful means of compassion through the lens of wisdom awareness in everything—in meditation and post-meditation—from the greatest to the smallest. You turn even neutral activities, like eating, walking, and drinking, into ways of opening. In more advanced practices, there is even dream yoga, where you turn sleep into practice. There is no part of life outside the realm of practice. Everything is turned into a virtue-generating activity, and everything is fused with positive intention and action.

In this way you *take the fruit of the path of virtue as the path of virtue.* You sow your basic goodness to reap your basic goodness. You purify your essential nature by practicing your essential nature. *Your path models the desired result.* In putting this into practice, you begin to replace your useless and confused thought processes with your inherent, good, merit-generating ones and that opens you to blessings and good fortune.

Understanding karma and how it works gives you the perspective for making sense of and applying the Buddhist philosophical perspective in your everyday life. Instead of operating from a rule book of dos and don'ts, you are empowered to work with the principles of basic goodness in making your own choices.

As your practice matures, your greater spirit emerges too, and the laws of karma and cause and effect begin to reveal themselves more clearly as you move up the hierarchy of needs to psycho-emotional wholeness and compassionate wakefulness. You become more open, attuned, and adaptive, and synchronicities begin to appear that further guide your choices. Then, the teachings say, in approaching transcendence, karma itself begins to dissolve along with the ego that drives it. You transcend the duality of subject and object—you and it—as well as cause and effect. In the meantime, you work the law of karma and the positive aspects of your nature to move upward along that path.

Supportive Post-Meditation Practices

To help maintain a continuity in your practice, you take everything on as path in your daily activities. The following points provide a few methods for your post-meditation time that help to deepen and extend your practice beyond the cushion and integrate it in whatever activity you are doing. Based on the same meditation principles as before, you simply shift the area of your Shamata focus to other sensory objects of awareness—body sensations, taste, seeing, or even hearing. In this way, you gradually *learn how to let the echo of your meditative awareness come back to whatever you are doing* in post-meditation.

Walking Meditation

Here, you focus on the body's movements and physical sensations with every step as you walk. You use the sensations on the bottom of your feet to anchor in Shamata, and then practice Vipassana as your mind wanders from it.

Begin by selecting a quiet place where you have room to move comfortably without distraction. Take ten to twenty steps in a straight line, moving much more slowly than your normal pace. You want to be deliberate with your steps, putting one foot in front of the other in a slow, rhythmic fashion. When you reach the end of those steps, turn around and walk back the same way, keeping the same slow pace.

As you walk like this, notice the sensations on the bottom of your feet as you lift them up, move them through space, and place them back on the ground. Try to follow and focus on them through the entire step. When your mind wanders, use the sensations of your steps to refocus your attention. If there are noises in the distance that you can't block out or another disturbance, simply acknowledge it with equanimity, and then return your attention to your steps.

As you gain comfort, pick up your pace. Take a walk around the block at a normal pace, and just be aware of the general movement and sensations of your body while anchoring on your feet. Or split your focus, 20 percent on the sensations of your feet and 80 percent on a panoramic awareness of everything around you in equanimity. Take the time that you have, and as you gain comfort with it, try to incorporate the practice any time you walk alone.

I personally love this practice and do it almost every day.

Eating Meditation

Eating meditation is very similar—you simply shift your Shamata focus to the sensations of your body and your mouth as you chew and swallow, and then practice Vipassana as your mind wanders from it.

Especially in the beginning, it is important to be precise in following all your bodily movements. So from a still position, notice your intention to eat, and as you do, focus your awareness on the slow ambulatory movements of the arms as you scoop up and insert food into your mouth. Don't start chewing until the arms are back at rest. Then shift your attention to the chewing—slowly—and notice the explosion of sensations inside your mouth as you do. Don't react in any way; just appreciate the enhancement of your taste function that you so often take for granted. Then, notice your intention to swallow as it forms, swallow, and again notice whatever sensation follows as the food travels to your stomach.

Then repeat. If your mind wanders at any time, then just bring it back to the process of the chewing and swallowing.

The tradition typically starts you off with raisins, but anything will do. Take one slow bite and chew at a time until you get the ebb and flow of the movement and the process. Always begin slowly, and then, as in walking meditation, pick up the speed as you grow accustomed.

You may want to pick a meal to do this daily. Before you begin your meal, do Shamata for a few minutes, and then move to your normal eating speed while trying to maintain a general awareness of the process.

Again, as above, with practice you will simply learn to eat within the backdrop of awareness.

Seeing Meditation

With this, you use looking at an object to practice becoming a neutral observer of a plant, a house, a tree—anything—by just gazing without reaction and without numbing out. You are there, just fully there.

Like the practices above, with seeing meditation you direct your full attention to the present moment of seeing. Just be aware of what your eyes are receiving in each moment of perception with equanimity. This means without labeling, without reacting, without following thoughts and feelings of pleasing, unpleasing, or indifference in each moment. Just be present in the moment as you take it in, without reacting to whatever is in the realm of your sight. You just shift your focus of awareness from your breath or your body to your eyes, while resting in equanimity. As your thoughts interrupt, note it simply, and return to seeing, as with the other two post-sitting methods.

Begin with something simple, and then broaden your gaze. I started with the trunk of a tree. I noticed how my mind wanted to label it—tree, bark, brown, mesmerizing patterns, and so on, but then returned to just simply seeing again and again. As I grew comfortable with it, instead of just doing walking meditation when I walked, I also incorporated seeing meditation by taking in the sights mindfully and openheartedly. I notice my reactions and let them fade away.

Random Acts of Kindness
This may sound trivial, but another very simple and easy thing to do is practice random acts of kindness. Open the door for someone, ask someone about their day, be a good listener, give a compliment, give up your seat, and so on. This engages your Bodhicitta by warming your heart and connecting with others.

Dedicating the Merit
As an act of selflessness and compassion, it is customary in many Buddhist traditions to dedicate the merit at the end of practice. Generally, merit means doing something that is worthy and creates value. When you meditate, perform rituals, practice the six paramitas, and so on, you create karmic merit that benefits this life and your future lives. Dedicating this value—this wholesomeness, your basic goodness—to all sentient beings expands this merit even more. When you do, you realize that your efforts are not just about you at all, and that further opens your practice. All beings are interdependent, so dedicating the merit to all beings aligns with the truth of what is, and the benefits just multiply.

I repeat the following slowly at the end of each practice to internalize it as I chant it. It is a brief dedication authored by both Patrul and Trungpa Rinpoches. The first stanza is chanted twice.

> By this merit, may all obtain omniscience,
> May it defeat the enemy, wrongdoing,
> From the stormy waves of birth, old age, sickness,
>   and death, (twice).
> From the ocean of samsara may I free all beings.
> By this merit, may all obtain omniscience,

> *May it defeat the enemy wrongdoing,*
> *From the stormy waves of birth, old age, sickness,*
>   *and death,*
> *From the ocean of samsara may I free all beings.*
> *By the confidence of the great eastern sun,*
> *May the lotus garden of the Rigden's wisdom bloom,*
> *May the deep dark ignorance of beings be dispelled,*
> *May all beings enjoy profound brilliant glory.[1]*

Take Everything as Path

A Systematic and Integrated Approach to Awakening

With that framing and understanding, you now have a systematic and wholistic approach for your growth and awakening. You have an intellectual understanding, you have meditation practices to approach that understanding in experience, you have post-meditation instructions to align your behavior to support it, and with discipline of steady practice you begin to feel the results. These are summarized in the following framework of principles adapted from the more formless practice of Dzogchen, but applied here in the context of Shamata Vipassana.

View. You have a view. With your analytical investigation you begin to understand that thoughts, feelings, emotions are not solid, concrete, as you supposed them to be. You have caught a glimpse or a taste of the universal truth of emptiness. This loosens your grip on what you believe is real or not real. Instead of feeling trapped by your feelings, you know you can let them go and fade like letters drawn on water.

Meditation. You have meditation techniques to practice and reinforce this view. You can experience it. In understanding the view and practicing equanimity, you let thoughts and emotions pass like clouds in the sky. You see everything as changeable and realize nothing is solid or permanent. Instead of being trapped by your thoughts and feelings, you let them disappear to discover and nurture your basic goodness—your awake and compassionate inner essence.

Conduct. You support this meditation with your *thoughts and actions* by practicing the skillful means of the Six Paramitas and leveraging the law of cause and effect through the lens of wisdom awareness to support the view on and off the cushion. You learn to conduct yourself in ways consistent with your inner nature of basic goodness and behave your way into a new way of being. In doing so, you enter a virtuous cycle—where your behavior affects mind and mind affects behavior in modeling the conduct of a Bodhisattva right as you are.

Result. As you gain stability in your practice, your basic goodness shines through more and more. The discipline transforms your life's difficulties and preoccupations, and you become happier and more grounded in a sense of well-being. As you grow, you also gradually let go of all the constructs of the path itself—the techniques and the methods, along with the pitfalls and spiritual materialism—and just relate from that space of basic goodness wherever you are.

In short, you change your view through your analysis and reinforce that view and your meditation through your conduct. You work from the inside out and the outside in. In both directions, you nurture basic goodness to reveal that inherent basic goodness naturally residing within. *The path and the result are of the same stuff.*

The Two Wings of Practice

You now have all the tools and techniques to model what is known as the two wings of practice of meditation and post-meditation, right where you are. The metaphor of two wings is often used to convey the two aspects necessary for taking flight in your practice. This expands on the metaphor presented earlier about wisdom awareness and the skillful means of compassion to now include meditation and post-meditation practices. It is adapted from one presented by Khenpo Tsewang Dongyal Rinpoche during a spring retreat in 2016.

Meditation

1. Motivation: Cultivating the spirit of awakening
   a. Reflect on the ground of compassion: Sacredness, Faith, and Basic Goodness, and
   b. The four thoughts that turn the mind toward the dharma
2. Shamata Vipassana practice
   a. Shamata
   b. Sweeping Shamata Vipassana
   c. Vipassana
   d. Open Vipassana
   e. The three allies: mindfulness, alertness, and carefulness
3. Tonglen
4. Dedicating the merit

Post-meditation

1. Motivation is the same
2. The six paramita practices
3. Walking, sitting, eating, and seeing practices

Practice with "it's there and not there"

1. What you see is like an illusion
2. What you experience is like a dream
3. What you hear is like an echo
4. What you think is like a passing cloud in the sky

It's worth repeating a quote from Shabkar shared earlier.

Now I have some heart-advice to give to you: a sky needs a sun, a mother needs a child, a bird needs two wings. Likewise, emptiness alone is not enough. You need great compassion for all beings who have not realized emptiness—friends, enemies, strangers. You need to have compassion that makes no distinctions between good and bad. You must understand that compassion arises through meditation, not simply waiting, thinking that it may come forth by itself from emptiness.[2]

Meditation Instructions: Open Space Vipassana Meditation II

Picking up from the last chapter, begin again with Shamata on the outbreath. Once you have settled for a few minutes, stop following it and just rest into the vast open space that it dissolves into. Let go and let your awareness follow the outbreath and rest in that vivid, vast open, wakefulness of *nowness*. When thoughts return, or you get lost in them, just return to the outbreath and repeat. The only focus in following the outbreath into space is the stillness and bigness of the mind and awareness itself.

Again, your eyes should be open and unfocused, gaze resting in space a few feet in front of you, to help you feel, appreciate, and relax in that openness and even vastness of space.

This can be a challenging practice, so experiment with it. When a distracting thought or emotion occurs, return to the outbreath to anchor and recalibrate. Then try again.

As you settle in, when your outbreath dissolves into space, imagine you are no longer holding onto anything, that you have let go of all or any attractions and aversions as they dissolve into space with the outbreath. Then just rest there, fully present and openheartedly vulnerable. You might even experience that the vast open emptiness mirrors the mind itself. It is uncontrived and empty and reflects the true meaning of insight—Vipassana—into the ultimate truth.

To provide some perspective, this practice approaches the choiceless awareness practices of Dzogchen and Mahamudra, but it is not those. There, Shamata and Vipassana merge and empty into the vast open space of pure beingness, and this requires more instruction, preparation, and commitment for fully experiencing the mind in a true resting place. It includes an empowerment, pointing-out instructions, and completion of preliminary practices. One purpose of this book has been to guide and inspire you to want to do that and to find a qualified teacher to help you.

When to Use the Different Techniques

Generally, always begin with Shamata. Then:

> Use Shamata again to settle and calm an agitated mind.
>
> Use Sweeping occasionally to increase concentration and to ward off an agitated or dull mind.
>
> For most of the time, especially as you are developing your discipline, remain in Vipassana.
>
> As you develop comfort and stability in Vipassana, move into Open Space Vipassana, and drop back to Vipassana as needed.
>
> Open Space Vipassana is the apex in the sequence of these meditation methods.

These methods move from the structured to the more formless and subtle. As you progress in them, you are gradually learning to practice first with and then without concepts or conceptual framing. As you do, you are learning three different levels of awareness that you experience and work with on your path, as often pointed out by Joseph Goldstein.

Awareness 1. This is a mentally fabricated awareness-development technique that is dualistic, where there is an observer and the observed. These contain the mental constructs of following the breath, sweeping, and noting an object—breath, sensations, thoughts—to become aware. There is a *doer* (the one making the effort to become aware) and an *object* (the thought or sensation as the vehicle to become aware).

Awareness 2. This is a nonfabricated (formless) technique that we began to explore in these last two chapters. This is where, once that object of your meditation dissolves—thought, emotion, sensation—you just rest in the nature of that awareness itself. *There is no doer, there is no object.* You have, hopefully, tasted it already in your practice. You experienced this intellectually by "looking at the looker" and investigating the source, dwelling, and destination of a thought and of mind. You have also experienced it with the outbreath in Open Space Meditation.

Awareness 3. Use the fabricated awareness of the technique to bring you back to the unfabricated nature of awareness itself—awareness of awareness. Here compassion begins to emerge naturally.

In working with the four Shamata Vipassana methods, you experience all three types of awareness. It's important to know when you are using each so that you do not confuse them.

Suggested Practice Schedule

As recommended earlier, try to maintain two twenty-minute periods of practice per day. It could be more or less based on the ebb and flow of your daily life. The most important thing is to maintain some momentum by practicing at least once per day. You may miss a day here and there, but try to bounce back into the schedule.

Begin each session with a few moments of reflection to raise your spirit of awakening, followed by a few minutes of Tonglen. Then start Shamata Vipassana, with a few minutes of Shamata followed by whatever Vipassana practice you are doing (see advice above). End each session with a few moments of dedication, appreciation, and thankfulness.

Mix in the post-meditation practices occasionally where your routine allows.

Finally, try to work in one three-to-seven-day retreat a year if you can. This deepens and strengthens your practice.

Seven Metaphors for Practice

Reflect on the following seven similes help guide you in both meditation and post-meditation practices. They come from eighteenth-century

Buddhist master Jigme Lingpa, and they help develop, support, and glorify our practice.

Be like a honey bee. A honey bee sustains itself and the flowers by collecting, spreading, and sharing nectar with others.

Be like a deer. A deer is always alert, peaceful, and focused in going about its business, and it avoids all distractions and unsettling places.

Be like a mute. A mute person does not waste time by speaking idly or saying unnecessary things, particularly gossip, a nonvirtue that can quickly grow out of proportion.

Be like a Thibja bird. A Thibja bird only nests in safe and secure locations so they can come and go with confidence, courage, and fearlessness. We want to be like this in our practice.

Be like a crazy person. A crazy person has no attachments to objects or things; they are free from clinging, and they act beyond the constraints of convention.

Be like a lion. Lions go forward free of hope and fear and conduct their activities without being manipulated by clinging emotions.

Be like a dog. A dog is never hung up on the worldly concerns and constant activity of everyday life, nor is it promoting its ego by neglecting and criticizing others.

Parting Advice

Finding a Spiritual Friend and Virtuous Companions

> *If you rely upon an authentic spiritual teacher, their positive qualities, virtues, and excellences will naturally saturate you. This is similar to placing an ordinary piece of wood in the midst of sandalwood. The scent of the sandalwood will naturally infuse it. In the same way, you should rely on virtuous spiritual teachers and virtuous companions.*
>
> LONGCHENPA

I want to offer some general advice on finding a teacher or a guru. Generally, if you have and maintain an abiding interest, sooner or later your heartfelt intent and synchronicities will lead you to one. This means an intention that is imbued with an openness for different possibilities is almost necessary for having the receptivity and tranquility to find one. One reason the Vajrayana in particular is secret is that most do not have enough wakeful, love-nurturing basic goodness to pursue or find it. For those who do or who have such motivation, however, the precious means of this vehicle eventually mysteriously arises in your life. It did so for me. Then, once there, examine the teacher's understanding of the dharma, their alignment with a lineage, their humility in spreading the dharma, their availability to meet one on one, and their heartfelt authenticity in modeling Bodhicitta. In my case, my interest gradually led me through a progression of Vipassana, Shambala, and Mahayana-Vajrayana teachings that unfolded naturally and resulted in following different Nyingma gurus who were closely aligned in lineage and monastic tradition. Above all, your heartfelt interest is key.

The Four Possible Ways for Practice to Unfold

As a reminder of all we have covered in how to apply and abide by these teachings, I offer the following benchmarks for gauging and guiding our progress.

Authentic Presence. First is authentic presence. As we progress on the path, we develop some merit and virtue that is reflected in our presence. Following the law of cause and effect, we become more open, adaptive, giving, and compassionate. This magnetizes and draws attention as our view, practice, and actions align in a way that makes us genuinely authentic, believable, and trustworthy.

Spiritual Materialism. Second is a reminder that if we fail to generate genuine warmth for our practice, all the subsequent practices will simply reinforce the ego. We may practice but never sever our attachment to things in life—friends, relations, food, clothes, and the like. Instead, we puff ourselves up with pride, find fault with others. . . . It is easy to fall prey to counting up the years of practice and to reinforce the ego without any diminution in afflictive emotions.

Trap of Convention. Third, if we work toward a goal, make our experience conform to expectations, and place ourself in a box of method, we fall into the trap of convention. Wanting to become the agent of our own awakening becomes an obstacle, so we need to recognize this and develop confidence and patience to do nothing. When the habits of practice arise, still do nothing. Let them arise and subside. This both deepens the practice and releases our investment in them. We do not want to objectify our practice, nor do we want to observe it; instead, just be aware while being inside it. We don't want to be like a spider caught in its own web—remain vulnerable and open. This is a key and subtle point.

Tracelessness. Finally, we want to be somewhat of a hidden yogi and simply blend our mind tracelessly with the dharma. Like the footprints of a bird in the sky in flight, we do not want to make a spectacle or an issue of our intent and practice. We want to distill the teachings to their essence in our being and be a quiet yet compelling inspiration to others.

> *The crane, the cat, or the thief, moving silently and covertly achieves its desired goal. A sage should always move in such a way.*
>
> SHANTIDEVA

Notes

Introduction

1. Rumi, *The Essential Rumi*.

1. What Makes You a Buddhist

1. Sidle, "What Makes You a Buddhist."
2. Lily Tomlin quotes, Goodreads website, accessed March 28,2023.
3. Tilopa, "Top 8 Tilopa Quotes," Quotefancy website, accessed March 25, 2023.

2. The Cosmic Fool

1. Trungpa, *Cutting Through Spiritual Materialism*, 15.
2. Welwood, "Principles of Inner Work: Psychological and Spiritual."
3. Wilber, *Sex, Ecology, Spirituality: The Spirit of Evolution*.
4. Jim Rohn quotes, Goodreads website, accessed March 28, 2023.
5. Trungpa, *Crazy Wisdom*, 147.
6. Goethe, *Faust: A Tragedy*, 12.

4. My Experience: Ceremonies and Reflections

1. Welwood, *Love and Awakening: Discovering the Sacred Path of Intimate Relationship*.
2. Pearce, *The Crack in the Cosmic Egg: New Constructs of Mind and Reality*.
3. Trungpa, *Shambhala: The Sacred Path of the Warrior*.
4. Trungpa, *Shambhala: The Sacred Path of the Warrior*, 160.
5. Shabkar, *The Life of Shabkar: The Autobiography of a Tibetan Yogi*, 294.

5. The Three-Year Cycle Ends: Some Takeaways

1. Pierre Teilhard de Chardin quotes, Goodreads website. (There is some disagreement over whether Chardin or George Gurdjieff made this quote and whether it is an accurate reflection of the original.)
2. Shabkar, *The Life of Shabkar: The Autobiography of a Tibetan Yogi*, 422.

6. Longing and the Spirit of Awakening

1. Sidle, *This Hungry Spirit: Your Need for Basic Goodness*. Used with permission.
2. Rinpoche Dudjom, *A Torch Lighting the Way to Freedom*, 154.
3. Rumi quotes, Goodreads website, accessed March 28, 2023.
4. Patrul Rinpoche, *The Words of My Perfect Teacher*, 195.

7. Meditation Benefits and Myths

1. Trungpa, *The Myth of Freedom*, 45.

8. The Monkey Mind

1. Khenpo Tsewang Dongyal Rinpoche, Unpublished commentary on *The Flight of the Garuda by Shabkar*, 2014.

9. The Grip of the Lesser Spirit

1. Khenchen Palden Sherab, *The Vajra Sound of Peace*, 150.
2. Dilgo Khyentse Rinpoche, *Pure Appearance*, 62.
3. Sidle, *This Hungry Spirit: Your Need For Basic Goodness*.
4. *Dhammapada*, 3.
5. Sam Foss, "The Calf-Path," Academy of American Poets website, accessed March 23, 2023.
6. Yongey Mingyur Rinpoche, *In Love With the World: A Monk's Journey Through the Bardo of Living and Dying*, 105–106.

10. The Freedom of the Greater Spirit

1. Dante, *The Divine Comedy*, 16.
2. Castaneda, *The Teachings of Don Juan: A Yaqui Way of Life*, 87.
3. William James quotes, Goodreads website, accessed, March 25, 2023.
4. Ralph Waldo Emerson quotes, Goodreads website, accessed March 22, 2023.
5. Winston Churchill quotes, Goodreads website, accessed March 25, 2023.

11. The Cosmic Joke: Peering into Transcendence and Who Am I?

1. Yongey Mingyur Rinpoche, *In Love With the World*, 140–41.
2. Dzongsar Khyentse Rinpoche, *Poison is Medicine*, an online book at the Khyentse Foundation website.
3. Salzberg, Facebook post, March 2022.

12. Bodhicitta and the Six Paramitas

1. Peck, *The Different Drum: Community Making and Peace*, 13–15.
2. Traleg Rinpoche, *The Essence of Buddhism*, 1.
3. Shantideva, *A Guide to the Bodhisattva Way of Life*.
4. Dzongsar Khyentse, *Poison is Medicine*.
5. Yongey Mingyur Rinpoche, *In Love with the World*, 36–37.

13. The Bodhisattva's Way of Life

1. Macy, "The Wings of a Bodhisattva."
2. Wrzesniewksi, "Jobs, Careers, and Callings: People's Relations to Their Work," 21–33.
3. Williamson, *A Return to Love: Reflections on the Principles of "A Course in Miracles,"* 55.
4. Solomon, *Finding Joe*.
5. Chodron, *The Wisdom of No Escape and the Path of Loving-Kindness*, 67.
6. Buber, *I and Thou*.
7. Buber, *I and Thou*.
8. William James quotes, Goodreads website, accessed March 28, 2023
9. Chodron, "How to Practice Tonglen," Lion's Roar website, January, 2023.
10. Trungpa, *Training the Mind and Cultivating Loving-Kindness*, 47.
11. Trungpa, *Shambala: The Sacred Path of the Warrior*, 39–40.

14. Karma and Taking Everything as Path

1. Trungpa Rinpoche, *Daily Chant Book*, translated by the Nalanda Translation Committee, 1994.
2. Shabkar, *The Life of Shabkar: The Autobiography of a Tibetan Yogi*, 422.

Bibliography

Buber, Martin. *I and Thou*. Translated by Walter Kaufman. New York: Charles Scribner's Sons, 1970.

Castaneda, Carlos. *The Teachings of Don Juan: A Yaqui Way of Knowledge*. New York: Washington Square Press, 1985.

Chodron Pema. *The Wisdom of No Escape and the Path of Loving-Kindness*. Boston: Shambhala Publications, 2004.

———. *When Things Fall Apart: Heart Advice for Difficult Times*. Boston: Shambhala Publications, 2016.

———. *Becoming Bodhisattvas*. Boulder, Colo.: Shambhala Publications, 2018.

Collins, Jim. *Good to Great: Why Some Companies Make the Leap and Others Don't*. New York: Harper Business, 2001.

Crowley, Mike. *Secret Drugs of Buddhism*. Hayfork, Calif.: Amrita Press, 2016.

Dalai Lama. *From Here to Enlightenment*. Boston: Snow Lion, 2012.

Dante. *The Divine Comedy*. Translated by John Ciardi. New York: Berkeley, 2003.

Dhammapada. Translated by Dharma Publishing staff. Berkeley: Dharma Publishing, 1985.

Dilgo Khyentse Rinpoche. *Pure Appearance*. Edited by the Nalanda Translation Committee. Translated by Ani Jinba Palmo and the Nalanda Translation Committee. Boulder, Colo.: Shambhala Publications, 1996.

Dudjom Rinpoche. *A Torch Lighting the Way to Freedom*. Translated by Padmakara Translation Group. Boston: Shambhala Publications, 2011.

Eliot, George. *The Essays of George Eliot*. Edited by Nathan Sheppard. New York: Funk & Wagnalls, 1883.

Eliot, T. S. *Collected Poems, 1909–1962*. London: Faber and Faber, 1974.

Goethe, Wolfgang. *Faust: A Tragedy*. Translated by Walter Arndt. New York: W. W. Norton & Co, 2001.

Khyentse, Dzongsar Jamyang. *The Guru Drinks Bourbon?* Boulder, Colo.: Shambhala Publications, 2016.

Khyentse, Dzongsar. *Poison is Medicine: Clarifying the Vajrayana.* Khyentse Foundation and Siddartha's Intent, 2021.

Longchenpa. *Natural Perfection.* Translated by Keith Dowman. Wisdom Publications, 2010.

———. *Finding Rest in Illusion: The Trilogy of Rest, Volume 3.* Translated by Padmakara Translation Group. Boston: Shambhala Publications, 2018

Macy, Joanna. "The Wings of a Bodhisattva." *Insight Journal* (Spring 2001).

Mingyur, Yongey Rinpoche. *In Love With the World: A Monk's Journey Through the Bardos of Living and Dying.* London: Bluebird Books for Life, 2019.

Nhat Hahn, Thich. "The Sunlight of Awareness." *Lion's Roar,* March 28, 2023. *Lion's Roar* website, accessed June 25, 2021.

Patrul Rinpoche. *The Words of My Perfect Teacher.* Translated by Padmakara Translation Group. San Francisco: Jeremy P. Tarcher/Putnam HarperCollins, 1994.

Pearce, Joseph Chilton. *The Crack in the Cosmic Egg.* Rochester, Vt.: Park Street Press, 2002.

Peck, M. Scott. *The Different Drum: Community Making and Peace.* New York: Touchstone, 1998.

Powell, Gerald. *Sh*t the Moon Said: A Story of Sex, Drugs, and Ayahuasca.* Deerfield Beach, Fla.: Health Communications, 2018.

Richo, David. *How to Be An Adult in Relationships: The Five Keys to Mindful Loving.* Boulder, Colo.: Shambhala Publications, 2002.

Rumi, Jalal Al-Din. *The Essential Rumi.* Trans. Coleman Barks and John Moyne. New York: HarperCollins, 1995.

Salzberg, Sharon. *Real Happiness: The Power of Meditation.* New York: Workman Publishing, 2019.

———. Facebook post, March 2022.

Shabkar. *The Life of Shabkar: The Autobiography of a Tibetan Yogi.* Translated by Matthieu Ricard. Ithaca, N.Y.: Snow Lion Publications, 2001.

Shakespeare, William. "The Tempest." In *The Yale Shakespeare: The Complete Works,* edited by Wilbur L. Cross and Tucker Brooke. New York: Barnes and Noble, 1993.

Shantideva. *A Guide to the Bodhisattva Way of Life.* Trans. Vesna A. Wallace and B. Alan Wallace. Boulder, Colo.: Shambhala, 1997.

————. *The Way of the Bodhisattva*. Translated by Padmakara Translation Group. Boulder, Colo.: Shambhala, 2006.

Sherab, Khenchen Palden and Khenpo Tsewang Dongyal. *The Vajra Sound of Peace*. Sidney Center, N.Y: Dharma Samudra, 2020.

Sidle, C. Clinton. *This Hungry Spirit*. Burdett, N.Y: Larson Publications, 2009.

————. "What Makes You a Buddhist." *Huffington Post*, October 2011.

Solomon, Patrick. *Finding Joe*. Film. Hillsboro, Ore.: Beyond Words Publishing, 2011.

Traleg Rinpoche. *The Essence of Buddhism*. Boston: Shambala Publications, 2014.

Trungpa Chogyam. *Cutting Through Spiritual Materialism*. Boston: Shambhala Publications, 1973.

————. *The Myth of Freedom*. Boston: Shambhala Publications, 1976.

————. *Shambhala: The Sacred Path of the Warrior*. Boston: Shambhala Publications, 1988.

————. *Crazy Wisdom*. Boston: Shambhala Publications, 1991.

————. *Training the Mind and Cultivating Loving-Kindness*. Boulder, Colo.: Shambhala, 1993.

Welwood, John. "Principles of Inner Work: Psychological and Spiritual." *Journal of Transpersonal Psychology* 16, no. 1 (1984).

Welwood, John. *Love and Awakening*. New York: Harper Perennial, 1997.

Wilber, Ken. *Sex, Ecology, Spirituality: The Spirit of Evolution*. Boston: Shambhala Publications, 2001.

Williamson, Marianne. *A Return to Love: Reflections on the Principles of "A Course in Miracles."* San Francisco: HarperOne, 1996.

Wrzesniewksi, Amy. "Jobs, Careers, and Callings: People's Relations to Their Work," *Journal of Research in Personality* 31, no. 1 (March 1997): 21–33.

Other Suggested Reading

Campos, Don Jose. *The Shaman and Ayahuasca*. Studio City, Calif: Divine Arts, 2011.

Goldstein, Joseph. *Insight Meditation: The Practice of Freedom*. Boston: Shambhala Publications, 1993.

Hart, William. *Vipassana Meditation, As Taught by S. N. Goenka*. New York: HarperOne, 1984.

Luna, Luis Eduardo, and Steven F. White, eds. *Ayahuasca Reader: Encounters With the Amazon's Sacred Vine*. Santa Fe, N. Mex.: Synergistic Press, 2016.

Metzner, Ralph, ed. *Sacred Vine Spirits of Ayahuasca*. Rochester, Vt.: Park Street Press, 2006.

Moyne, John, and Coleman Barks, trans. *Open Secret: Versions of Rumi*. Putney, Vt.: Threshold Books, 1984.

Narby, Jeremy. *The Cosmic Serpent*. New York: Jeremy P. Tarcher/Putnam, 1998.

Sogyal Rinpoche. *The Tibetan Book of Living and Dying*. New York: HarperOne, 2002.

Index

becoming the serpent, 44–45
biography, 261–62
Buddhist background of, 6
changes mental models, 144–45
early practice of, 125–26
findings about Ayahuasca, 2
journal entries, 40
learns about Peruvian shamanic
    culture, 26–29
and longing, 122–23
mother's passing, 61–63
and personal stagnation, 24
rock climbing event, 148–49
training in Vipassana, 76
skillful means, Ayahuasca as, 1–3
sow and reap, 231
spirit in action, 20
spiritual bypassing, 19–23, 37–39
    defined, 19
    examples of, 21–22
spiritual materialism, 16–18,
    245–46
    defined, 18
stagnation, personal, 24
stereotyping, 138–39
sublimation, 136
suffering, 93–94, 98
    caused by clinging, 13–14,
        87–88
    and monkey mind, 109–10
    the truth of, 135
suppression, 136
Sweeping Shamata Vipassana, 141–42,
    160–62
sympathetic joy, 223–24
synchronicity, 232

Tantra, 88–90
    defined, 88
    and physics, 89
Tenga Rinpoche, 90
there but not there, 195–99, 210, 222,
    240
thingies, 133
thought, is not solid, 143–45
thoughts, noticing, 227–28
Tibetan Buddhism
    challenges for Westerners, 4–5
    and Shamata Vipassana, 3–6
Tilopa, 8
Tomlin, Lily, 10
Tonglen, 223–36
tooth of the Buddha, 82–83
tracelessness, 246
Traleg Rinpoche, 186–87
transcendence, premature, 22
transcendental, defined, 187
Trungpa, Chogyam, 18, 47, 84, 133,
    223, 226–28
    on becoming human, 22
    on observing thoughts, 107
trust, faith and, 83
truth, relative and absolute, 195–99
Tulkus, 89–90

unshakeable faith, 83
Urgyen, Tulku, 52–53

Vajrayana
    challenges for Westerners, 4–5
    defined, 3–4
Vasudeva, 208–9
victimization, feeling of, 147, 151–53

About the Author and Suggested Retreat Centers

C. Clinton Sidle is the former and founding director of the Roy H. Park Leadership Fellows Program at the Johnson Graduate School of Management, Cornell University. Clint's nationally recognized leadership programs focused on servant leadership and discovering one's basic goodness as the basis for "doing well by doing good in the world." He argues that leading from such a place is the pinnacle of the authentic self and ensures personal effectiveness. His books include *The Leadership Wheel: Five Steps for Achieving Personal and Organizational Greatness*, a view of leadership through the lens of the Five Buddha Families, and *This Hungry Spirit: Your Need for Basic Goodness*, which advocates nurturing basic goodness as a premise for both happiness and success.

Clint's professional work was based on his thirty-plus years as a practicing Buddhist. Beginning with his first teacher, Sri S. N. Goenka, he practiced for seventeen years in the Hinayana tradition, attending annual week-long Shamata Vipassana retreats, many of them at Insight Meditation Society. He followed that with Shambhala Training and the

Terma teachings of Chogyam Trungpa Rinpoche, and since 1998 he has studied and practiced the Vajrayana with Tibetan Buddhist masters Thinley Norbu Rinpoche, Kenchen Palden Rinpoche, Khenpo Tsewang Rinpoche, and Tulku Sang-nyak Rinpoche, all within the Nyingma lineage. Over that time, he has spent one to two months per year in intensive meditation retreat. He has also edited three books by the Khenpos based on their commentaries on the *Dudjom Tesar Ngondro*, *Yeshe Lama* by Jigme Lingpa and *The Flight of the Garuda* by Shabkar Tsokdrug Rangdrol. Finally, he is on the board of Namgyal Monastery, HH Dalai Lama's only Western monastery, where he has been teaching Shamata Vipassana since 2017.

Suggested Retreat Centers

Sweeping-Style Shamata Vipassana

Dhamma Dhara Vipassana Meditation Center, Shelburne Falls, Massachusetts

Dhamma Mandala, Kelseyville, California

Open Shamata Vipassana

Insight Meditation Society, Barre, Massachusetts

Spirit Rock Meditation Center, Woodacre, California

Open Space Shamata Vipassana

Shambhala Training at Karme Choling, Barnet, Vermont

Samadhi Integral, Boulder, Colorado

Centro Espiritual Mama Abuela's, Idaho Springs, Colorado